*The publisher gratefully acknowledges the generous support
of the Joan Palevsky Literature in Translation Endowment
Fund of the University of California Press Foundation.*

*This translation is partially supported by the Norway House
Foundation, a California non-profit corporation dedicated
to honoring the Norwegian seafarers who risked their lives
for the Allied cause in War World II. The Norway House
Foundation carries its mission by promoting, encouraging and
supporting educational, professional and cultural exchange
between Norway and Northern California.*

*This translation has also been published with
the financial support of NORLA.*

The Immigrant and the University

The Immigrant and the University

PEDER SATHER AND GOLD
RUSH CALIFORNIA

Karin Sveen

Foreword by Kevin Starr
Translated by Barbara J. Haveland

UNIVERSITY OF CALIFORNIA PRESS
BERKELEY LOS ANGELES LONDON

University of California Press, one of the most distinguished university presses in the United States, enriches lives around the world by advancing scholarship in the humanities, social sciences, and natural sciences. Its activities are supported by the UC Press Foundation and by philanthropic contributions from individuals and institutions. For more information, visit www.ucpress.edu.

University of California Press
Berkeley and Los Angeles, California

University of California Press, Ltd.
London, England

Library of Congress Cataloging-in-Publication Data

Sveen, Karin.
  [Mannen i Montgomery street. English]
  The immigrant and the university : Peder Sather and gold rush California / Karin Sveen ; translated from the Norwegian by Barbara J. Haveland.
      p.   cm.
  Translation of the author's Mannen i Montgomery street : portrett av en norsk emigrant.
  Includes bibliographical references and index.
  ISBN 978-0-520-27648-2 (cloth,)   — ISBN 978-0-520-95712-1 (electronic)
  1. Sather, Peder, 1810–1886.   2. Businessmen—California—San Francisco.   3. San Francisco (Calif.)—Emigration and immigration
I. Title.
HC102.5.S38S8413   2014
979.4'604092—dc23   2013016623
[B]

23   22   21   20   19   18   17   16   15   14
10   9   8   7   6   5   4   3   2   1

For Liv Duesund

Therein lies, to some extent, the foundation of Man's future circumstances. Personally, I have often regretted that I did not have better Opportunity to acquire Learning when I was young, since Youth is the Right Time for this.

PEDER SATHER on education, from a letter to
his brother Christoffer in Odalen, written
in San Francisco on December 7, 1867

CONTENTS

ILLUSTRATIONS

ACKNOWLEDGMENTS

This book was published in Norway in 2011. Since then I have made fresh discoveries that shed more light on Peder Sather's early years in New York. Chapters 4 and 5 have therefore been completely rewritten and more details added elsewhere.

Liv Duesund has been my tireless mentor throughout. Liv is a professor at the University of Oslo and the moving spirit behind the establishment of the Peder Sather Center for Advanced Study at UC Berkeley. Without her there would have been no book. It was at her instigation that I first visited Berkeley, and I have been back there many times since then. She has read countless drafts of the manuscript closely and critically commented on them. This book is dedicated to her with my gratitude.

In the fall of 2010 a seminar was held at UC Berkeley to mark the bicentenary of Peder Sather's birth. It was at this that I first presented my research to the staff of the university. The seminar was chaired by Carla Hesse, Peder Sather Professor of History; and Jan de Vries, professor of history and economics, gave his comments on my work. A big thank you to you both!

Barbro Osher, the Swedish Consul-General in San Francisco, has followed my project with the keenest of interest. On the evening after the seminar she hosted a grand bicentennial dinner. I will always remember her generosity and the part she played in rescuing Peder Sather from oblivion. Through her work Barbro Osher has shown herself also to be Scandinavia's consul-general.

As coarranger of the event Sten Arne Rosnes, the Norwegian Consul-General in San Francisco, did his part to strengthen the historical ties between UC Berkeley and Norway. Rosnes is a true man of learning and it is a privilege to have his support.

Barbara J. Haveland has transformed my whole perception of the art of translation. She has checked every fact, every detail, and has restored to their original language quotes from letters, documents, and newspapers on which the years have taken their toll. Equally enriching is her feel for the tone of the narrative, for everything that allows the reader scope for interpretation. Armed with this skill she has set course through the foreign waters of the story, just as a sea captain in 1832 once steered across the ocean to America with a single passenger on board—the young Peder Sather.

I want to express my profound gratitude to Niels Hooper at UC Press for his editorial prowess and passion for this project; also, his assistant Kim Hogeland, project editor Cindy Fulton, and copy editor Andrew Frisardi, well-known poet and translator, deserve my heartfelt thanks.

Sather's descendants have also been of great help, contributing pictures, letters, and papers. Sparse documentation, but as vital to me as the kindness of the givers. My sincere thanks to Kathleen Bruguiere Anderson, Wenche Sæther Håtun, Eva Helle, and David Prestemon.

Over the past many years I have been fortunate in receiving financial support from the Norway House Foundation in San Francisco for the work involved in the writing of this book and its translation. The Foundation made all of my journeys possible, both those of a physical nature and those that carried me back in time. Thus I have had the pleasure of walking where Peder Sather walked, of searching there, thinking there, writing there.

Do I neglect to thank NFFO, the Non-Fiction Writers' and Translators' Organization in Oslo? Oh, no. Have I forgotten NORLA, Norwegian Literature Abroad? How could I?

Karin Sveen

FOREWORD

Writings by Norwegians and Norwegian-Americans frequently exhibit a minimalist style that ranges from reticent to enigmatic. This tendency can be noted without fear of cultural stereotyping, for it reflects something deep and abiding that goes back to the Norse sagas; hence, it constitutes a frequently noted characteristic of the Norwegian temperment.

In this biography, the noted Norwegian writer Karin Sveen employs a typically Norwegian restraint as she sifts through the meager documentation connected to her subject, banker Peder Sather (1810–86): trustee of the College of California, which was the forerunner of the University of California, whose widow donated to the university the well-known Sather Gate, the Sather Tower (or Campanile), as well as three professorships (two in history and one in classical literature) that keep Sather's name alive. Indeed, Sveen herself enters the narrative, as she wrestles with the spare documentation and personal statements surviving Sather, one of the most important financial figures of mid-nineteenth century United States, based in San Francisco and the West Coast primarily but maintaining connections to Wall Street and the national banking establishment. How could such a wealthy and influential man, Karin Sveen asks, have remained such a private figure—indeed, remain in significant measure in the shadows—despite her years of scrupulous research, retrieving a record that only her extraordinary industry and devotion to her subject made possible for her to assemble?

Was it a crime or some lesser malfeasance? Balzac, after all, once noted that behind every great fortune lies a crime. No, there was no crime; but there had been a young Norwegian housemaid who had become pregnant by an equally young and obscure clerk just off the farm; and this clerk, not ready to marry the girl who bore his child and to face a bleak future with her, had fled to New York; entered personal service; edged into the world of money and banking; become a devout Baptist; and built a major New York financial firm, which he brought to frontier San Francisco, where it prospered and evolved into the Bank of California. In middle age, this Norwegian immigrant, now a pillar of the community, helped to found a university for his adopted state. But, despite his prominence—his fortune, his homes on Rincon Hill in San Francisco and across the bay in Alameda, his reputation as a churchman and social activist—there remained something elusive about him, secretive even, as if he were hiding from something associated with his native Norway, which he never revisited despite numerous continental and Atlantic crossings. Sather wrote to his older brother, who had inherited the family farm and dispossessed Sather into an ill-paying clerkship, only after twenty-four years of silence.

Karin Sveen recovers the enigmatic story of Peder Sather by scouring the available public record. With skill and a disciplined sense of personal involvement, a concern for the man behind the enigma, she deftly employs the details she can muster. She documents Peder Sather's long first marriage, notable for his extended absences in San Francisco while his wife remained in New York; and, later, his frequent trips to New York while she remained in San Francisco. Sveen notes the lack of surviving correspondence between husband and wife during these intervals. With economy and drama, she chronicles his three children who died young, the surviving son unable to engage the opportunities presented to him, the daughter who was lost to insanity—and who died before fifty, it must be added—because her father banished from her life the man she loved and wanted to marry. The son, failing to connect, survives as little more than a shadowy figure, even more elusive, if that were possible, than Peder Sather himself.

This biography, however, is not a melodrama. Rather, like a saga, Sveen's narrative possesses a drama of external event that manages to suggest interiority even when details are wanting and hence must be tentatively conjectured. In most cases, Sveen allows the facts, the personal tragedies, the silences, to speak for themselves, with a minimum of speculation. Even when it comes to public events, because Peder Sather always remained so elusive, so devoid of personal commentary, Sveen must track him down in sparse newspaper clippings and contextual evidence—as if she were a detective and Sather a missing person in his own life. Nevertheless, however it was managed, Sveen does assemble a compelling narrative: banking, city building, university founding, fires, accidents, depressions, runs on banks, vigilance committees; all played out against Sather's personal struggles, such as tuberculosis, loss of children, conflicts over questions of love and marriage, and much else. Herein, then, is a biography situated in the rise of New York City and San Francisco as financial centers, the story of a gilded age whose major figures make cameo appearances in this biography because they were colleagues and friends of Peder Sather. Yet even these public events often happen offstage, like so much in Sather's life, and thus rarely yield personal statements from Sather himself. Never straying from the record, Sveen does her best to suggest the possible psychological and emotional content of a life lived, paradoxically, so long in the public eye yet so privately. The young man who fled Norway in obscurity becomes, by middle age, one of the founders of the modern banking industry, a well-connected New Yorker, whose friendship and business circles were at the center of high finance; and, in San Francisco, a contributing founder of both city and state, as banker, real-estate developer, public-spirited activist, philanthropist, civic leader, and counselor to the powerful and great.

And yet—because of a reticence animated at once by a Norwegian habit of mind and the personal circumstances that drove him from Norway—Peder Sather so successfully covered his tracks that, were it not for this biography, he would have remained as he had always been, one of the Great Unknowns of nineteenth-century California: known only because a gate, a campanile, and two professorships at the University of California bore his name—and even the record of these bequests only now comes fully to light. Peder Sather survives in memory, ironically, because his second wife made these bequests after his death. Peder and Jane Sather were briefly married, a mere four years or so, but she understood him so well, and appears to have loved him with such a lavish outpouring of supportive emotion and physical presence, that the four brief years they shared together before Peder Sather's death most likely were among his happiest. Not since the 1850s, when he was living as a bachelor banker atop Rincon Hill in San Francisco—working long hours, true, but in the evenings enjoying cigars and champagne amid the convivial company of his fellow bankers, talking of the city and state in which they were investing—had he been as happy as he seems to have been in these final years.

Like so many high-achieving Americans of the nineteenth century, natives and immigrants alike, Peder Sather regretted that his education had not been better. He certainly knew his arithmetic, however, especially when the numbers were aligned neatly on a ledger, leading to a favorable bottom line. He read constantly, Sveen tells us, and he loved to keep fine furniture, paintings, and objets d' art in his home, which he inventoried meticulously, for they represented an aesthetic expression of all that he had achieved professionally following his precipitous flight from Norway. He traveled in Europe to enjoy himself and to improve his mind, as well as to conduct business, like many self-made Americans in that age, and he learned from what he saw there. In the great universities of Europe and the eastern United States, Peder Sather— so we learn from one of his few statements of appreciation and regret— encountered alternate scenarios to his own interrupted youth and circum-scribed middle years. There, he suggests, he might have studied, might have expanded his horizons, might have been happy. What an American story! Had an aspiring novelist met him on one of these European journeys, Peder Sather might survive today in a novel as well as in a gate to a university cam-pus through which innumerable young men and women have entered and exited in their own pursuit of that more complete life through higher educa-tion that eluded Sather. Yet the life he did find in America, in New York City, in the San Francisco Bay Area, possesses its own grandeur, and now, at long last, the life of Peder Sather receives due recognition in this distinguished biography.

Kevin Starr

ONE

Monuments and Mysteries

I learned to read through my mother reciting to me the wording on shop and street signs in the town of Hamar, when we went shopping there. To me, words such as *Londonerbasaren, Festiviteten*, and *Biografen* were not merely the names of a store and couple of cinemas; they were mysterious doors into unknown stories. We stopped to look at the old paddle steamer, *Skibladner,* and the memorial to the fallen, and when my mother told me the stories behind these, Hamar was no longer just a place where we bought light bulbs, soap, and reels of thread; it was also a world full of tales and legends.

Later I would hear enigmatic words at school, but when my teachers took it for granted that we all knew what they meant I didn't dare to reveal my ignorance by asking. One of these words was *university*, and the shame of not knowing what a university was moved me to conjure my own images out of the thrill that ran through the classroom when this word flew from the teacher's lips. In my mind I saw the university as a palace in which young people like princes and princesses wandered through great halls in the company of sages who confided the secrets of their universe to their students.

My father worked in an iron foundry and no one in the family had had what you could call an education. But in our house we would listen to a radio talk by a historian as intently as we followed the work of a seamstress, from the moment she threaded the needle until a happy figure was twirling in a new summer dress. If we found a book that spoke to us we would wash our hands before starting to leaf through it, and give a lot of thought to what we read. Knowledge was something we longed to acquire, but the desire for learning and the places of learning belonged to two separate worlds.

This ingrained way of thinking was put seriously to the test seven years ago when I first visited the University of California at Berkeley, across the

Bay from San Francisco. The sense of being on someone else's home ground was in no way lessened by the knowledge that this university is ranked as one of the best in the world. It has fostered twenty-two Nobel Prize winners and at any given time there is at least one Nobel laureate on the faculty. I was going to be at Berkeley for a year, on a visiting scholarship, so I would have plenty of time to explore my inner contradictions, but it was not long before I came across something which made me view the university in a quite different light.

California is as far west as you can go without ending up in the Far East, and the physical effects of traveling such a long distance are palpable. I was still jangling inside well after landing, and the feeling of being airborne had not yet left me when I drove away from the airport outside of San Francisco in a minibus, setting out on the last leg of my journey to Berkeley. This took me over the enormous bay lying inland from the Golden Gate, on the thundering Bay Bridge—as high at its midpoint as a mountain ridge and overlooking shimmering hills, blue and silent. The sun was descending into the Pacific Ocean, red and alarmingly big, appearing to swell as it sank. White sailboats bobbed in the bay and a steady stream of freighters slipped through the Golden Gate strait, heading for the port of Oakland, where long-legged container cranes waded in the water like huge birds.

While the metropolis of San Francisco reared up on its windswept heights, looking as though it was about to plummet into the sea, Berkeley lay snug and sheltered, a town the size of Norway's Trondheim. Its streets sloped gently from the marina on the bay up to a wreath of wooded hills. The buildings were small and low, like the buildings in Norwegian towns fifty years ago. There was not a mall in sight, no high-rise apartment blocks to speak of, and only a handful of buildings in the center of more than five storeys. Only one structure rose high into the air: a majestic tower, pointing heavenward like a great granite finger.

Berkeley is a university town in the original sense of the term, having grown up around the university built on that spot, the first on the American west coast. This was in 1868, and there was no town here then, just meadows and pine trees and oak groves with a little river running through them, and mountain lakes in which turtles paddled contemplatively, their shells barely breaking the surface. The university's founders chose this spot because they considered such surroundings more conducive to mental reflection than the restless city of San Francisco with all its many distractions. The founders also had to come up with a suitable name for this peaceful stretch of countryside, eventually agreeing to name it after George Berkeley, an Irish Enlightenment philosopher whose thinking embodied their own ideas on education. Knowledge without the wider perspectives of enlightenment served neither the individual nor society.

The tower at Berkeley stands on the university campus, close to the main entrance, and is so tall that it can be seen for miles around, even from the Golden Gate, where incoming ships can take their bearings from it. So when I set out the next morning, my feet still throbbing faintly from the flight, I had no difficulty in finding my way to the campus. At precisely twelve noon a peal of bells rang out from the tower, first a dozen booming kettledrum chimes sounding the hour, then a carillon so delicate and penetrating that it drove the din of cars and motorbikes to the back of my mind.

I found myself caught up in a crowd of young men and women, and followed them along an avenue of plane trees to the university's main entrance, a monumental gateway which, like the tower, has achieved the status of a historic landmark. In front of the gateway was a sunlit circular plaza full of stalls and musicians, people sitting reading on benches, others giving free tango lessons. Tourists, freshmen, and graduates were busy taking pictures of the gateway or having themselves photographed posing between the massive pillars of granite and white marble. Like a roof above their heads, there stretched a green patinaed bronze arch on which the gateway's name was picked out in capitals. This was Sather Gate, the university's and the town's most iconic feature, along with the tower. I stood for a long time gazing at this venerable gateway to the world-famous seat of learning, a portal designed to inspire humility and sharpen both the wits and the senses.

Sather Gate consisted of three gateways, a wide one in the center and two narrower ones to either side, all ornately framed in bronze. Mounted on the apex of the central arch was an oval, laural-wreathed medallion bearing the inscription "Fiat Lux," Latin for "Let there be light." These words are taken from the Book of Genesis and have for centuries been used as an expression of the ideals of enlightenment. This I learned in my Latin studies at Hamar Cathedral School, and standing there, surveying Sather Gate, suddenly I was a schoolgirl again and this monument a book just waiting to be read and interpreted.

On two of the granite pillars flanking the gate hung marble plaques stating that the gate had been donated by Jane K. Sather in memory of one Peder Sather, born 1810, died 1886. Behind me I heard someone wondering aloud whether Sather might be a Jewish name, since it sounded rather like Seyder.

I took a picture of the gate and had my own photograph taken in front of it before going on to have a closer look at the bell tower. My walk led me along a path known as Campanile Way, a sign told me that the tower was called Sather Tower.

The campanile was 307 feet tall. Such a lofty structure is best viewed from a distance; nonetheless, newcomer that I was, I had to go there, press my palm against the granite and lean my head back, walk round the foot of the tower, and observe the other people doing the same. On one side of the tower was a bust of Abraham Lincoln, but a Chinese couple in the crowd of sightseers thought it must be a portrait of this Peder Sather.

Sather Tower is an almost exact replica of the campanile on St Mark's Square in Venice. It was built on a hill alongside Sather Esplanade, a paved rectangle adorned with trees and shrubs, white-painted benches, and color-ful, exotic flowers. Too late I discovered that I had wandered into a gathering of people in smart dresses and dark suits; I beat a retreat as the bridal couple appeared on the scene and a flurry of clapping and cheering filled the air.

I hurried on into the tower, where an intricate system of elevators and stairways led to an observation deck two hundred feet above the ground and thirty-three feet below the belfry itself. From the deck you could see the whole of the university campus, with paths and walkways winding between buildings and around green lawns, granite facades here, reddish-brown red-wood walls there, oaks with dark-green tops. Out on the horizon I could see the Golden Gate Bridge shimmering in the sparkling light of the Pacific and San Francisco drowsing in the sunshine, silent and motionless, as if distance had transformed the actual city into a still photograph.

Two kettledrum booms above my head made my whole body reverberate, and for a second the world was nothing but sound; then it became visible once more, with its roofs and chimneys, solitary walkers, groups of people streaming out of a door, gleaming windows. It struck me that Berkeley, with its campus and the campanile at its heart, was not unlike a medieval monastic village, then had to laugh at this foolish comparison when champagne corks began to pop down below on the Esplanade, a sea of voices filled the air, and a jazz trio struck up. I made my way down from the tower and strolled on across the campus, past magnolia trees and silver firs, beneath cedar boughs and the lobed leaves of lime trees.

I went over to the university library to have a look around: a gray granite building, the rooms inside lined with bookshelves of golden walnut and floored in marble and oak. In a vast reading room on the second floor, where the bright light from bottle-green reading lamps fell over open books and the slightest cough resounded in the silence, I presented myself to a librarian who showed me around, speaking in hushed tones. During this little guided tour I happened to ask who the monuments I had seen commemorated. The librarian told me that Peder Sather had been one of the university's founders, a New Yorker and, as far as he knew, Norwegian-born. When he told me this I realized that the surname Sather could be a slight Anglicization of the Norwegian *Sæther*. The *æ* was the only letter in his name that had not followed him to America; it was of no use in the new world. When the librarian heard that I was from Norway he suggested that we go down to the archives to see what else we could find out, and so I followed him through doors, down flights of stairs, and along corridors.

The university records were kept in a room in the maze of basements and subbasements: the domain of the archivists, each in his or her own little cubbyhole, surrounded by old books and papers. Eventually I found myself clutching a document which confirmed that Peder Sather had been involved in the establishment of the university in the 1860s, he was one of its founding fathers. The sound of paper was all I could hear, the rustling of the sheets I gently turned. The tower and the basement, the name of a Norwegian inscribed both high and low.

There is a wealth of literature on immigration from Norway to North America; accounts of farmers in the Midwest and seamen and shipbuilders on the West Coast, but that a Norwegian immigrant had had a hand in the establishment of one of the finest universities of our day, this was news to me, and I cannot deny that this fact made me feel surprised and proud. According to the records, Peder Sather was also the only foreign-born member of these educational pioneers, something that made him quite unique. This still did not explain, however, why the main entrance to the university should bear his of all names.

While the obliging librarian was showing me back to the reading room, I tried to put Peder Sather into his historical context. He had been born in 1810, which is to say four years before the dissolution of the union between Norway and Denmark and a year before Norway acquired its first university. Peder Sather was also a contemporary of such great Norwegian artists and intellectuals as Ole Bull, Henrik Wergeland, Camilla Collett, Ivar Aasen, Peter Christian Asbjørnsen, and Jørgen Moe, all of them nation builders and champions of the Enlightenment. If Peder Sather had been a founding father of the oldest university in California, it seemed reasonable to assume that he had cherished ideals closely akin to those of his fellows in Norway. The inscription on Sather Gate, "Fiat Lux," seemed to bear out this theory, but was there, in fact, a connection?

I asked whether the library had any books or articles on Peder Sather, because this was a man I wanted to learn more about. But after some searching, the librarian had to confess that there was nothing and asked me to let them know if *I* came across any literature on him elsewhere. I was amazed that so little seemed to be known about Peder Sather, despite the fact that his name cropped up all over the place. The university had two professorates in history, the Sather Chair in History, and one in classical literature, the Sather Chair in Classical Literature. Then there was a law library, originally known as the Sather Law Library; and a scholarship foundation, the Peder Sather Memorial Fellowship; not to mention a computer-programming language, the Sather Language. For more than a century the chairs of history and classical literature had been occupied by leading scholars from all over the world. Over the decades the praises of Sather Tower have been sung in cantatas and odes, and more recently it has figured in a poem by Ishmael Reed entitled "Sather Tower Mystery." Sather Gate, too, has been immortalized in poetry— "Sather Gate Illumination," by Allen Ginsberg, for example. But who was Peder Sather?

I got in touch with Sigvor Hamre Thornton, a leading figure in North American Scandinavian circles and a famously hospitable hostess to Norwegian students and academics. Sigvor, who had been made a member (first class) of the Royal Norwegian Order of St. Olav for her work, was able to tell me that Peder Sather had been a successful banker and that Jane Krom Sather was his wife and a generous benefactress. In my mind I pictured an industrious gentleman with a pince-nez on his nose, poring over ledgers, but what did the day-to-day business of a bank have to do with the university, why had his wife built a gate to his memory and what had brought Norwegian Peder Sather to the American west coast sometime during the mid-nineteenth century?

Sigvor's first husband, Haakon Hamre, a professor at the university's Department of Scandinavian, had known a lot about Peder Sather, she told me, but Hamre was long dead. In 1990, Professor Ingrid Semmingsen, senior lecturer in the history of Norwegian emigration at the University of Oslo, had visited Berkeley to search for biographical material on Peder Sather, but was taken ill during her stay and died soon after returning to Norway. In Berkeley Ingrid Semmingsen had stayed with Sigvor Hamre Thornton, and

Sigvor remembered the historian coming back from libraries and archives with lots of notes in her bag. Word had it that Sather was a native of Trøndelag in central Norway, Sigvor said, but Ingrid Semmingsen had had the idea that he might, in fact, have hailed from Stange in the Hedmark region. I knew that Ingrid Semmingsen herself was from Hedmark and might, therefore, have had access to local historical sources that could confirm his origins. But if this were true, then it seemed odd that I had never heard of Peder Sather, since I too am Hedmark born and bred, I spent thirty years of my life there and have always been interested in the history and the stories of that area.

I can just picture those two elderly ladies in Sigvor's house high up in the Berkeley Hills, with the Pacific a narrow band far off on the horizon, fragrant eucalyptus trees in the woods behind and rambling roses climbing the wall around the front door. On the couch, Sigvor, probably with her knitting, and in the armchair Ingrid Semmingsen: from there you can see the view. Cups and saucers on the coffee table, and on the floor next to the leg of the armchair a bag with a sheaf of handwritten notes on Peder Sather sticking out of it, notes that I wished I could have read. No one knows what became of them, but they may have disappeared after Ingrid Semmingsen's death.

I had come all the way from Norway to Berkeley to get to know a new world, to experience life in the far west, in the present, but now here was this gateway, like a mysterious door back into Norway and the past. Each day I passed through Sather Gate; and morning, noon, and night the chimes of Sather Tower reminded me of Peder Sather. During my year at Berkeley I attended lectures by the philosopher Hubert L. Dreyfus and wrote the manuscript for a collection of essays entitled *Frokost med fremmede* (Breakfast with Strangers), but still, I couldn't get Peder Sather out of my mind. I started dipping into books on Norwegian and American eighteenth-century history, hoping to find some trace of him and form a picture of his day and age. At other times I would let Peder lie for a while, but research into him gradually began to occupy more and more of my thoughts and my time, and there came a day when I realized that there was no way back. A new world had indeed revealed itself to me, but not at all in the way I had expected.

After my stay there as a visiting scholar I went back to California once a year, partly in order to learn—I am one of life's eternal students—but also secretly hoping to find a huge and hitherto unknown archive that would divulge information about the life of Peder Sather. With a man of whom so little was known the tiniest new nugget of information was an event: the discovery, for instance, of a home address, a picture of a house he had lived in, a part of a sentence, a whole sentence, or, if I was very lucky, a passage in which his name was mentioned. Because the fact was that I never did come upon any public or private archives, no piles of faded letters that could provide the answers to my questions. So I bit the bullet and proceeded to search for Peder Sather in American census reports, passenger lists and employment records, newspaper archives and other public documents, and eventually I made contact with one of his descendants.

It was a while before I found a picture of him. It was stored in the archive of the California Historical Society, which is housed in premises in the center of San Francisco, behind a front door so unassuming that if you didn't know what lay behind it you would walk right past. On the day that I made the trip across from Berkeley to see this photograph rain was pouring down, so I came dripping in off the street, peeled off my soaking-wet raincoat, and went up to the reception desk, my sneakers squelching across the floor. Before going to fetch the photograph a forbidding-looking archivist motioned me to take a seat at a table in the tiny reading room. Apart from a man with a very bad cold who coughed and sneezed more than he read, the room was empty. Minutes later the archivist returned carrying a slim file which she solemnly handed to me. She wanted to know whether my fingers were clean and dry, because if not I could borrow a pair of white gloves. I accepted this offer, and slipped the gloves on as she returned to her post behind the reception desk, with a look that seemed to say she didn't trust me not to steal this document.

The photograph looked as if it had not been touched since the day when an unknown owner had brought it to the archive. I turned back the innermost sheet of paper and for the first time laid eyes on the face of Peder Sather. I gazed at it as though, if I just waited long enough, he would proceed to tell me all about his life. What I saw was a grave-faced man, probably in his mid-fifties, which would mean that the photo had been taken around 1865. His hair was smooth, thin, and almost white, parted on the left. The short, neatly trimmed beard was still dark, except around the chin. Peder Sather looked slim, bordering on thin, and a doctor to whom I later showed the picture thought his gaunt features might be evidence that he was suffering or had suffered from a serious illness.

His forehead was high and broad, his eyebrows fine, dark, long, and straight. There was a tight set to the mouth that was reinforced by the rather staring eyes, although this could perhaps be ascribed to the powerful flash and the long exposure times of early photography. But as I looked I began to see

FIGURE 1. Peder Sather, 1865. Photographer: William Shew, 421 Montgomery Street, San Francisco. Courtesy of Eva Helle.

that his expression was more complex than I had first thought. It was not only an authoritative face, it also had an air of reticence and of sadness about it.

A year later I was back at Berkeley again, and this time I visited the Bancroft Library, the university library which specializes in the history of California. There I found another photograph—there would be no more.

Peder Sather, One of the Founders of the
Old Banking House of Drexel, Sather &
Church

FIGURE 2. Peder Sather, 1885. In *San Francisco Chronicle,* October 17,
1909. Courtesy of the San Francisco Public Library.

This too was a portrait, taken of an elderly Peder Sather, possibly around
1880 when he was in his early seventies. This photograph had appeared in
the *Overland Monthly* magazine, established in San Francisco in 1868 and
edited by Bret Harte, a well-known writer of the day and a close friend of
Mark Twain. The photograph was grainy and indistinct; even so, I could

tell that this was a different Peder Sather from the one in the first photo. His hair and beard were now completely white, he looked confident and benign, his cheeks were plumper, and he came over as being both jocular and affable.

I obtained a copy of this photograph, took it back to Berkeley, and arranged to have it enlarged at ZeeZee Copy in Sather Lane, a narrow passage near Sather Gate. Ever since, these two photographs have hung on the wall above my desk, to remind me that these represent a real person and not a fictional character. There is a line between these two, although as soon as we start to recount something, we inevitably also start to invent. My friends were always keen to know what new details I had unearthed, but to them my discoveries sounded, they said, like chapters in a novel, even though my descriptions were based on pure fact; because between the facts and the recounting of them there are always the words, and the narrator's interpretation of both facts and words.

Peder Sather's face is also an interpretation of a face, shaped by the photographer, colored by the camera lens and assessed by my own eye, homing in first on one feature, then another. Two pictures are not much to go on, though, when one considers the shifting expressions that passed over that face during a lifetime. Nor are these photographs like the snapshots of our own time; instead they appear to have been intended for the public eye and for posterity, as documentation of an individual's existence. And yet they are as silent as standing stones. The silence that hangs over these portraits corresponds to the silence surrounding the monuments at Berkeley and that which fell when Peder Sather died and disappeared into the fringes of history. When, in writing the following account, I attempt to bring him back, I do so by means of my own discoveries, while the pictures on my wall hold their peace.

TWO

Sole Passenger

Peder Sather was born Peder Pedersen Sæther and he came into the world at Nordstun Nedre Sæter farm on September 25, 1810. This, at any rate, is the date recorded a month later by the local vicar in the register of baptisms for the parish of Strøm, in the diocese of Ulleren. His date of birth is, however, still a bit of a mystery because in 1869, when immigrant Peder Sather applied for an American passport, he gave his date of birth to the notary public in New York as September 17. Had the vicar's mind been elsewhere for a moment? Had he confused one baptized infant with another? Who can say. Had Peder Sather been living abroad for so long that his memory was failing him? Surely not. But the date of birth so neatly entered in the register by the vicar when the baby boy Peder was baptized does not appear in any other official record. Born twice in September, christened once in October, so begins the story of Peder Sæther or Sather.

In Norwegian, a *sæther* or *sæter* is a summer pasture in the mountains. Nordstun Nedre Sæter, often known simply as Nordstun, lay near the village of Disenå, a few kilometers from Skarnes and bounded by the Glomma, the Disen, and the Sæter, waterways that ran through cultivated fields and wild forests, rivers and streams that frothed and swirled in the spring and flowed smooth and sparkling on fall days. Nordstun was larger than a smallholding, but nothing like the size of the big farms around the vast Lake Mjøsa, although it did employ a handful of workers. The farm is still there, but of the original buildings the only one left is the *stabbur,* the raised wooden store-house. Old photographs show that Nordstun consisted of a low, white-walled farmhouse with two doors on the one side, a barn, a hayloft, a woodshed, a washhouse, and a cowshed. A pond in the farmyard with water lilies floating on it; a garden surrounded by a white picket fence; tall birch trees flanking

FIGURE 3. Peder Sather's birthplace, Nordstun Nedre Sæter, date unknown. Courtesy of the California Historical Society, MS 3829.001.

the farmhouse; shorter, stubbier trees elsewhere in the yard. The fringes of a forest in the background, and beyond them, hilltops. Bumble bees in the meadows in summer, swishing scythes, frost-covered walls in winter, roaring fires, a wood box next to the iron range—the perfect spot for children with frost-bitten fingers to sit. Golden-brown stubble in the fields in September, ploughed furrows, poles propped up against a wall, and tools lying in the grass, a harrow. But not a soul to be seen. These are pictures of the farm, taken as documentation and as mementoes. Some of them were sent across the sea; I found them in an archive in San Francisco.

Peder Sather's father was Peder Larsen, his mother Mari Kristoffersdatter, she too born and raised at Nordstun. The couple had six children, daughters Anne, Berte, and Marte; and sons Lars, Christoffer, and Peder, the youngest. Anne, the oldest, was married in 1816 to Ole Olsen Dysterud, a man known for being something of an eccentric. He tried, among other things, to build a perpetual motion machine. After working on this for ages he turned up at the smithy one day, all cock-a-hoop, and announced: "Now all I need is a wheel, now all I need is a wheel!" The perpetual motion machine ended up in a bog, or so the story goes.

Ole Olsen Dysterud became the first mayor of the district, so his eccentricities cannot have damaged his reputation. He must also have taken an interest in public enlightenment, because in the late 1820s he received a visit from the writer and poet Henrik Wergeland, who was at that time establishing public libraries up and down the country. In May 1830, at the vicarage in Eidsvoll, the writer penned a report on his work for the Royal Norwegian Society for Development and took the occasion to make special mention of the contribution made by certain countrymen toward the setting up of the libraries and "in particular Dysterud in Oudalen." The very next day Wergeland would hitch up his horse and cart and set off to visit Dysterud and help him organize his books. Henrik Wergeland also made particular reference to Anne's husband on another occasion. In a catalog of "Worthwhile Enterprises" the writer praised Dysterud for his plans to build a forge for the production of scythes. There was no knowing, Wergeland noted, whether his plans would come to anything, but it was high time that Norwegians freed themselves from their dependence on Swedish steel!

Already we see that, within Peder Sather's close family in Odalen, there was much interest in both literary and technical matters. Åse Sæter, a descendent of Christoffer, told the local newspaper *Glåmdalen* in 1999 that the sons at Nordstun had a name for being clever. The young people on the farm had their own private tutor, she said, something which was extremely unusual at a time when others had to make do with a circuit teacher who traveled from hamlet to hamlet, never staying in any one spot for more than a few weeks. Only around 20 percent of school-age children in the country learned to read and write. That Peder and Mari Larsen arranged private tuition for their brood testifies to a certain level of prosperity, and to a couple who could see beyond corn and cattle. The practical skills were supplemented by theoretical knowledge, reading, writing and arithmetic, the catechism, history and natural history, and general knowledge. But there was to be no schooling of any sort for Peder Sather. This we know because, in 1867, while involved in the work of establishing the university at Berkeley, he wrote the following words about education to his brother Christoffer.

> For, as I am sure you know, therein lies, to some extent, the foundation of Man's future circumstances. Personally, I have often regretted that I did not have better Opportunity to acquire Learning when I was young, since Youth is the Right Time for this.

Tragic circumstances dictated that the young Peder Sather would receive no schooling or any other form of education. When he was eight his father died. His mother remarried the following year, but died two years later at the age of thirty-eight. This was in 1821, when Peder was eleven. There is reason to believe that his sixteen-year-old sister Anne took him under her wing after the loss of his parents. The farm went to Christoffer and Lars, but in 1825 Lars sold his share to a third party who in turn sold it, later that same year, to Christoffer, with the result that Christoffer became sole owner of Nordstun Nedre Sæter. A photograph reproduced in the local gazetteer shows Christoffer to be an elegant, refined-looking man, with long, dark, curly hair and fine-drawn features. It is hard to imagine him behind a plough or in the cowshed, and not behind a quiet desk in a government office. Nonetheless, a farmer he became, and lived at Nordstun until his death in 1872.

As the youngest, the prospects for Peder Sather in little Disenå were not great, unless, like other country boys with no land of their own, he found himself a smallholding or contented himself with being a tenant farmer. Some time after his Christian confirmation, at the age of fifteen, Peder Sather left Disenå and the farm never to return; and seven years later, in 1832, left Norway altogether. Not until twenty-four years after he emigrated did he reestablish contact with Christoffer. Nor did the latter ever get in touch with Peder during this period, according to the first letter Sather wrote to his brother, in 1856. It is hard to construe this as anything but a sign of a rift between the brothers, so serious that neither would stoop to make the first move. But from 1856 onward they wrote to one another regularly. For Peder Sather this correspondence must have filled a great need, one which seems to shine through in the aforementioned letter to Christoffer, from 1867, where he warmly styles himself "your devoted brother." The family member with whom Peder had kept in touch in the first years after his emigration was his brother-in-law, Ole Dysterud, his oldest sister, Anne, having died in the early 1830s.

Åse Sæter, now dead, was known to be an expert on Peder Sather's early life in Norway. She maintained, correctly, that he had lived for a while in Christiania, as the Norwegian capital was then called, before emigrating. One of her descendants, Wenche Sæther Håtun, has stated in interviews and in an outline for a biography, however, that Peder also worked in the city then known as Trondhjem, where he is said to have worked for some years as a trainee in a bank. This may explain why, until now, he has been identified as a native of Trøndelag, both in Norwegian-American circles in the United States and in those written sources in which he is mentioned.

Why Peder Sather should have wound up in Trondhjem of all places might have something to do with the consequences of the dissolution of the union between Norway and Denmark in 1814. Norway had to establish its own national bank, and there were fierce discussions in the Norwegian parliament as to where the bank's headquarters should be located. The choice lay between the capital (Christiania) and Trondhjem, and one of the main arguments for choosing the city in central Norway was that such a location would help to prevent too much fraternization between members of parliament and bank officials. For the Norwegian parliament this consideration tipped the scales in Trondhjem's favor, and in 1816 Norges Bank opened its doors, first in the fine eighteenth-century wooden mansion of Stiftsgaarden, and later moving to Kongens gate 1.

It seems not unlikely that this was where Peder Sather eventually served his apprenticeship. As an employee with the country's national bank this young man must have shown a not inconsiderable knack for finance. And the records show that his position there would have included training in the reading and writing of business correspondence in English. From a professional and an economic point of view, the future must have looked bright, certainly not giving cause for thoughts of emigration.

There was not much emigration from Norway, actually, until around 1840, and the few who did leave the country tended to travel in groups, like the "sloop people," a party of fifty-odd Quakers who sailed from Stavanger in 1825 on the sloop *Restauration*. Letters from these and other emigrants did circulate in the years that Peder was in Trondhjem and Christiania, and the subject of emigration was discussed in the press, but not as a frequent, topical matter.

Peder Sæther must, however, have taken a close interest in these newspaper articles, because by 1832 he had made up his mind to emigrate. At that time there was no regular, direct sailing route from Christiania to America, so in the late summer he set off for Gothenburg, Sweden, in hopes of securing a passage. And one day he boarded the *SS Herald,* an American cargo vessel bound for New York, probably with a cargo of iron ore, weighing about 250 gross tons. Iron was a major Swedish export, and American vessels shuttled back and forth to Gothenburg to pick up the raw materials.

According to the manifest presented by Captain William Samson to the New York port authorities on arrival, Peder Sæther was the sole passenger on the *SS Herald.* I have looked through a great many passenger lists, from both passenger ships and cargo vessels. The majority are very lengthy, and not one has been limited to just one name. It was also a clear departure from the norm for an emigrant to travel completely alone, unaccompanied by family, neighbors, or at least a friend—which does make one wonder whether Peder urgently needed to leave the country, and in a hurry at that.

What we call wanderlust or a taste for adventure was never, generally speaking, a motive for emigrating. In Peder Sæther's day some people left the country for religious reasons, others because farmland was cheap in America, something which was of great interest to anyone who wanted to have their own farm, but couldn't afford to buy land in Norway. Both of these motives are well known, and during the nineteenth century thousands of Norwegians traveled to the settlements of the U.S. Midwest. But Peder Sæther clearly had no intention of being a farmer. It had been years since he left Odalen and became a city boy in Christiania and the Trøndelag capital. As the youngest son of his family, he could never expect to take over the farm, but he might well have had a good future in banking, if that was the career he chose to pursue.

There are also other factors which make one wonder why Peder Sæther should have been in such a hurry to emigrate that he would set off alone. Early in 1832, New York was struck by a massive and much-dreaded cholera pandemic; notices in the press warned everyone against coming to the city. When the SS *Herald* sailed from Gothenburg the pandemic was at its height, and it would be surprising if Peder Sæther had not been aware of the situation. The disease had made itself felt throughout Europe, spreading even as far as Norway. It originated in the Indian subcontinent and was carried from Asia to Europe on navy and merchant ships. In 1831 it hit Britain, where tens of thousands died. Right to the last, Americans had hoped that the Atlantic Ocean would protect them, but cholera reached America in the same way as Europeans had seen it reach them: by boat.

The doctors did not realize this, though. Some of them were convinced that the epidemic was caused by bad smells, bad air, or "poisonous miasma," while others believed the dead had only themselves to blame, since it was primarily the poor who were affected. No wonder they got sick when they lived in stinking, damp hovels, all because they were too shiftless to work and earn the money to pay for more salubrious accommodation. The streets of the slums ran with sewage and were knee-high in garbage. As one upper-class resident, the respected civic leader John Pintard commented of the cholera: "It is almost exclusively confined to the lower classes of intemperate, dissolute and filthy people huddled together like swine in their polluted habitations."

One of the hardest hit neighborhoods was the Manhattan slum known as Five Points, where, according to Kenneth T. Jackson, professor of history at Columbia University: "African-Americans and immigrant Irish Catholics were crowded in squalor and stench."

New York, in short, was a deathtrap, from which only the well-to-do, who owned their own carriages and had family or friends outside the city with whom they could live, were able to escape. *The New York Evening Post* reported that all roads out of the city were jam-packed with the exodus, and compared the panic to that of the people of Pompei as lava rained down on their houses. New York became a ghost town. According to one eyewitness, an assistant to the painter Asher B. Durand, "There is no business doing here if I except that done by Cholera, Doctors, Undertakers, Coffinmakers & c. Our bustling city now wears a most gloomy aspect—one may take a walk up & down Broadway and scarce meet a soul." In the desolate streets nothing stirred, except for carts laden with corpses, drawn by sick-looking people who knew that their own days were numbered. Norway, too, was hit by the pandemic; not so severely, but still badly enough for Henrik Wergeland to make it the subject of a play, *The Indian Cholera,* in which he presented the pandemic as being India's revenge on the British colonialists.

Peder Sæther could not have picked a worse time to emigrate, but a document found in the Norwegian National Archive might go some way to explaining his sudden departure. In this, a list of infants christened in Aker during the years 1828–32, there is an entry stating that on April 8, 1832, "housemaid" Ingeborg Marie Knudsdatter, residing at Lakkergaden, in one of the poorest quarters of Christiania, and in service with a certain Ole Simonsen, had brought for baptism an illegitimate child who was christened Petrine Frantsine. The father was known and his name entered in the baptismal register as Peder Sæther, sales clerk.

Another source links Ingeborg with Trøndelag. In a census taken in 1875, Petrine and Petrine's children by stonemason Christian Encke were registered in the small village of Soknedal, south of Trondhjem. According to the census report Petrine was resident in Christiania, and in all probability had been visiting her relatives in the village when the census was taken. So Peder Sæther could have met Ingeborg while he was working in the bank in Trondhjem.

But plenty of men had fathered children out of wedlock without considering this a reason to leave the country. The difference in station between a farmer's son and a "housemaid" or domestic servant in Lakkergaden was great, however; so Peder was to father a child out of his class, unless Ingeborg was actually a girl of good family who had run away from home to conceal the shame of expecting a child by a man who would not marry her. For Peder Sæther's part, the church register would forever testify that he was the father, and he may have been afraid that his having got the girl pregnant would bring disgrace upon him and his family in Odalen if the truth were to get out. So it must have been a very unhappy Ingeborg who took the infant Petrine to be baptized, and a desperate Peder Sæther who waited on the quayside at Gothenburg, hoping for some ship's captain to come along who would take pity on him and offer him passage to America.

The sloop *Restauration* took fourteen weeks to cross the Atlantic Ocean in 1825, and seven years later ships were still powered by sail, so such voyages took time, even when conditions were favorable. Peder Sæther celebrated his twenty-second birthday on board the *SS Herald,* on his way from a mother country he did not necessarily have any wish to leave to a city which everyone was being advised to stay well clear of. Nor was this merely a reconnaissance trip for him; in the ship's manifest Captain Samson has noted that the young Norwegian was intending to settle in America.

The decision to emigrate is one of the hardest a person can ever make, since it changes one's life forever. The fact that Peder gave his name to the New York port authorities as Peter Sather is clear proof of the impact emigration had on an individual's identity. Although the changes to his name were not great, and were made only to render it easier to pronounce, nonetheless they marked the beginning of a new life in a strange new world, in which Peder would be the same man as before but also quite different from the man he might otherwise have become. In principle, as an immigrant he now had the chance to reinvent his past and compose the next chapter himself, as if his life were a story, subject to his own personal laws.

Captain Samson registered Peder Sather as a cabin passenger. If the *SS Herald* had been a passenger ship, the fact that the young man from Odal had his own cabin would have ranked him among the wealthy immigrants, since the poor folk traveled steerage, crammed together in the hold. But the *SS Herald* was a cargo vessel and it may be that the captain had nowhere else to put this lone emigrant except in a cabin, possibly even one of his own. Even so, Peder must have had the wherewithal to pay for his berth, and this seems to support those sources in American literature which maintain that he had amassed a bit of capital by working for a while as a fisherman on the Trøndelag coast.

Weeks at sea, days and nights in his cabin, gave Peder plenty of time to think about what he had left behind and what lay ahead. He was traveling not only to a new country and a new name but also to a new language. And if he was as bright and quick to learn as Åse Sæter held the Sæther boys to be, I can well imagine Peder spending his time on board learning enough English to be able to talk to the captain and make himself reasonably well understood when he reached New York.

I picture him in his cabin, head bowed over his grammar book and dictionary, in calm weather and when storms tore at the sails and tugged at the rigging. I picture him up on deck, his dark hair blown back by the wind, his face splashed by the cold salt spray. There had been no parents to wave him off, only pride and sorrow. But he had been fending for himself for at least five years, saving up the money for his fare by himself.

In my mind's eye I see him in the galley at daybreak, as the ship slices through the waves, wallowing from side to side. He sits down at a table bolted to the floor, alongside American seamen and deckhands, and leaving his mother tongue behind him he extends his hand and says: "Hello, I'm Peter." This was the Christian name he meant to go by from now on, and he was going to have to remember to use it and answer to it.

And then there were the approximately sixty evenings alone in his cabin, his head buzzing with thoughts that would not be quelled. He felt bad about Ingeborg; in his mind he saw his brothers and sisters, as if he were dead and looking down on them from some nonexistent place. Images of his home kept returning to him, silent pictures. He was far out at sea, and yet he felt as though he were in the little grove of trees, secretly observing his own childhood home, nestling between the three rivers, the Sæter, the Disen and the Glomma. There it lay, in a fall landscape in which everything seemed to be over. The potato field had been ploughed up and the black earth brooded over the grain that was gone. Of the barley field all that remained was a swathe of faded, jagged stubble. The woodshed was clearly no longer in use and the washhouse looked abandoned, as if no one would ever again fire up the boilers until the wooden walls were baking hot and steam billowed out of the window. The farmyard was deserted, as though everyone had gone inside or gone away. The flagpole looked gray, the house was gray, everything seemed to have aged. The barn was nothing but a shell, empty, so it seemed, of winter fodder, and the horses and the other livestock fled. The maple trees looked black, as if a darkness had risen out of the earth and wrapped itself around their murky tops. A pole was propped against the wall of the hayloft, as if no

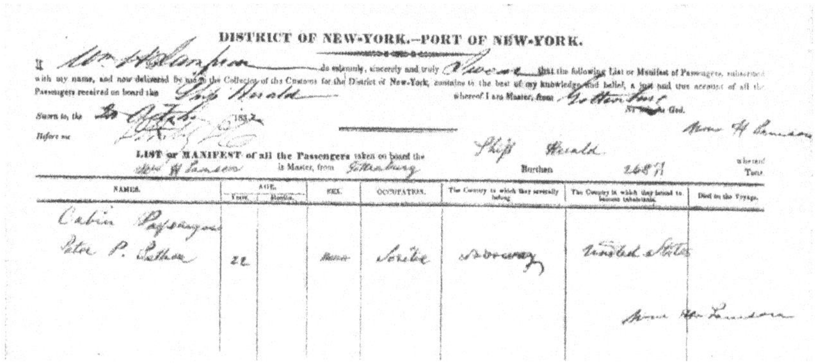

DISTRICT OF NEW-YORK.—PORT OF NEW-YORK.

do solemnly, sincerely and truly … that the following List or Manifest of Passengers, subscribed with my name, and now delivered by me to the Collector of the Customs for the District of New-York, contains to the best of my knowledge and belief, a just and true account of all the Passengers received on board the Ship Herald whereof I am Master, from … So help me God.

Sworn to, the 20 October 1832

Before me

LIST or MANIFEST of all the Passengers taken on board the Ship Herald whereof … is Master, from … Burthen … Tons.

NAMES.	AGE. Years.	AGE. Months.	SEX.	OCCUPATION.	The Country to which they severally belong.	The Country in which they intend to become inhabitants.	Died on the Voyage.
Cabin Passenger							
Peter P. Sæther	22		Male	Scribe	Norway	United States	

FIGURE 4. Captain William H. Samson's passenger list. Port of New York, October 20, 1832. Courtesy of Ancestry.com.

one had had the strength to carry it inside. The well-house was locked, hiding a spring that must surely have run dry.

When he took a few hesitant steps forward in his mind, everything he saw vanished. But he had to hold onto this image of his home, and so he kept his distance. He lifted his eyes to the hills behind the farm. They were cloaked in the mist of streams and rivers: raw and chill. It occurred to him as he sat there by the porthole in his cabin that this was how he had viewed his home on his last visit there, from a distance, as if he were already a stranger, as if he were gone, banished from this world.

On October 20, 1832, the *SS Herald* sailed into New York Harbor. She anchored offshore amid a forest of ship's masts. The crew couldn't wait to get unloaded and go ashore, but no one was allowed to leave the vessel until the ship's inspector, the customs treasurer, and a representative of the immigration authorities had made their rounds and registered the passengers. On the deck all was quiet, with no one but the newly dubbed Peter Sæther out there, surveying the scene. Gulls rode the gusts of wind and there was rain in the air, a few drops peppered his face, but came to nothing more. Christiania was a hamlet compared to what awaited him here, a city of 250,000 people. The ship seemed to have plucked him out of past and present and transported him straight into the future. He had read about New York, of course, and studied drawing and maps, but what match were they for what he was now seeing and hearing, what he was now feeling?

Immigrant ships and cargo vessels were anchored so close together that it was hard to believe that fear of the cholera epidemic could have stopped anyone from coming here. Schooners and brigs were continually gliding into the harbor and edging their way into vacant berths. German, Irish, and Italian voices rang from ships' decks, where crewmen clambered out of holds and down masts. The quayside was crawling with slumlords on the lookout for potential tenants among the gullible, homeless new arrivals. Extortionate rents were charged for the most miserable corners of draughty lofts or damp-ridden basements. Wily travel agents foisted expensive, counterfeit tickets onto confused immigrants planning to travel on across the country by wagon.

Peter had been warned by the captain and was not about to be hood-winked. He meant to go straight to the Norwegian-Swedish legation to ask for help in finding lodgings. While the inspectors were making their rounds and twenty-two-year-old Peter Sather was being registered as an immigrant, darkness began to fall. The lanterns on the ships were lit and so were the gaslights on the quayside. The young Norwegian had never seen streetlamps like these before; it was as if the day was only just beginning, even though it was drawing to a close. He heard horses neighing there on the docks, saw shadows flitting back and forth between the warehouses. Soon he too would be one of those figures, there one moment, gone the next. When the transfer boat was ready to take him from the *SS Herald,* the ship's deck seemed to heel over in the heavy swell and for a moment he felt as if he was drowning. Peter clutched at a suitcase, needing something to hold onto.

"You're trembling," Captain Samson said.

"Yes."

"You've been warned," Captain Samson said.

"Yes."

And so they parted. The last Captain Samson saw of Peter Sather was his back as he stood on the quayside under a gaslight, negotiating a fare with a cab driver. Then he disappeared into the maze of warehouses and the clatter of horses' hooves and the rattle of carriage wheels on cobbles was all that could be heard.

THREE

Baptism and Marriage

The world to which Peder Sather had come was not exactly waiting to lavish its bounty on him.[1] Unemployment was high in New York City in the 1830s, and the population was exploding. The number of inhabitants rose from 200,000 in 1830 to 350,000 in 1840, making New York the largest city in the country. Fourteen hundred immigrant ships sailed into its port every year: American merchant ships which sailed to Europe with cargoes of cotton, tobacco, and timber, and filled their holds for the return journey with what was callously referred to as "human cargo." The immigrants came primarily from Germany, Ireland, Poland, Russia, and Italy. Thousands of them died en route, their bodies committed to the deep. They died mainly of typhus, or "ship fever" as it was called, cholera, tuberculosis, or diphtheria. Of those who made it to New York alive, most had no money, no education, and no knowledge of English.

The immigrants were by no means welcomed with open arms. At best these newcomers were greeted with total indifference, at worst with open hostility. Opponents of immigration formed their own party, the "Know Nothings," a notorious anti-immigrant movement set up to put a stop to immigration and make life in general as difficult as possible for all immigrants, and for the Irish in particular. Members of the party marched through the streets, attacked new arrivals after dark, and did all they could to bar their entry into polite society.

The movement's name derived from the standard reply which, under the dictates of their manifesto, its members were bound to give when asked what they stood for and what they did: "We don't know." In those cases where,

---

1 For simplicity's sake Peder will be used from now on.

nonetheless, immigrants did receive financial support for food or lodgings this was done purely out of self-interest, to prevent robberies and rioting. As a rule, though, immigrants could not count on financial support, goodwill, or acceptance. Consequently, the new arrivals had no choice but to stick with their own kind. They helped one another with odd jobs and shared what they had. As a result many of the ethnic groups became more or less self-sufficient and this led to the development of parallel societies.

While the immigrants poured into Lower Manhattan, the American middle classes were escaping uptown, to reside at a safe distance. Gangs of newcomers burgled homes and scared people off the streets, but many immigrants were themselves robbed as soon as they set foot on American soil. On the docks they risked being charged deposits on accommodation at nonexistent addresses, or being offered basement rooms, which were often cut off from all daylight and overrun with rats. This was particularly true on the Lower East Side, where immigrants could find themselves living under the most appalling conditions.

When Peder Sather arrived in New York, the city was in the midst of a massive process of industrialization that was radically transforming working life. Jobs once done by hand were now mechanized, a development which came as a serious blow to skilled craftsmen. The invention of the sewing machine, in 1832, devalued the work of the countless tailors in the city, consigning them to hard and badly paid piecework in the clothing factories and putting them on the same footing as unskilled workers. The sky-high costs of food and lodgings drove people to desperation. The 1830s saw a number of "bread riots." Workers attended political rallies in the parks of Manhattan, then marched in a body to the flour stores, where they rolled the barrels out onto the sidewalks, broke them open, and helped themselves to the bread flour until the police appeared on the scene and chased away the famished demonstrators.

A newly moneyed middle class had sprung up, consisting of industrialists who were now elbowing the old merchant aristocracy aside and demanding political influence. So too were the workers. By 1829, their discontent was so great that they formed their own "Working Men's Party." The number one issue on their agenda was free public education, since it was felt that the key to a better future lay in schooling for all children. In the words of the workers: "Next to life and liberty we consider education the greatest blessing bestowed on mankind."

Throughout the 1830s the struggle continued, against the monopolization of production brought about by industrialization and against the banks, which had introduced the use of banknotes. When it then transpired that the value of paper money had sunk like a stone, wages were drastically affected. President Andrew Jackson was reelected the month after Peder Sather arrived in New York, but incurred the wrath of the wealthy by claiming that the profits from the banks were going straight into the pockets of the elite or disappearing out of the country.

Many immigrants, both women and men, wound up in the factories. They worked a ten-hour day and had no rights or protection. One can't help wondering why, if conditions were so bad, they didn't all move further inland and settle in places where the cost of living was lower. But New York City's big size alone led immigrants to assume that it would be easy to find work there. We might also think that Peder Sather, farmer's son that he was, would have gone into farming in the Midwest. But he must have dismissed all thought of a life in the country before leaving Norway, since on his arrival in New York he gave his profession as "scribe," that is, secretary or clerk. According to some reports he then opened a small money exchange somewhere in Manhattan.

A twenty-two-year-old newcomer intent on establishing himself in the world of finance all on his own would need to have a good, solid knowledge of English, some initial capital, and more than a nodding acquaintance with American and international finance. All the signs are that Peder Sather was eminently qualified on all these counts, and with several years of banking experience from Trondhjem under his belt, a money exchange may well have seemed a reasonable undertaking. Immigrants came to New York carrying every form of currency, as did merchants from all over the world. No national banking system had yet been created, so exchange rates varied from state to state. Competition was stiff and times were hard, but still, there ought to have been a market for a money exchange. Nevertheless, I have now been able to ascertain that the twenty-two-year-old Norwegian immigrant did not start out by setting himself up as an exchange broker. First he took a job as a servant with a wealthy Manhattan family. Which family this was I have been unable to discover, but this piece of information is, in itself, interesting. Not only was he now assured of clothing, bed, and board—the serving staff usually lived in their own wing of the house—but in a grand house Peder Sather was introduced to a social environment very different from that encountered by most immigrants, and possibly made some good connections. The servants came into close daily contact with the family and were eyewitnesses to what went on in the upper levels of society.

There was also a certain prestige attached to being in service in such a house, especially for those who enjoyed the privilege of being indoor servants, as opposed to outdoor servants such as gardeners, odd-job men, coachmen, or stable lads. An indoor servant could act as secretary to the family, take care of correspondence, be entrusted with confidential information, become an ally. He was always on hand, whether inside or outside the doors to the inner chambers, when the tea was served in cups of the finest china. Peder Sather's position as a servant exposed him, in other words, to impulses from an American way of life far removed from the street gangs and immigrant ghettoes down on the Lower East Side.

During his first years in New York Sather also became a member of the Baptist Church, one of the innumerable religious bodies in a country with no official state church. If he was a practicing Christian before he emigrated, then it seems likely that he came from a God-fearing family—as tradition has it the Sather's were. In Norway the ties between farm and church were generally pretty close. The vicar normally lived on a farm himself, and farmers often donated land to the church. But probably just as important here is the fact that, as adherents of the Good Book, the faithful could read, and one book tended to lead to others. This fits with the fact that Peder Sather's parents had a private tutor for their children.

This hypothesis may be wrong, of course. In which case Peder Sather's religious devotion may have developed while he was struggling to find his feet in New York. A young man who had emigrated, or possibly fled, from Norway in desperation at the threat of unwanted fatherhood, must himself have felt like an outcast and found life hard at times. But that he should have chosen baptism as the haven for his exiled soul is something of a surprise, since earlier Norwegian immigrants had established their own churches, founded on the teachings of the Lutheran faith they knew from home. In a report from the Baptist Church in New York he is, what is more, cited as being an exceptionally loyal member of the congregation. So to Peder Sather's story, which began with two dates of birth and one date of baptism, another baptism is now added. I have had my work cut out for me, trying to picture that baptism ceremony, a sturdy Hedmark man being totally immersed in a pool or a river in the presence of a singing, rejoicing congregation. It would have been easier to imagine Peder Sather as a Catholic in the confession box, remorseful and contrite, with an invisible, merciful ear close by.

Peder Sather was not your average man from rural Hedmark, though. He was, in fact, the first person to emigrate from that district, and he had said goodbye to Odalen long before he left the country. That he, as a grown man in a foreign land, chose to be saved and baptized by clothing himself in a white robe and being symbolically cleansed and born again, into a new life in the hands of the Lord, is an indication of the deepest commitment. As a phenomenon, conversion is not unlike emigration, representing as it does a break with the past and a fresh start in new life, under unaccustomed conditions. The act of conversion is, moreover, not only about the relationship between an individual and God, but also about that between a single person and a religious community. To be saved was to be received into a socially binding fellowship, and for a solitary immigrant like Peder Sather this must have been a huge benefit.

"A stranger taking up residence in any city in America must think the natives the most religious people on earth," wrote the English authoress Frances Trollope (1780–1863). The country abounded in Methodists and Baptists, Episcopalians and Presbyterians, Calvinists and Quakers, Universalists and Swedenborgians, not to mention a host of splinter groups from these denominations. Trollope visited America in the late 1820s and made careful note of her observations on the customs and manners of the American people. These copious notes provided the basis for a book entitled *Domestic Manners of the Americans,* published in 1832—the year in which Peder Sather arrived in New York.

This book sold in the thousands on both sides of the Atlantic and brought the penniless Frances Trollope wealth and fame. But it was very badly received in America, and not without cause one might say. With wit and wry humor she exposed what she saw as the American people's complete lack of good manners: middle-class gentlemen who chewed tobacco and spat out the juices anywhere and everywhere, who belched and picked their noses; guests at dinner parties who bragged and bellowed and seemed to have no interest whatsoever in what anyone else had to say. Americans, she said, believed themselves capable of achieving the impossible and were almost farcically optimistic. Jokes were lost on them: they lacked wit and took everything literally. The women were extraordinarily subservient, they seemed content simply to look after their homes and their children and otherwise to just nod and smile. And as to their table manners: "The total want of all the courtesies of the table, the voracious rapidity with which the viands were seized and devoured ... the frightful manner of feeding with their knives, till the whole blade seemed to enter into the mouth; and the still more frightful manner of cleaning the teeth afterward with a pocket knife, soon forced us to feel that we were not surrounded by the generals, colonels, and majors of the Old World; and that the dinner hour was to be any thing rather than an hour of enjoyment."

Almost everyone Frances Trollope spoke to was a member of one church or another, apart, that is, from those living in the most impoverished urban and rural areas, where, according to the residents themselves, they had no money to build churches. Only in America, Mrs. Trollope remarked caustically, could people not afford to be Christians. She also hinted that the middle classes also had a rather odd attitude toward their religion. Men and women with whom she could be having the most interesting conversation would suddenly up and leave in order to attend a religious meeting, and when she took them up on this she invariably received an evasive answer, even from highly educated individuals who normally had no difficulty in expressing themselves. Normally it never would have occurred to them to mix with the general public, but in church high and low sat side by side. Frances Trollope took exception to this double standard.

Equally incomprehensible was the way in which perfectly sensible people readily accepted such activities as speaking in tongues, exorcism, and mass conversions, all of which were normal fare at the festival-style revival meetings held by traveling preachers who could set towns and villages abuzz for days at a time. Did they all simply turn a blind eye to these irrational goings-on? Mrs. Trollope wondered. How else could people settle themselves quietly on the grass with their picnic baskets and gossip and chatter afterward as if nothing had happened?

Nor did Frances Trollope know of any other country in the western world where religion let men off so lightly while their wives were subjected to such strict discipline. As she says: "I never saw or read of any country where religion had so strong a hold upon the women, or a slighter hold upon the men. . . . Almost every man you meet will tell you, that he is occupied in labours most abundant for the good of his country; and almost all of the women will tell you, that besides those things that are within (her house) she has coming upon her daily the care of all the churches." For the men to leave all work for the church to their wives may have been the rule, but there were exceptions. After some years Peder Sather was, for example, made an honorary member of the local Baptist church in gratitude for all he had done for his fellow Baptists.

When Frances Trollope attempted to discuss what the life of the congregation meant to them they would stutter and stammer and seem embarrassed. Her explanation for this was that in America religion had to be a very worldly affair. Americans seemed to regard the church as a useful social arena to which one had to belong. Because the fact was that even though people flocked in their hordes to revival meetings, they seemed more concerned with the socializing as a means to worldly advancement and happiness than with the riches that might await them in Paradise. American society was, quite literally, a church society, with each church ruled by its own "government." What is more, the members of one church seemed to care remarkably little about whatever rules and laws might apply in other "small states." The various congregations lived side by side in the most pragmatic fashion, all of them wrapped up in their own worlds.

Frances Trollope writes with a dry and malicious wit, but she was not the only one to be struck by the piety of the Americans. Frenchman Alexis de Tocqueville, who also visited America around this time, could not help noticing what power the churches had. In his classic work, *Democracy in America,* published in 1835, he did, however, take a more positive view of them than Frances Trollope had done. In Tocqueville's opinion the churches could be good breeding grounds for a democratic frame of mind. Here people learned to organize themselves, to abide by the rules agreed on by the congregation, and to pull together. At the same time they adhered to the principle of Scripture that all men were equal in the eyes of God and that no one was better than anyone else. To become a part of American society you pretty much had to join a church, Tocqueville observed. To belong in America seemed to be synonymous with belonging to a religious community. All social life revolved around the church, this was where people made friends, obtained work, and found help with babysitting, schooling for their children, comfort, and support when it was needed.

Both of the books I've mentioned here may help to explain why Sather should have joined the ranks of the Baptists so early on. As a newcomer he was doing everything he could to become assimilated into the society. Discoveries I have made relating to a later period in his life indicate, however, that his was an enduring faith and that for him the church was not merely a social hub. On May 26, 1849, Sather wrote a letter to a friend who had embarked on a dangerous voyage to the West Coast by way of Cape Horn, concluding it with pious sincerity: "May God in his mercy bless you with good health and keep you safe. He alone can protect us in any place and He alone wherever we may be. Only trust in Him."

But it was not just his background as a bank clerk in Norway, his time in service in a grand house, and his membership of the Baptist Church that saved Peder Sather from ever ending up in the immigrant ghettoes. Still more significant was his marriage into an American family. The lady in question was not, however, Jane Krom Read, as the inscription on Sather Gate might suggest, but Connecticut-born Sarah Thompson.

The wedding took place on April 14, 1835, in the Reformed Protestant Dutch Church in Manhattan. So says the marriage certificate, a copy of which I was given in 2008 when I visited Sarah and Peder's great-great-granddaughter, the American diplomat Kathleen Bruguiere Anderson. The certificate, one of her few memorabilia, was lying on the coffee table surrounded by books and newspapers when I walked into her living room. It soon became evident that up till then Mrs. Bruguiere Anderson had not been nearly so preoccupied with her great-grandfather's Norwegian origins as I was: subsequent generations of the family had intermarried with too many different nationalities for that. And the fact that he had come from a small farm in Odalen was more of a parenthesis than a headline in the family history.

The marriage certificate was a neatly penned document addressed "To whom it may concern." The text was framed by an ornate border, and headed with a vignette of a devout couple standing before the minister. The two were married by Pastor Thomas de Witt, a leading theologian and later professor. This was surely not mere coincidence: a minister of some standing and a quiet wedding.

I felt quite flustered to think that I now held in my hand the marriage certificate handed to the newlyweds by Reverend de Witt on an April day in 1835. This was, for me, a thrilling and historic moment. The marriage certificate also confirms that at this time Peder was still calling himself Peter, although he would revert to his original Christian name some years later, perhaps as a way of reaffirming his Norwegian origins.

The succession of crucial decisions taken by Sather during his first years in New York speak of a man who did not sit around twiddling his thumbs. The question is whether there was any logical progression between the different links in the chain of choices. Did Peder Sather meet Sarah while he was in service, for example? Did she stay in the house where he worked? Did the enterprising young Norwegian make up in talent and charm for his lack of financial wherewithal? What is certain is that he did not meet Sarah through the Baptist Church, since she was a member of the Dutch Church, which was more akin to the Norwegian Lutheran Church in which Peder had been baptized.

Sarah was twenty-eight when she married—quite old, in those days, for a first-time bride. In wealthy families, an unwed daughter past the first flush of youth was often condemned to a life of boredom, cooped up in her childhood

FIGURE 5. Peder Sather and Sarah Thompson's marriage certificate, April 14, 1835. Courtesy of Kathleen Bruguiere Anderson.

home with no work to go to and nothing to do but embroider, go for walks, practice on the spinet, and dress for the evening's social events, being sure always to keep a smile on her face in case some eligible bachelor or widower happened to be on the guest list.

So, the need to find a spouse may have been as urgent on Sarah's part as it was on Peder's. And what was she like as a person? On my visit to Kathleen

FIGURE 6. Sarah Sather, née Thompson, 1807–81. Married to Peder Sather 1835–81. Undated daguerreotype. Courtesy of Kathleen Bruguiere Anderson.

Bruguiere Anderson's home I was shown a picture of Sarah as a young woman—a daguerreotype in a costly little ivory frame with a cracked glass. I recognized her straight away, from another picture of her in an archive at the university in Berkeley, but Mrs. Bruguiere Andersen herself had no idea that the lady in the daguerreotype was her own great-great-grandmother, Sarah. I have been able to unearth very few written sources offering any information about Peder Sather's first wife, although she was married to him for forty-six years.

I thought Sarah looked rather reserved and tight-lipped; my first impression that of an aristocratic face. In the picture she is wearing an elegant, turban-style hat with some sort of veil or train falling down her back. No housemaid, market woman, or factory worker could ever have afforded such a piece of headgear. This doesn't necessarily mean that Peder Sather married above his station, but it is a possibility.

July 28, 1836, saw the birth of the Sathers' first child, Caroline Eugenia. Carrie, as she was called, was born with a deformity of the spine and suffered from serious, lifelong health problems as a result. The little family was living at the time at 46 James Street, a few blocks northeast of Wall Street and the Financial District, where they stayed for three years. Local history books describe sections of this street as no more than an alleyway, and the area in which it lay was a mix of detached homes and tenement buildings. New York was divided into wards or districts, the worse the area the lower the number. James Street was in the Fourth Ward in Manhattan, so not too high up the scale, but the mayor of the city had lived for a while in this same part of the city, on Rose Street, and it was during these years that the middle classes had begun to move uptown.

The year after his marriage Peder Sather was no longer in service. In the employment records for New York City he is registered as a clerk. Did Sarah Thompson's parents help him to obtain employment more befitting his station? I feel bound to at least consider this explanation, and closer investigation reveals that there were a number of bankers on Wall Street by the name of Thompson. Of these, one John Thompson is of particular interest due to specific details to which I will return later. Here I will simply say that before coming to New York in 1832, this John Thompson had worked both as a teacher and as a clerk . In the city he went into business as a money changer and banker, and in 1836 he founded the influential financial quarterly *Thompson's Bank Note Reporter,* often seen as the forerunner to the *American Banker.* Thompson regularly ruffled feathers by announcing in his newspaper that the paper money in circulation was not worth its face value, although this was a crucial piece of information.

American financial history has it, however, that in 1836 Peder Sather became an agent for the celebrated banker Francis Martin Drexel, from Philadelphia. But is this true? If it is true, after four years in a city in the grip of poverty, disease, and economic recession, he had been more fortunate than anyone could possibly have dreamed.

FOUR

1837

So, by marrying into the Thompson family did Peder Sather have everything handed to him on a plate? And are the historians correct in claiming that it was Francis Martin Drexel who gave the Norwegian his big break in 1836? We may indeed all be history makers, but when it comes to writing history, we still do have to hunt for documentation, study it, and give thanks when we manage to retrieve primary sources from the dim recesses of the past. As far as the early stages of Peder's career in New York are concerned, I have found evidence that the answer to both of the above questions is no.

In a letter to the Norwegian Justice Department dated August 21, 1838, Ole Dysterud, then mayor of South Odal, mentions that his brother-in-law, Peder Sather, was working for Farrar's Exchange at 164 Nassau Street, New York City. Dysterud knew this from his correspondence with Peder at that time. Sadly these letters have been lost, but this snippet of information about Farrar has survived and can be confirmed by an American source to which I will shortly return.

And what of Francis Martin Drexel? He was to play an important part in Peder Sather's life, but was Drexel an up-and-coming banker in 1836? Not at all, says his biography. Drexel too was an immigrant, born in 1792 in the Austrian town of Dornbirn, where his father was a merchant. Young "Franz" had a gift for drawing and painting and wanted to become an artist rather than follow in his father's footsteps. When France invaded Austria during the Napoleonic Wars, Francis Drexel left his native land for good. He roamed around Europe, making a living as a portrait painter and attending art classes in Milan and Paris.

Several of his artist friends had emigrated to Philadelphia, and in 1817 Francis Drexel followed them. Philadelphia was the third largest city in the

English-speaking world, after London and New York, a cosmopolitan metropolis and a favorite haunt of artists, known for its leading academies within such fields as art and science, philosophy, and the classical languages.

The city was also home to opera companies and symphony orchestras, and Francis Drexel adored classical music. He taught himself English by reading poetry and novels, and soon began to feel quite at home. So much so that in 1818, after only a year in the city, he held his first exhibition, at the Philadelphia Academy of Fine Arts. Like Peder Sather, it was not long before Francis Drexel married an American woman. Her name was Catherine Hookey, the daughter of a merchant with many influential connections. The marriage got off to a bad start, however, when it was rumored that he had rather too fond an eye for his female art students.

In 1826, gossip and slanderous accusations drove Francis Drexel, by then the father of two, to take off to South America. Catherine was pregnant with their third child, and in her husband's absence she gave birth to a son, who was christened Anthony Joseph. Anthony was to become one of the greatest financiers and philanthropists in American history, but for the first four years of his life he was a quiet little boy who had never met his father.

Francis Drexel set out to support his family by painting portraits and in this he was extremely successful, not least due to his choice of models. He became friends with Simón Bolívar, among others, and painted a famous portrait of the Latin American freedom fighter and liberator of Venezuela, Colombia, Bolivia, and Peru from Spain.

Francis Drexel spent four years traveling around South America, living the life of an adventurer. He regularly sent money to Catherine in Philadelphia and eventually returned home for a while, before embarking on a new trip to Mexico in 1836. After that, and after a brief detour to New Jersey, he finally settled down with his family. By this time Francis Drexel was something of a linguist, speaking fluent Spanish, German, French, Italian, and English.

He did not, however, have enough money to support his steadily growing family. He tried going into business as a brewer, along with four Irishmen, and then—when that didn't work out—as a small goods trader, working from a room in his home. But he had no luck with that either. So one day he sat down and took stock of his skills. He could speak five languages, had made a lot of contacts, quite a few of them with people in high places. And his travels had given him valuable insight into foreign currencies and money broking.

FIGURE 7. Francis Martin Drexel, 1792–1863, artist and Philadelphia banker. Self-portrait, ca. 1820. Courtesy of the Drexel Collection, Drexel University, Philadelphia.

So why not try banking? And if he made a go of it as a broker, why not offer loans to his customers? This was a totally new concept; generally, loans were arranged privately, man to man, for obvious reasons. For one thing, transporting cash long distances by boat or on horseback was far too risky; for another, loans taken up in one state rose or fell in value when the money crossed state lines. Loans had, therefore, to be negotiated in person, anything else was a pure gamble.

No sooner said than done. In 1836 Francis Drexel opened a money exchange in Philadelphia, no more than a hole in the wall, 150 square feet all told. People shrugged and laughed at the artist turned bank man. Drexel was a completely unknown name in finance circles, and there was no talk here of an agency in Manhattan.

In 1836 Peder Sather's name appeared in the employment records for the first time, his profession given as "clerk," but with no business address provided. Francis Drexel was old enough to be his father and had been in America for years. Peder was a newcomer, no linguist, no seasoned traveler, no expert in foreign currency; he had no knowledge of American banking practices and no contacts except those he might have made through Sarah.

But Peder Sather had done all he could to make a place for himself in his adopted country. He had learned the language, steered clear of the immigrant districts, married an American, and, unlike most Scandinavians, become a Baptist. He was here to stay, and there is no trace of any correspondence with his brothers and sisters in Norway during these years. His brother Christoffer was running Nordstun Nedre Sæter farm, but never wrote to his young brother, and Peder sent no word to him either. This speaks of a serious estrangement, and of the need to live with this estrangement.

In 1836 Peder Sather was twenty-six years old. He was newlywed, residing at 46 James Street in Manhattan and working as a clerk—but where? There's no mention of any bank at 164 Nassau Street at that time, no Farrar's Exchange. Was Peder stuck behind a shop counter, selling milk and bread? Or was he installed in a lucrative banking business with John Thompson?

Most certainly not. All the indications are that Peder Sather started out as a lottery seller. There were around sixty lottery offices in New York in 1836. One of these, established in 1832, was located at 164 Nassau Street and run by a man named John Farrar. So it seems reasonable to suppose that Peder was selling lottery tickets for Farrar.

Now Nassau Street was not just any street in New York. It lay in the Financial District, a side street to Wall Street, but was better known for its newspaper and publishing offices. The newspaper the *Maine Cultivator* wrote at the time that Nassau Street was

> the short cut to the city's business, the path down from breakfast and home to supper, for all who go afoot. It is the most used street in New York for transit, (after Broadway) and quite the most influential and indispensable street, looking at the pursuits of its miscellaneous rent payers. Most of the newspapers of the metropolis are published in Nassau Street, it is thick with printers and paper-makers, stuck with lawyers like a paper of pins, savory with eating-shops, cosy with hosiery windows, swarming with news-boys,

full of everything but dandies and ladies. We doubt whether there is any sleep done in Nassau Street.

Number 164 was a four-storey red-brick building. It was owned by a wealthy widow, Elisa Bloom, from whom John Farrar had leased office space on the ground floor. The other occupants of the building included a bar, a printer's, a publisher, a couple of law firms, and various small businesses. On his right side Farrar had the Brother Jonathan publishing house and on his left the legendary Tammany Hall, a notorious social club frequented by often corrupt members of the Democratic Party.

John Farrar ran his lottery office from 1832 until 1837, but then he gave up selling lottery tickets. From one year to the next he switched to money broking, a surprising move, but not unusual. The aforementioned celebrated banker John Thompson also started out as a lottery agent before setting up in business on Wall Street.

Peder Sather, too, became an exchange broker in 1837, but evidently not with John Farrar, since the employment records give his work address as 24 Catherine Street. This suggests that Peder tried to make a go of it on his own as an exchange broker before, in 1838, taking a job with John Farrar in Farrar's Exchange at 164, Nassau Street. Here Peder Sather appears to have been the only employee.

But who was this John Farrar? I can give no conclusive answer to this question. But where I had expected to find a New Yorker, my sources sent me to Pepperell, a small town in Massachusetts. The Farrar family had lived there for generations, and while some of them were farmers, others became merchants, ministers of the church, or lawyers. In the early 1820s, however, three young Farrar men, John, Samuel and Charles, moved to New York, where Charles opened a shop on South Street, down by the harbor. He then helped the other two to get started.

And who should have been living at 46 James Street when Sarah and Peder moved there in 1836, but one Charles Farrar? Whether Charles was John's brother, cousin, or uncle is less relevant than the fact that he was the real entrepreneur of the three, and the most active socially. In May 1874 the *New York Herald* would write in retrospect of Charles Farrar something that made me think how fortunate Peder Sather was to have met this man: "Mr Farrar was a man universally beloved by the large circle of his friends and acquaintances. He was quiet, unassuming, considerate, generous. His whole life was filled with deeds of charity and love. His sympathies were freely given to the young, and many a poor boy has been helped up and started on a prosperous career by his friendly hands, and many others whose poverty and misfortune have been brightened by the timely aid that came often unasked and always in full measure, will not forget the worth of one who did his alms not to be seen or heard of men."

Until it can be proved otherwise, it is my contention that it was through Charles Farrar that Peder Sather was given his chance with Farrar's Exchange. So was Peder "a poor boy" when he arrived in New York City in 1832? On balance, the answer is probably yes. He certainly did not come armed with any great inheritance. The farm had passed to his brothers on the death of his parents and the estate had not yet been settled.

It was a wonder, really, that Peder Sather did so well, since 1837 has gone down in American history as one of the nation's worst years, marked by sky-high inflation that led to a seven-year financial slump. The seeds of the crisis were sown in the early 1830s, when the government sold vast tracts of public land to private individuals at knock-down prices in order to finance the expansion of the railway network and the building of the Erie Canal, which would connect New York City with the Great Lakes. But, contrary to what had been agreed, speculators then resold the land and made fabulous profits, and President Andrew Jackson was held responsible for an economy that had run amuck.

Rampant inflation of paper money ensued, and with no bullion reserves to back it up hundreds of banks collapsed. The fact that the different states did not have and were generally against a national financial system also played a part in causing undue losses and gains for banks and their customers.

Despite the financial chaos that reigned among the private banks, President Jackson was fiercely opposed to the only federal bank in operation, the Second Bank of the United States, in Philadelphia. Jackson believed that this bank was concentrating all finance on the East Coast, and it did not matter to him that it was partly government-owned. The president of the bank was the legendary Nicholas Biddle, reputed to be a consummate Renaissance man. Biddle was highly educated in the classics and had a keen academic mind; one minute he could be discussing the differences between ancient Greek and modern Greek dialects, the next having meetings with government leaders about the nation's finances. Both Francis Drexel and Nicholas Biddle were undeniably rare birds among the fauna of the world of finance, and proof of just what a weird and wonderful menagerie the banking business of the early nineteenth century could be.

During this time of economic crisis President Jackson found himself caught in an increasingly insoluble dilemma. Faced with a choice between the federal bank, run by Biddle, and the rogue private banks which he detested, the president reluctantly came down in favor of the latter. This he made dramatically clear when he vetoed the renewal of the federal bank's charter by Congress. When it was forced to close, a host of banking people saw their chance to profit from the vacuum thus created. Countless new banks opened up and the uncontrolled issuing of credit expanded to bursting point. As a result, President Jackson became more and more unpopular, and in 1835 he narrowly escaped being assassinated. An unemployed house painter tried to shoot the president while he was attending a funeral on Capitol Hill—a mite ironic when one considers that the president himself came from a humble background and saw himself as the voice of the common man.

The crisis reached its height in 1837 when the banks refused to accept what were often totally worthless banknotes and instead demanded settlement in gold or silver, both of which were in short supply. And this in the same year in which Peder Sather was for the first time able to call himself an exchange broker. Were John Farrar and his sole employee speculators, taking advantage of the crisis? Who can say?

In any case, 1837 marked a turning point for Peder Sather. It was now five years since he had left Norway; he was married and had a family, he had a job and a place to stay. That fall he received a visitor from his birthplace, Odalen, on the arrival in New York of nineteen-year-old Peder Olsen Dysterud, son of his sister Anne and Ole Dysterud, who had by then been a widower and the local mayor for a year. The young man stayed with his uncle until late fall, when he set out to travel west, across the state of Indiana to a Norwegian settlement near Chicago—a journey which, by horse and cart at such a chilly time of year, would take weeks. The young newcomer spoke no English, so Sather sent his nephew off in the company of an American who knew the country and supplied him with everything he needed in the way of clothes, provisions, money, and equipment.

What followed has been recounted in a history of Lake County in the state of Indiana, written by historian Timothy Ball and published in Chicago in 1872. Ball describes how an entry in one of the documents that formed the basis for his book had made him stop and wonder. The document in question was a report from the local Overseers of the Poor, dated Red Cedar Lake, January 1, 1838. In this report it was noted that four men, all of them named, had presented a request for the refund of thirty-one dollars. They claimed that they had had dealings with "a transient pauper" by the name of "Peter O. Dijsternd" and that they had thereby incurred expenses which they now expected the county to cover. Four accounts had been presented: one for the sum of thirteen dollars, one for twelve dollars, one for four dollars, and one for two dollars. The report stated that the Overseers of the Poor had reimbursed the men's expenses the very next day. Their demands were pretty barefaced, Ball thought, and rather suspicious. What was the real story behind this?

While Ball was pondering this report it dawned on him that he had actually witnessed the events described in it, on Christmas 1837, when he was eleven. That fall the Ball family had moved from New York to Red Cedar Lake, a small township south of Lake Michigan. The Balls were planning to open the township's first school. Mrs. Jane Ball had been educated at one of the best schools in Hartford, Connecticut, and her husband, Harvey, was a lawyer.

Timothy Ball was shocked by the report and saw it as his duty as a human being to record for posterity the real circumstances surrounding the request for payment made by these four men. The incident had been branded on his memory, he wrote. Ball went on to tell of a bitterly cold evening just before Christmas when a stranger from New York drove into Red Cedar Lake in a buggy. In the back he had a young man who had fallen seriously ill along the way. The young man was Norwegian, people in the township were told. He didn't know a word of English and was therefore unable to speak for himself. The two were just passing through, but his companion now felt that it would be unwise for the boy to continue. So he left him in the care of an acquaintance in Red Cedar Lake, a man named Aaron Cox. The other traveler left again that very same day, taking with him all of the sick Norwegian's belongings. Where he went no one ever knew.

In the course of the next few days, Peder Olsen Dysterud grew weaker and weaker; his chances of survival seemed slim. No one could understand what he tried to say and Aaron Cox just let him lie there, Ball writes. Four days later the nineteen-year-old was dead. Some of the men made him a rough wooden coffin. Eleven-year-old Timothy watched as four men carried the dead youth to a hastily dug hole in the woods, between a cedar tree and an Indian burial mound by the banks of Red Cedar Lake.

Timothy felt so sorry for this strange boy, falling ill with no one there to care for him, dying with no hand there to hold, and buried with no parent or friend present, in a land far from home, alone and forsaken by all. He was later to say that he had witnessed many burials in his life, but none as heart-breaking as this one.

Ball was furious when he realized who the men were who had made the claim for expenses. He felt they should all have been above such a thing, Aaron Cox included. Cox had left town shortly after Peder Olsen Dysterud's death, heading in the same direction as the boy's companion. When Cox returned he was extremely secretive, refusing to say where he had been, leading the townsfolk to suspect foul play of some sort.

Ball felt that the young Norwegian had been badly done by and totally misrepresented. Thirty-four years after the event he proposed to have his name deleted from the list of the paupers of Lake County. "Justice was not done to him by those in whose hands he died," he writes. "I claim for his memory and resting place the respect and care which are justly and richly due." He remembered the youth as being smartly dressed, very polite and well-mannered, quite clearly from a respectable, genteel family.

Only after he had been buried was it discovered that the Norwegian had an uncle in New York City. Some weeks later Peder received word that his nephew was dead, and, Ball tells us, he immediately set out on the long journey to Red Cedar Lake. The uncle spent a good while there and was anxious to know all the details of his nephew's illness, death, and burial. He visited the makeshift grave in the woods several times, paid the county for the little plot of land, and recompensed it for the money paid to the four men.

Ball describes the boy's uncle as "a broker of means, intelligence, and culture"; everyone in Red Cedar Lake found him to be courteous and gentlemanly, he says. This gentleman, he adds, had given him a slip of paper which he had kept all these years. On the slip were the following words: "Peter Sather, exchange broker, 164 Nassau Street, New York. Peder Olsen Dysterud, from Norway." Ball concludes this detailed account by reiterating what charming people both uncle and nephew had been. Ball then urges the authorities in Lake County to do everything in their power in the future to prevent anyone from being laid to rest in such an unworthy fashion as the solitary Norwegian.

That year, which had begun so well for Peder, thus ended in shock and horror. It would be months before anyone at home in Odalen learned what had happened to the lad. First, Peder Sather had to get back to New York. Then he had to write the difficult letter explaining how it had all come about. Then he would have to go down to the harbor and dispatch the letter on a ship which would sooner or later set course for Gothenburg. From there it would take days for the sad missive to be carried by boat up the coast to Christiania. A father would come out onto the front step, all unsuspecting, when he saw the postman swinging into the yard. Spring would be in the air, melting snow dripping from the roof, birdsong in the trees, the days growing longer and lighter. The branches would no longer be decked with white, but with green. Water gurgling under the ice on rivers and streams, everything would be fragrant and rippling. Did the postman bring a letter from America? Oh, perhaps some word from his son.

How hard Peder Sather had taken the death of his nephew only became clear some years later: in 1845 he had a son, his only son, and named him Peder Dysterud Sather.

FIVE

New Yorker and Norwegian

The Sather's daughter, Caroline Eugenia, was born in the house on James Street, July 28, 1836, at eight in the evening, according to the Sather family register. Such registers were public documents; they had grown out of a European tradition brought to America by immigrants in the seventeenth century. They provided the authorities with a clear account of the members of a household and of where a family was living when a new member was born. The entries in the Sather family register are neatly inscribed and surrounded by an ornamental border. From the handwriting it is clear that they have been made by two different people, but their identities are long forgotten. Peder Sather's name appears first, at the top of the page, and after his comes that of Caroline Eugenia, his firstborn.

Forty-six James Street was not such a shabby address, not when one considers who else was living in the building: for the most part merchants and grocers like Charles Farrar and his long-standing associate Henry Lyon. At the end of 1837 or the beginning of 1838 the Sathers moved, though, to a ground-floor apartment at 164 Nassau Street—the address given on the slip of paper handed to Timothy Ball by Peder Sather at Red Cedar Lake. So this was, in fact, his home address as well as his business address, which means that the family was virtually living in the bank, or rather, the broker's office. Peder Sather did not have far to go to work now; only a door separated him from his wife and children. The family register gives the same place of residence for the following year, and informs us that on Thursday, November 6, 1839, at ten in the morning—that is, during office hours—the Sathers' second child, Mary Augusta, was born there, in the small bedroom behind the broker's office.

After 1838 there is no trace of John Farrar in the employment records. Does this mean that he left the broker's office to his only employee? A court report cited in the *Weekly Herald* on December 25, 1841, may help to shed some light on this matter. The newspaper reported that James Gidelman, a relative of Elisa Bloom, the deceased and childless owner of 164 Nassau Street, had gone to court to have two tenants, Peder Sather and Martin Flowers, evicted. The latter ran a bar on the property, while exchange broker Peder Sather lived and worked there. Both of the premises in question were owned by John Farrar, and together they amounted to one-third of the building's space. So in actual fact, the newspaper explained, the lawsuit was being brought against John Farrar. But why did Farrar have to leave? Elisa Bloom's relative laid claim to the property on the grounds that the bill of sale was invalid.

The court report seems to suggest, therefore, that John Farrar rented the office to Peder Sather, who then ran it alone. Eventually the Sathers were evicted and had to move, this time just a little way down the street, to 69 Nassau Street. This was a basement flat, which leads one to believe that it was merely a temporary solution. Norwegian Søren Bache visited Peder Sather there and mentions it briefly in his diary. But how had John Farrar fared? Badly, I suspect. Before starting Farrar's Exchange he had tried his hand at one thing and another: he had been a lottery agent, we know, and done stints as a shopkeeper with Charles Farrar in South Street. In 1842 he appears on a list of bankrupts, and after that things went from bad to worse. Letters of Administration issued by the City of New York in 1849 name Samuel Farrar, then a lawyer, as executor of the estate of John Farrar (deceased), and state that any creditors should contact him. John Farrar left no will and it looks as though he may have died suddenly.

Peder Sather fared much better. According to Timothy Ball, by 1838 he was already a well-established exchange broker, and that in a city to which he had come only six years earlier and which boasted sixty-one banks. It is tempting to attribute his speedy rise to backing from his parents-in-law, but his first job as a lottery agent and the family's basement dwelling are hardly signs that they smoothed his path for him. On the other hand, he was in a good location, right next door to Wall Street, and ambition, flair, hard work, and luck must all have played their part.

Peder Sather was also a cultivated man, according to Timothy Ball. How can Ball have been so sure of this? After all, he was only eleven when the tragedy at Red Cedar Lake occurred, and Peder Sather was just twenty-seven when he visited the township. But the case had caused quite a stir in the little town, and fortunately another account of these events also exists, almost identical to

Ball's but including one additional interesting piece of information. Apparently it was Ball's parents who sent Sather word of his nephew's death, which means that they must have known him and known where he lived.

Timothy Ball was not, then, merely a chance witness to those events in the winter of 1837–38. And, since he would later become a well-known figure in Indiana, we also have recourse to his biography. Ball's parents were Baptists and so was their son. He was later ordained as a minister of the church, but also taught school in Red Cedar Lake and proved in fact to be such a good teacher that to this day the school bears his name: the Timothy Ball Elementary School. Jane and Harvey Ball and little Timothy had moved to the township from New York in 1837, so it seems quite likely that they knew of Sather's standing and his occupation through the Baptist Church. Not only that, but my research revealed that Jane Ball also hailed originally from Hartford; she was the second woman I had come across who was a native of this state, the first being Sarah. So Jane must have been the link between the Ball and the Sather families. This tells us not only where in Connecticut Sarah came from, but also which social class she belonged to. This might also explain Ball's indignant denunciation of the Overseers of the Poor Center Township—to give it its full name—thirty-four long years after the young man's death. How dared they call the nephew of the august Peder Sather a "transient pauper."

But if business was surpassing all expectations for Sather the exchange broker, sickness and death were casting shadows over his private life. Within three years he lost his sister Anne, who died in 1836, and saw her son suffer a tragic death after bidding farewell to his uncle in New York. As if that weren't enough, Peder and Sarah's firstborn, Caroline Eugenia, was handicapped due to a congenital curvature of the spine and before the end of 1841 two-year-old Mary Augusta was dead of dysentery, one of many dreaded diseases at that time. Death in early childhood was very common and women were said to bear their children with resignation and dread.

For Sarah this must have been a terrible time. When Mary Augusta died, Sarah was heavily pregnant with their third child, Josephine Frances, who was born on January 11, at ten in the evening in the apartment at 164 Nassau Street. The feud with Elisa Bloom's relatives must have been over, at least for a while.

It was nine years since Peder Sather had left Norway and Petrine, his daughter by Ingeborg Knutsdatter. Did he confide this secret to anyone? There is nothing to suggest that he did. He worked hard, he suffered from headaches, he had become a Baptist and a highly respected Christian; he had wanted to make a new life for himself. In just five hectic years the farmer's son had become a servant, the servant a lottery agent, and the lottery agent an exchange broker. The family's frequent changes of address testify to an unstable domestic situation and a daily life marked by somewhat fluid boundaries between Sather's work and his private life. The same could be said of many, but not of all. While Manhattan had become so overpopulated that immigrants were being put up in disused churches and breweries, Peder Sather was already enjoying another, very different life.

A new line of thought at that time advocated the benefits of keeping work and home life separate. A home should be a place where the head of the house could find rest, renewed energy, and a breath of fresh air. The middle classes had been steadily moving northward for some time, of course, but now they were also drawn to the idyllic countryside of Brooklyn—later considered to be America's first suburb. By 1840 approximately thirty-five thousand people were living out there, in row houses and detached homes with ivy-clad facades and small-paned windows, surrounded by neatly tended gardens and white picket fences. Most of the buildings were of brick, an expensive building material but resistant to fire, and among the mass of wood-frame buildings in Manhattan the danger of fire was ever present.

Only six months after their marriage in 1835 Peder and Sarah had witnessed one of the worst fires in the city's history. It started in a warehouse and, fanned by gale-force winds, rapidly spread until the conflagration covered seventeen blocks. It left almost seven hundred buildings in ruins, and the flames were so fierce that the glow from them could, it was said, be seen in Philadelphia. The firemen were assisted by reinforcements from other cities, but they could do little to help. The weather had been bitterly cold for some time and the East River was frozen over, something which rarely if ever happened. The firemen hammered away at the ice, desperately trying to get at the water, but when they did eventually manage to make a hole in it and start pumping, the water froze in the leather bags. Thousands were left homeless, and the material losses were colossal. To make matters worse, word spread afterward that the fire had been started deliberately.

There were, therefore, many good reasons for making one's home in Brooklyn, for those who could afford it. Among these were Charles Farrar and his wife, Mary, and the Sather family. In May to June of 1842 the Sathers moved to 111 Nassau Street—Nassau Street in Brooklyn, that is, not Manhattan: a number of streets had been called after counterparts in

Manhattan, thus forming a symbolic metropolitan connection. It wasn't as if they were living in the sticks.

But a new home brought with it additional financial responsibilities and Peder now saw fit to take on extra work, for a fellow Norwegian named Hans Rees, from Christiania, where Peder had worked as a sales clerk. Rees had been a shoemaker by trade when he came to New York in 1839 with his two brothers, one of them a saddler, the other a carpenter. According to the description in his passport Hans Rees was a strapping young man with thick dark hair, plump cheeks, and blue eyes. He and his brothers set up a leather goods business, with a shop and workshop at 49 Ferry Street. Here Peder Sather assisted him, probably with the accounts, and the fact that in 1845 the firm was registered "Rees and Sather" tells us that Peder had become a partner in it.

The two were more than just partners, though. Hans Rees was to become Peder's best friend in the Norwegian community. Like Peder, Hans soon found himself an American sweetheart, a young woman named Lucinda Krom, who was from a humble farming family in Ulster County in New York State.

Other than his brother-in-law Ole Dysterud Peder Sather had little or no contact with his family in Norway. But in New York he did not shun the company of other Norwegians. Sather was a gregarious character who became something of a social linchpin for fellow countrymen visiting New York or just passing through.

Peder Sather has left few traces of himself, even in literature pertaining to immigrants from Norway, but since I know, for example, that the family moved to Brooklyn around midsummer in 1842, I also know of at least one reliable source among his Norwegian visitors, namely Søren Bache, the man who had called on Peder at the basement apartment in Nassau Street in 1839. Bache was a farmer's son from Store Valle farm outside the town of Drammen, roughly forty miles from Christiania. He made three trips to America, visited Norwegian settlements, and kept a diary of his stays there. This was translated into English in 1951 under the title *A Chronicle of Old Muskego*.

Søren's father, Tollef Bache, was a wealthy farmer and timber merchant. He considered young Søren to be a bit of a layabout and felt that he might learn something from a trip to America. Tollef himself was a sworn adherent of the famous preacher Hans Nilsen Hauge, and became so taken up with the revival meetings which he organized at the farm that Mrs. Bache eventually rebelled and demanded a divorce.

Søren Bache sailed first class to New York in the spring of 1842, having been supplied by his father with a substantial sum of money and an English-speaking companion. According to his diary, he called on Peder Sather in Nassau Street every day while he was in the city. On June 6, Peder invited him over to Brooklyn; and since Bache notes in an entry from May 30 that the family was at that point living on Nassau Street in Manhattan, they must have been in the midst of moving during that period.

Bache did not make richly detailed notes, but he does tell us a few things, such as how, from the deck of the Brooklyn ferry, Peder Sather pointed out to him the house where he had been in service. On one trip to Brooklyn, on June 6, 1842, Søren Bache was accompanied by tanner Hans Rees. They spent the entire day there with the charming Sather family. Bache wrote in his diary: "That evening we returned home after enjoying the beauty of the day and the generosity of this rustic place. Many of the houses in Brooklyn are surrounded by beautifully planted trees."

The trees were doubtlessly beautifully planted, but surely there must have been other things to write about. While I am glad to have such a source as Søren Bache, I am bound to say that his diaries testify either to an awfully prosaic observer or a man with no gift for writing. He seems more concerned with making the acquaintance of successful Norwegians than in opening his mind to the new world. He is also much concerned with his trunks, which he finds it such hard work lugging about. After a dinner party he comments on the quality of the food served and makes much of his host's high social standing.

His notes on New York are like something straight out of a tourist brochure. The reader is informed that the city has one mayor and ten deputy mayors, and that City Hall is situated not far from Wall Street, as are the Stock Exchange and Astor House. These are diary entries, it's true, but Bache was intending to present the finished product as a memorandum to the Norwegian parliament! Tollef Bache could well have been right in thinking that his son had much to learn. But pride goes before a fall, and this I too must remember. Am I not writing a book about Peder Sather, a man who has, for generations, been as silent as the grave?

Søren Bache made his third trip to America in 1843, and again visited Peder Sather in Brooklyn, again remarking on the hospitality of the family and the beauty of the surroundings. Here I cannot help thinking of Sarah, who was pregnant with the couple's fourth daughter. Mary Emma, named after little Mary Augusta who had died, was born on September 24 at 111

Nassau Street, Brooklyn, at exactly 5:30 A.M. But Bache makes no mention of his hostess, the young mother with yet another baby on the way. There is not a word, either, about Caroline, the little handicapped girl, but he is pleased with the warm welcome and the attention he receives.

All doors seem to be open to Peder Sather in Brooklyn. He is a practicing Baptist, he has a wife and three daughters—Caroline Eugenia, Josephine Frances, and Mary Emma—he has a nice house, friends, and colleagues. He does not lie idle, this man; he crosses the East River every morning and evening on the ferry. But the Sabbath had to be honored and kept holy. Every Sunday he went to church, alone, because Sarah was not a Baptist. And after the service: blue skies and walks in the hills of Brooklyn. Did he still think of Petrine, did he know that she was growing up with a stonemason as stepfather, now that her mother Ingeborg, the former housemaid, was married?

The Sather family took on some help in the house, first one servant, then a second. Might one of them have been a governess, and the other possibly a trained nurse, to help Caroline Eugenia? And what about Sarah? I would like to have seen her out of doors, on those quiet residential streets, strolling along the paths with Peder on a Sunday afternoon, under a big, hot sun, with her bonnet dangling from one perspiring hand by its long ribbons, and wearing skirts so long and wide that no one could get past her. I imagine that the servants have been charged with keeping an eye on the children in the garden, finding them a place in the shade, feeding them lemonade and cake, rocking Mary Emma to sleep under an apple tree, and staying outside so long that the children are left fortified and freckled, brown and happy.

When the work week comes around again it's all "hush" and "Father's busy" if the children are awake when he comes home. In my mind's eye I can see him getting off the ferry, as the paddles come to a halt and the water stops frothing. He strides up Fulton Street and onto Nassau Street: tall, slim, and dark, wearing a knee-length waisted coat, tight-fitting trousers, and black lace-up boots, with his hat on his head or under his arm—dressed, in other words, like all other middle-class men in Manhattan. He was not a dandy, quite the opposite one might say. Born and bred in Odalen he still had something of the farmer in him. According to one letter, Peder Sather was a proud and principled man, exceedingly so at times.

In 1844 he still had no one working for him at the broker's office and had more than enough to do besides, what with acting as accountant for Hans Rees in Ferry Street as well. Rees too was making great strides, on all fronts. Hans Rees and Lucinda Krom were married on January 16. It was his leather business that had brought them together. Twenty-four-year-old Lucinda came from the little township of Shokan in Ulster County, which was surrounded by great forests consisting mostly of pine trees. Pine bark contained a substance that could be used in the tanning of hides and skins. This had made Shokan a center for the tanning industry, and several of Lucinda's sisters had married tanners. Eventually, though, the forests were decimated. Hundreds of tanners were left without work and many of them moved to New York.

Lucinda had eight brothers and seven sisters. One of her sisters was Jane Krom, born in Ulster County in 1824. And in January 1844 she became the sister-in-law of Hans Rees, Peder Sather's closest Norwegian friend. Peder must have met Jane at the wedding, if not before. She was a strong-minded young woman with a pert tongue and a mordant wit: Jane Krom was nobody's fool. She was also single. Sources say that she stayed with each of her married sisters in turn. This means that she would also have stayed with Hans and Lucinda. Through them she soon became a close friend of the Sathers in Brooklyn, where her sister and brother-in-law also moved—to Williamsburg to be exact.

Lucinda and Jane had grown up on a farm, where the family lived in a traditional stone house. The women spun, wove, and made all their clothes, which, in such a large family, must have been quite a job. According to some biographical notes they had a library consisting of thirty-eight books and several Bibles. That such information should have been handed down does make one think. Why should these particular details—a stone house, home crafts, books and Bibles—have been saved from oblivion? Possibly because they were so atypical of the time and the place. These things have been passed on by word of mouth and eventually someone has seen fit to write them down.

Shoemaker, tanner, and leather goods merchant Hans Rees, his brothers, and his sisters Lucinda and Jane Krom all became friends of exchange broker Peder Sather and his wife, Sarah. Over in Brooklyn, with the house constantly full of Norwegian-speaking guests, Sarah must have felt like a complete foreigner. Or did she learn Norwegian? And what about the Krom sisters? It is a known fact that Hans and Lucinda visited Norway more than once. The thought that Jane might have spoken Norwegian is an alluring one. Did it surprise Sarah that Peder never went back to Odalen, or took her to see his native land? He could have done, if he had wanted to—he could certainly afford it.

In 1845 Hans and Peder were still working together on Ferry Street, but on Nassau Street new opportunities were knocking on the door. The broker's office was no longer simply offering exchange services; its activities were becoming more and more bank-related. The economy was booming. The building at 164 Nassau Street was under new ownership, and in 1846 it was completely renovated and had three new floors added to it. Peder Sather obtained a permanent lease on his ground-floor premises and hired his first member of staff, thirty-one-year-old bachelor Edward W. Church, born in New Jersey and living at 438 Pearl Street in Manhattan. In his passport he is described as a tall, thin, dark man with a lantern jaw, narrow brow, and ruddy cheeks. Prior to this he had worked for some years for Sather's friend and mentor Charles Farrar, on South Street. Peder made Edward a partner in the business, thereby endowing it both with an injection of fresh capital and a new name: Sather & Church.

The business expanded and so too did the Sather family. On Friday, October 3, 1846, at 8:20 in the evening, Sarah gave birth to a baby boy, Peder Dysterud Sather, named after his cousin, who had been named after his grandfather in Norway. Peder junior, a boy with three sisters, a son. By then the family had moved again, this time to 81 Pineapple Street, high up on Brooklyn Heights, the best neighborhood in Brooklyn. From there one had a panoramic view of Manhattan and the East River, and it was only a short cab ride down to the harbor and the ferries that sailed several times an hour.

Edward W. Church said goodbye to bachelorhood two months before Peder became a father for the fifth time. On August 14, 1846, he married Letitia H. Pearsall, an elegant New York girl. It was not long before the Churches, too, would move to Brooklyn, not far from the Sathers and the Farrars.

These really were new times. The seven years of depression, with a sagging national economy and a general financial slump, were finally at an end. Nassau Street was alive with hackney cabs and newspaper boys, bookshops and concert houses, taverns and offices—and all manner of clubs and societies. Number 142 was the home of the Anti-Slavery Society. Slavery was still sanctioned in the southern states, and represented a constant source of discord and tension between north and south. It had been abolished in New York State in 1827, but black people were still being discriminated against.

In 1840 the Anti-Slavery Society began to publish a newspaper, the *National Anti-Slavery Standard,* edited by the writer Lydia Child, the most famous human rights and antislavery campaigner of the day. Peder Sather was not unmoved by the newspaper's message and the society's adept moving spirit. He was an avowed opponent of the slave trade in the South and of any discrimination against black people.

Lydia Child was a highly influential public figure, who moved in the same circles as leading politicians, cultural figures, and artists. One of these was the famous Norwegian violinist Ole Bull, who toured America several times and always gave a number of concerts in New York. Lydia Child wrote ecstatic articles about his virtuoso performances and the two became close friends after he visited her at 142 Nassau Street in 1843. Sather's office was only a few doors further down the street, and Ole Bull and Peder Sather met and became friends—an interesting alliance. Ole Bull was no puritan, no moralist, no faithful father, no self-sacrificing husband and breadwinner. He was an impulsive adventurer who could be on cloud nine one minute and down in the dumps the next. He would often include popular melodies in his program, bringing the house down with tunes such as "Yankee Doodle." He was a handsome man who had the ladies swooning in their seats. And afterward, there was always a party, and people flocked around Ole Bull eager to hear his fantastical tales from around the world. This man became Peder Sather's friend, a fact which prompts the question: behind the dignified mask, was Sather, too, a bit of an adventurer and a complex character?

And another thing I would like to mention, if only to better place Peder Sather in his setting and time. Right next door to the exchange broker's at 164 Nassau Street were the offices of the small newspaper the *New York Aurora,* which, in 1842, secured the services of a young writer by the name of Walt Whitman to be its leading editor. Peder Sather must have seen Whitman nearly every day. Whitman was an extremely productive editor, and wrote innumerable articles himself, particularly on slavery and immigration. He was as fierce in his denunciation of the former as he was in his defense of the latter. Eventually he was fired, not because of *what* he wrote, but *when* he did so. Because Walt Whitman had an incorrigible habit of turning up at the newspaper office at the most irregular times: seldom in the mornings, occasionally around noon, but most likely not until well into the afternoon.

Whitman had grown up in Brooklyn. He moved back there in 1846 and spent two years as editor of the local newspaper the *Brooklyn Daily Eagle.* So after working in Nassau Street for some years he was now living, like the Sather family, in Brooklyn Heights. The population of Brooklyn rose sharply in the 1840s and, while I don't want to be accused of indulging in unjustifiable wild flights of fancy, I do like to think that over the years Sather's and Whitman's paths may occasionally have crossed, on the omnibus down to the ferry landing, on the ferry, walking up Fulton Street and onto Nassau Street. In *Leaves of Grass,* published in Brooklyn Heights in 1855, there is a famous poem which paints a wonderful picture of the trip by ferry across the East River. The poem, "Crossing Brooklyn Ferry," consists of twelve stanzas, and I would love to quote them all here. This poem has provided me with the most vivid source from which to form an image of the ferries, the people and the towns on both sides of the East River. Whitman scans the ample hills of Brooklyn, the gray walls of the granite storehouses by the docks; he shows us the numberless masts of ships on the river, the sailors at work in the rigging, the flags of all nations, the white sails of schooners and sloops, and the fires from the foundry chimneys burning high into the night. On the deck of the ferry sit Peder Sather, Edward Church, Hans Rees, Lucinda, Jane, Charles Farrar and his wife, Mary—and Walt Whitman. They sit there taking it all in, and the poet sits there thinking of them and all the other ferry passengers:

> how curious you are to me!
> On the ferry-boats, the hundreds and hundreds that cross,
>   returning home, are more curious to me than you suppose;
> And you that shall cross from shore to shore years hence, are more
>   to me, and more in my meditations, than you might suppose.

But no, Peder Sather never did meet Walt Whitman, or at least, I've found no evidence that he did. There is, however a documented link between a later close friend of Peder, George Childs, and Walt Whitman. George Childs (1829–94) was a bookseller and publisher in New York before becoming editor of the Philadelphia newspaper the *Public Ledger.* Childs turned this newspaper into the biggest and best in the country and became a legendary publicist. He was extremely well read, had a huge library, and was a charismatic key figure in political, financial, literary and artistic circles—a member of the country's elite. He was on close terms with the great writers of the day, such as Henry Wadsworth Longfellow, Charles Dickens—and, yes, Walt Whitman. *Leaves of Grass* was to become an international literary classic, but it received a mixed reception when it was first published. Childs recognized the outstanding quality of Whitman's poetry right away, though, and was full of admiration for his vibrant language, his modern style, and surprising

FIGURE 8. George Childs (left) and Anthony Joseph Drexel (right).
George Childs (1829–94) was editor of the Philadelphia newspaper
Public Ledger; Anthony J. Drexel (1826–93) was a banker, philanthro-
pist, and founder of Drexel University, Philadelphia. Both of them were
Peder Sather's close friends. Courtesy of the Drexel Collection, Drexel
University, Philadelphia.

choice of subject matter. He told the debutant poet this, gave him money, and
invited him to his home.

All the news of the day was reported from Nassau Street. In the latter half
of the 1840s nine newspapers had their offices there. The *New York Daily
Globe* was at number 164, the *New York Tribune* at 154, and elsewhere in the
street one had the *Evening Mirror,* the *Evening Post,* the *Morning Star,* the
New York Express, the *New York Herald,* the *Sun,* and the *True Sun.* It
was during these years—if not before—that Peder Sather's sense of social

commitment was aroused. Knowledge and culture had been of prime importance in his childhood home and his brother-in-law Ole Dysterud, with
whom he was by now corresponding, was a good friend of Henrik Wergeland,
Norway's most original writer and social commentator. Was money as
important as life itself to exchange broker Peder Sather? A fool may answer
more questions in an hour than a wise man can answer in seven years.

SIX

A Specimen of the Gold

In 1847, after fifteen years in the United States, Peder Sather became an American citizen. When you consider that an immigrant could apply for citizenship after just four or five years, he does not seem to have been in any hurry to take this step. And this could make one wonder whether his farewell to Norway had been as full and final as the information given to the immigration authorities in 1832 would have it. But by the late 1840s Peder Sather was so established that he can scarcely have envisaged having any future in Norway, where poverty and hardship drove thousands to emigrate.

Meanwhile, things were looking up in America. By 1847 the depression of President Jackson's time was a thing of the past. In the construction industry business was booming, thanks to the large-scale development of roads, canals, and railway lines. A new, modern age was on the way, and Americans regarded Europe, with its monarchies and feudal traditions, as hopelessly old-fashioned. Numerous government envoys came across to report on the American system of government, among them lawyer Ole Munch Ræder, who was sent from Norway to America to study the judicial system. Born in Kongsvinger near Odalen in 1815, Ræder had attended the Cathedral School in Trondhjem while Peder Sather was working in the bank there, so the two may have known one another from Norway.

Ræder arrived in New York in 1847. After paying a visit to Adam Løwenskiold, the Norwegian-Swedish consul general in the city, he embarked on a tour of the country. He recorded his observations on the land and the people in a series of letters that were published in the newspaper *Den Norske Rigstidende* and later collected in a book entitled *America in the Forties*. Of Norwegians immigrating to America he writes that they appeared to be welcomed with open arms and that they were quick to learn English and settle in there. They had no plans to return to Norway, even though they were often homesick. They seemed to take no great interest in politics, were much more taken up with their families and their work, and tended to keep to the Norwegian settlements, like that of Muskego in Wisconsin.

As a banker and a New Yorker, Peder Sather had taken a different road, although his friendships with other Norwegians in the city are proof that Norway was not a closed chapter for him. Nonetheless, as a new-fledged American citizen he had made a choice crucial to his future—and this was looking bright. Sather & Church was doing so well that they had taken on another member of staff, the young lawyer Luther Spaulding Lawrence. Luther, who came from Pepperell, Massachusetts, was Charles Farrar's nephew and lived with him in Brooklyn. The bank was small enough, though, not to appear on those lists of Manhattan banks that I have looked at. Even so, it provided Peder with a decent livelihood and ensured that he and his family did not have to worry about money.

Since the Sathers had moved there from Manhattan the population of Brooklyn had more than trebled, rising from thirty thousand to almost one hundred thousand in 1850. Many of the new residents were immigrants who, like Peder, had done so well for themselves that they could afford to buy a house there. Brooklyn was a town now, and 1847 saw the opening of its first park, Fort Greene Park. Its first school for black children was opened that same year. The credit for both the park and the school belonged largely to Walt Whitman, for his tireless efforts and countless newspaper articles in support of both projects. Whitman lived near the park himself, as did the Sather family; Fort Greene Park was only a few minutes' walk from Willoughby Street where the Sather family was now living, at number 81, with the Farrars as near neighbors.

The Sathers' eldest daughter required constant medical care, and from hints dropped in correspondence between a husband and wife who knew the Sather family it would appear that Caroline Eugenia spent spells in a succession of sanatoriums and hospitals. There was also a terrible dread at that time of infectious diseases, and the middle classes were much preoccupied with diet, fresh air, and hygiene. Ole Munch Ræder writes that there were two groups who tended to be regarded as dirty: the Irish and the Norwegians. But Ræder says nothing here of the inherent social and economic differences: of the immigrant communities, the Irish and Norwegian were among the poorest. Peder Sather was not one of them, however, and remarks made in the aforementioned letters indicate that he took care to eat fruit and vegetables and to go for walks on Sundays. The residents of Brooklyn now also had access to clean drinking water from the new Croton reservoir north of New York, and with a complete drainage and sewer system Brooklyn was less vulnerable to epidemics than large areas of Manhattan. In an age with no antibiotics or penicillin, to fall prey to sickness or one of the many diseases that were rife back then often meant certain death. The Sathers could not, therefore, have chosen a safer place to settle in than Brooklyn.

And yet all was not right. Peder Sather had begun to suffer from loss of appetite and would wake in the night bathed in sweat. He also coughed constantly, as if he had a cold that never got better. He chose to put it down to overexertion and began to take a day or two off every now and again. From May to September, especially, when the heat was at its most oppressive, it was all he could do just to get to the office. He was subject to more and more frequent bouts of fever and was sometimes confined to bed for weeks, too feeble even to hold a pen. The doctors he consulted eventually had to conclude that he was showing all the symptoms of tuberculosis. No drug existed to combat the disease, and the only remedy they could advise was a lengthy stay in a more clement climate. The best thing would have been for him to move away altogether. The winters in Brooklyn were bitterly cold and the summers scorching. He told friends that he was thinking of going to Norway; a few weeks of sea air might cure him. But he couldn't sit on the deck of a ship forever, hoping to get well, and so he dismissed this idea. That he actually went so far as to consider leaving his family shows just how serious things were, but it is also an indication of how strong the ties with Norway still were.

Sarah and the children were now in danger of losing husband, father, and breadwinner. As a last resort, therefore, the doctors recommended that Sather go to California, where the climate was mild all year round and ideal for him. They believed it would be best if he were to live there permanently, but a lengthy stay would also do him good. From the mid-nineteenth century onward many TB sufferers traveled to California on doctor's orders and reports from these invalids were clear and unequivocable: their health was permanently improved.

Until 1847, California had belonged to Mexico, but after a brief war in 1848 the region promptly passed into the hands of the Americans, and after that it was only a matter of time before the former Mexican province became the thirty-first state of the Union. Mexico had not cared much about this outpost of its territory and considered it no great loss. Neither the Mexicans nor, for that matter, the Americans thought it likely that anyone would settle in this wasteland in the foreseeable future. In 1847, on the spot where San Francisco would one day lie, there was only a little fishing village called Yerba Buena, after a sweet-smelling herb that grew in those parts.

Peder Sather could not bear the thought of going to California, even though he might have to. How was he supposed to live there—by hunting and fishing? And where would he live? In a tent? Or a log cabin? Apart from scattered tribes of Indians, Mexican mission stations and a handful of fishing villages, California was nothing but wilderness and wild mountain ranges. He had no wish to go there alone, and taking his family with him was out of the question. He could hardly expect Sarah to leave her family and friends on the East Coast. Peder Sather, in Brooklyn before the midpoint of the century, was gaunt and sallow, cooped up behind brick walls overrun by rambling roses, a sick and dying husband and father, and not yet forty. He had an ominously high temperature, a cough that never let up, and phlegm and blood in a basin on the floor next to him in bed, on freezing winter nights when no amount of blankets could warm him and in summer under a sheet hot and clammy as a sheepskin. Who would look after Sarah and the children? What was he to do?

The journey to California was in itself daunting enough to deter anyone from following doctor's orders. It took six months by boat, round Cape Horn; it would be sheer madness to take the alternative route through the Straits of Panama. Of those who had tried the latter many had died of tropical diseases, physical exhaustion, or venomous snake, reptile, or insect bites. Better, then, to put one's life in the Lord's hands and stay in Brooklyn.

Eighteen forty-eight was an election year in America and this overshadowed most other matters. The incumbent Democratic president, James Polk, who had waged war against Mexico, had promised that he would not run again if he won the war. And he was true to his word, so the Democrats chose Lewis Cass as their presidential candidate to stand against the Whig candidate, Zachary Taylor. The Whig Party had been formed in 1833 as a protest against President Andrew Jackson's economic policy. The Whigs were fiercely opposed to the admission of California into the Union; like the Mexicans, they regarded this stretch of the West Coast as an absolutely worthless wasteland. For tactical reasons, though, they went along with it. Zachary Taylor was not the ideal presidential candidate, he had only been nominated in the first place because he had been a general in the war and could attract votes. He had no political experience, either, but by the September, to everyone's surprise, he looked set to win the election. The *New York Herald* gave the whole of its front page to this sensational news for several days running and devoted countless column inches to the story in the days that followed. So, on September 15, very few people noticed a brief item at the back of the *Herald* in which the newspaper's editors apologized for an oversight. The item read: "INTERESTING FROM CALIFORNIA—We have received some late and interesting intelligence from California. It is to the 1st of July. Owing to the crowded state of our columns, we were obliged to omit our correspondence. It relates to the important discovery of a very valuable gold mine. We have received a specimen of the gold." The gold had actually been discovered back in the February, at Sutter's Mill, a sawmill roughly 110 miles northeast of Yerba Buena, the fishing village which had been renamed San Francisco after the war with Mexico. But the news had taken a long time to travel all the way from there to the East Coast, and was drowned by all the coverage of the forthcoming election. Space in the newspapers not taken up by the presidential election was filled by reports on crises and revolutions in Europe. There was outright war in Italy, rebellion against the king in France, and the most terrible famine in Ireland. Reports on developments in Europe hit the streets only hours after the ships sailed into port with the mail. Few people remarked on the news from California simply because it was marginalized by other goings-on.

That fall, more pieces about the discovery of gold appeared in the press, but still no one realized the magnitude of this news. Those who did comment on it paid little regard to the actual worth of the gold. Journalists were more interested in the extra income it would generate for eastern merchants, through the sale of provisions and equipment to the prospectors. To whet the appetite the papers cited the rumor that a shovel that cost ninety cents in New York could fetch ten dollars in California!

In Washington, too, it took the politicians a while to catch on to what was happening. Some of them believed that unemployment on the East Coast would fall if people left en masse for California, while others detected in the discovery of gold a good argument for reviving Nicholas Biddle's old idea about a state-owned national bank. Had such an institution been in existence the authorities could have cleared the debt incurred due to the war with Mexico. Comments on the find were, on the whole, sparse; varied widely in content; and if the subject of California did come up in the political debate, the focus tended to be on the question of how the new state ought to be governed.

By 1848, thirty-eight-year-old Peder Sather was so weak that there were fears for his life. To make matters worse he had also succumbed to a bout of cholera. But he knew that gold had been discovered and that many New Yorkers were now planning to head west. One day he received a visit from his friend Anthony Lewis Tasheira, an iron founder who had worked for some years in a foundry producing pipes and faucets for the drinking water supply from the Croton reservoir. Anthony never worked less than ten hours a day and earned no more than three to four dollars a week. The foundry was owned by a friend of his, William Metcalf, but Metcalf was in serious financial difficulties. Creditors were queuing up, demanding to have their accounts settled on the spot, and he was soon forced to shut up shop. This left Anthony out of work and with no idea of how he was supposed to manage. He was in his mid-twenties, married to an English girl, London born Eliza Stanley. The Tasheiras had three young children: ten-year-old Harriet, four-year-old Lewis, and two-year-old George. Since the death of his father, an alcoholic cabinetmaker, Anthony had also been supporting his widowed mother, who now lived next door to him and his family on Downing Street, which lay in one of the worst neighborhoods on the Lower East Side.

The young iron founder sat there in the parlor in Brooklyn, dreading the prospect of his children having to grow up on Downing Street. He wanted to ask his friend what he thought of his going to California to prospect for gold. And Peder Sather told Anthony that if *he* were as hard-up he would not hesitate to go. And that being the case he had a mind to help the poor man on his way by paying his fare for him.

Anthony sailed home on the ferry and presented Sather's offer to Eliza. They agreed that he should accept it, since he could never afford to go otherwise. The really poor never made it to California during the Gold Rush. In his book *The Public City,* historian Philip Ethington says that this ticket to the West Coast functioned as a social filter. It was one of the main reasons that class boundaries in San Francisco in the 1850s were fluid and difficult to define: here one had no distinct lower or upper class as one had in the cities on the east coast. Because the well-to-do did not get caught up in the race to find gold—they had no need to—they did not head west.

On March 10, 1849, twenty-seven-year-old Anthony Lewis Tasheira said goodbye to Eliza, the children, and his mother and boarded the *SS Helena.* None of them knew whether they would ever see one another again; the sea voyage was dangerous and no one had any idea what to expect in California. The New York Port Authority records state that there were 150 passengers on board the *SS Helena,* not many compared to what would soon become the norm. On August 23, after a six-month voyage that took it round Cape Horn, the ship slid through the Golden Gate and soon afterward Anthony Lewis Tasheira was striding down the gangway in San Francisco. A number of buildings had already shot up around the harbor: boarding houses, grocery stores, hardware stores, saloons, and a post office. Other than that, the place consisted of nothing but huddles of tents among the windswept sand dunes and a mission station, the Mission Dolores, where Franciscan friars worked among the rows of potatoes and other vegetables in the kitchen garden when they weren't preaching the gospel to a handful of Indians.

What were meant to be streets and roads were no more than alleys, ditches, and foul-smelling cattle tracks, and all of them were drenched in sand—fine and silvery, coarse and gritty—that swirled and flurried in the wind off the Pacific and rasped like gravel between your teeth if it got into your mouth. Anthony trudged doggedly along the waterfront, making for the post office, a low wooden building built out of roughly hewn planks. He wanted to send a letter to Eliza to let her know he had arrived safely. To his surprise he found a letter waiting there for him; it had been carried on another, speedier ship: wind and weather could make a big difference to the length of a sea voyage. Anthony instantly recognized the handwriting on the envelope: it was Peder Sather's. He had sent the letter so that Anthony would not feel totally alone when he landed in San Francisco.

Anthony Lewis Tasheira wasted no time in setting off on horseback for a mining camp at Tuolumne, a county some miles east of San Francisco. He spent a year there before returning to his family on Downing Street for a little while. Then he set off for California again, this time having arranged that Eliza and the children would join him once he had managed to save some money and find them a place to live. In the meantime, Anthony and Eliza wrote lots of letters to each other, she more than him, in the long quiet evenings when the children were in bed. Their correspondence is in the collections of the Californian State Library in Sacramento. This collection also contains three letters from Peder to Anthony, including the one mentioned earlier. Equally interesting are the unique glimpses that Eliza provides into the life of Peder Sather and his family in their home in Brooklyn, which she visited often with her children.

Apart from a few typewritten transcriptions, all of the letters in the collection are the original documents, handwritten and sometimes difficult to read. This is particularly true of Eliza's letters. She seems to have attached much less importance to the aesthetic appearance of the letters than Anthony did. He writes in an even, clear, and elegant script, although he feels that he writes very badly and excuses this by explaining that his fingers are swollen and stiff when he gets back to his cabin after twelve hours of laboring in the gold fields.

Peder Sather seems to write very freely, in a large, slanting hand that often allows for no more than a few words to a line. The word *whether* is consistently misspelled *wether,* a tiny mistake in letters that in all other ways show that Peder Sather's written English was excellent, but that still betray he was not an American. Three friends, three handwriting styles: one emphatic and impetuous, the second neat and elegant, the third practiced and flowing. The person who seems to weigh his words most carefully is Peder Sather. He deletes words and phrases he is not happy with, or parts of sentences that are going in a direction he no longer wants to take. It doesn't happen often, but it does happen. His letters are usually short and to the point, possibly written in haste in order the catch the mail steamer—the passenger ship which carried the mail to San Francisco.

A picture of Anthony Lewis Tasheira shows a young, dark-haired man, pale and somber, heavily built, cleanly dressed, already balding, and looking very much alone. The letters give no hint as to how the young founder met Peder Sather, but a remark about going to church might suggest that Anthony was also a Baptist. Frances Trollope wrote of American churches in which high and low sat side by side in the pews, who otherwise had nothing to do with one another, but this was not the case with Anthony Tasheira and Peder Sather. They were good friends and on high days and holidays such as Christmas or the Fourth of July the Tasheiras were always invited over to Brooklyn. I have not, however, come across any instances of the entire Sather family visiting Downing Street; Peder always went there alone.

Still, though, there is something baffling about this friendship. The tone of Sather's letters to Anthony is remarkably formal. It may be that this was the way in which men wrote to one another in those days—there is not much of a personal nature in Anthony's letters either. There is, however, a more obvious and quite central explanation: Peder Sather is writing as a person of some standing to an extremely grateful iron founder.

The difference in Peder's and Anthony's social stations was too great for this friendship to have come about simply as a matter of course, and the unearthing of one clue can have a sort of domino effect, leading to the discovery of a whole series of illuminating facts. In this case the trigger was an entry in the 1860 census, which revealed that Harriet had been born in 1839, and not in Manhattan but in Bridgeport, Connecticut: the third time that a trail had been traced back to this particular state; the first two having led to Peder's wife, Sarah, and to Jane Ball, the mother of historian Timothy Ball.

A fourth discovery, pertaining this time to Eliza Tasheira, also led back to Connecticut. In April 1832 she married William Bostwick Kirtland. The wedding took place in Bridgeport, only a few days before Peder and Sarah were married in Manhattan. Kirtland was a businessman from Bridgeport and came from a wealthy family which was linked by marriage to the Thompson family. The Thompson men held a variety of top posts in banking and commerce. One of these was Joseph Thompson, born in 1806. Thompson was the town druggist and he was married to Harriet Maria Kirtland, also born in Bridgeport in 1808. To cut a long story short: Joseph and Harriet Kirtland were William B. Kirtland's uncle and aunt. Within only a couple of days of each other, Peder Sather from Norway and Eliza Stanley from England had both married into the same large Bridgeport family.

In Eliza's case her marriage ended rather dramatically. Harriet, her daughter, was only five when Eliza sued William for divorce. Her first marriage may not have gone well, but Eliza was used to being well off financially, so being wed to Anthony really must have put her to the test. And he was a widow when they met, with two little boys from his first marriage to support: Lewis, born in 1845, and George, born in 1847.

In other words, in 1849 Anthony and Eliza were still relatively newly wed, and in Brooklyn Peder and Sarah were working on plans to help them out of their financial difficulties and, not least, to restore Eliza's social status. California's gold provided the solution. But it was no easy task that lay ahead of Anthony when he set sail from New York in March 1849.

The first letter from Peder Sather is dated May 26, 1849, at which point Anthony would have been on board the SS *Helena* for over two months and still had to round Cape Horn. Sather begins the letter "My dear Sir," almost as if he were writing a business letter. When writing to a close friend it might have been more natural to say, "My dear Anthony." In the letter's first lines Sather refers to himself in the plural—using what we call "the royal we"— and continues to use this form throughout, again as if he were writing to a fellow businessman. Here, in its entirety, is the letter of welcome which was waiting for Anthony when he arrived in San Francisco that August and was tucked away in his inside pocket when he rode off to Tuolumne.

New York, May 26th 1849

Mr A. L. Tasheira, my dear Sir,

With the intention of forwarding by the Ship Jaleon, which sails tomorrow, we have now thought to write to you, so that you may feel better when you arrive at San Francisco. I send herewith also your Passport, which did not arrive from Washington till several days after you had sailed.

Your family I am happy to say is very well, which you will probably see from your wife's letter, which I expect to get today and enclose with this.

An extract of a letter from a passenger on board the Ship Helena appeared in the Herald one day last week, which had been thrown on board of a Brig that had (been) in sight. I think it was dated April 10th, but am not certain, as I have mislaid the paper. This item informed us of the rappid [sic] progress your fine ship had made, stating that she made about 1500 miles the first week after leaving this port, also that she had made some days as many as 280 miles, meaning of course 24 hours. Reporting all well, but one passenger sick. This was the first we had heard of the Helena since she left, and it was very gratifying to see that she had proved herself, as we expected, a fine sailor.

Letters from California continue to be published from all quarters, and as regards the matter of Gold—all very generally agree in their statements, this leaving not a shadow of a doubt, about the unexpectable [sic] abundance of this metal.

We have not really had a direct account, nor reliable, about the state of the market for goods. Some letters have been published . . . representing the influx of merchandise so great that goods are actually selling in San Francisco at ordinary N.Y. prices and in the mines only at a small advance. How true it is, one cannot of course know and still it renders generally unsatisfactory and unadviceable [sic] to think of sending Goods, without knowing something definite to rely on.

The accounts we have had during the last few weeks have also been very extraordinary in regard to real Estate or Lots. It has been stated in several letters that building lots in the town are selling for from $5000 to $50000. This looks to me exceedingly absurd—even more so, than that goods should be as cheap there as here. A large overstock would naturally produce the latter, but I can conceive no . . . cause for so great a rise in Lots. Should there however be any truth in this, then I should think that it will be difficult to have a spot on any reasonable terms, where business can be done. I am therefore on this point entirely in the dark, and do not consider that it would be good policy to forward goods, haphazard, until I know what is convenient and proper.

When you have been there a while, you will soon discover what you can do among them, and then carefully inform me what kinds of articles will be the best for your purpose in that market. Should I in the meantime however receive letters from any of those which I am acquainted with who are gone there, I may send an invoice, and if so I should immediately on so doing write to you by mail, in order that you would have the letter several weeks before the arrival of the goods.

From the accounts which we have had lately, it appears that ships cannot get up to San Francisco to within half a mile. If this be so, I have my doubt, wether [*sic*] the present location will not be changed for another place on the Bay, which may be found more accessible for the Shipping. It will do no harm to have this in mind, and if any such movement should be attempted, I should not wonder if it would prove successful.

You will recall that I spoke to you about Capt. Simmons, who, as I understood, owns considerable Land about the Bay of San Francisco. He left N. York before you did, destined to San Francisco with his family, so Mr. Taylor, a neighbor, told me at that time. Mr. Taylor promised to give me a letter of introduction for you. He has since given up business, and I regret much that I cannot forward an introduction letter to Capt. Simmons. I think however that should it so be that you might wish to see him, you will be able to find him. As from Mr. Taylor's remark, he is not only a kind and clever person, he will be happy to afford information to any Respectable individual. I have written to Mr. Parker which I shall also send by this mail. You will have a letter to him, also if he may not be there much before you.

To Mr. Dometius, the Norwegian, who went out in the John P. Cutler, I soon want to send a few words. Your wife has just been here with the letter. She told me that she saw in the process account of the Helena from Rio that the Ship John P. Cutler had not departed. I shall therefore not write to him this time.

When she arrives at San Francisco, go on board and enquire for Dometius. I think you will find him. My health is not as good since the warm weather set in. I suffer very much from headaches.

Many sincere wishes for your future prosperity, and may God in his mercy bless you with health and keep you safe. He alone can protect us in any place, and He alone wherever we may be. Only trust in Him.

Most truly, yours P. Sather.

It is clear from this letter that Peder Sather knew several people who had already gone west. The Mr. Parker he mentions was William Parker, a gentleman who had gone to San Francisco to open a hotel there; he named it the St. Francis, considered by many to have been the first hotel in the city.

The letter also confirms that Sather had other Norwegian friends in New York besides the Rees brothers, among them the Captain Dometius whom he mentions and who was most probably Henrik Dometius, the son of a ship broker. What Sather did not yet know was that Captain Dometius's ship had left New York but had run into difficulties and sunk. Captain Dometius was among the dead; his body was never found.

Peder Sather appears to have been well informed on the situation in California, and, like others on the East Coast at that time, less interested in gold than in the prospects for trade. He wants Anthony to consider trying something in this line and provides him with a detailed description of the commercial possibilities as he sees them.

But Anthony had no chance to embark on any sort of business venture. He worked himself half to death in Tuolumne and was glad if he made two or three dollars a day. The only food he could afford to eat was bread he baked himself. Eliza was horrified when she read in the papers that there had been outbreaks of typhus and cholera among the prospectors, and that murder, robbery, and lynchings were common, as were clashes with the Indians. All of this was true. Anthony was not at all happy in what was, to him, a brutal world of gamblers, crooks, and drunks. He was a strict teetotaler, and for the most part kept to himself. Anthony in a draughty wooden shack in Tuolumne; Eliza in a slum in Manhattan; a wealthy but sick Peder Sather in Brooklyn. Eliza was afraid that their benefactor would die. Each time she stepped onto the East River ferry she feared that this was it, this time he would be gone, the only person she could turn to and trust.

SEVEN

A Particular Friend

By the spring of 1850 Peder Sather was so ill that he was unable to work and was confined to bed for several weeks. He hadn't the strength to write letters and apologized to Eliza on one of her frequent visits for not having dropped a line to Anthony. That evening she wrote to her husband:

> I went over to show him your letters and it relieved his mind greatly to hear your health was so good, as he had learnt of sickness and diseases among the miners from the newspapers. He asked me to tell that if you would spend about $1 per week on vegetables you would be sure to escape the dysentery and other illnesses. Mr. Sather is perfectly the gentleman in all his dealings with me, and evinces upon every occasion the greatest consideration for my feelings, my dread and my longing, and the utmost concern about you, so fearful you should neglect any precaution to preserve your health and seems perfectly satisfied if he can only learn you are well.

Sather had by now received reports from a number of acquaintances who had gone to San Francisco. Among these were Henry Wells and William Fargo, who had already opened a bank in Montgomery Street, the Californian city's main street. There was a big demand for loans as well as for depositing facilities and a gold exchange. A city was springing up and there was a market for everything. Building materials were almost impossible to come by. Before William Parker and his wife left New York they shipped the prefabricated sections for their hotel to San Francisco so that it could be erected as quickly as possible. The St. Francis Hotel was a wooden building which rapidly became too small and had to be extended by means of a makeshift annex with a canvas roof and walls. It was known as a stylish establishment that attracted a clientele which had the money to pay to stay there for long spells.

During the two years since gold had first been found, San Francisco had changed beyond all recognition. Thousands of young men had journeyed west on overcrowded ships, often with nothing but the clothes on their backs. No sooner had they stepped ashore and loaded up on supplies then away they went, taking the riverboats up to the mining camps in the Sacramento Valley or hitching rides to the foot of the Sierra Nevada Mountains. Sailors jumped ship and went off with the passengers, leaving hundreds of vessels to languish in the harbor dock, some for months, others until they sank or were turned into floating hotels.

The new arrivals all needed somewhere to stay, and that included those who had spied an opportunity to make money, not from prospecting but from setting up shop in San Francisco. "I do my digging here," as one man put it most aptly. A rough cot or a mattress on the floor in an eight-bed room could cost as much as a hundred dollars a week, and a single room could cost five times that. While gold was being found in such quantities that its worth sank like a stone, the cost of accommodation soared sky-high. Most of the newcomers were only intending to stay in California for a few months, and therefore had to rent rooms. Before too long there was a hotel behind every second door, and William Parker wrote to Peder Sather that he and his wife were making more in a month in San Francisco than they had made in a whole year in the same business in New York.

Eliza was frantic with worry when she heard that Parker was trying to persuade Peder Sather to come out west. She does not say why in her letters, makes no mention of Peder's health, and expresses no concern for Sarah or the children. What Eliza seems to have been scared of was the prospect of losing a helping hand, a father figure and a generous supporter.

Not that Eliza was in any imminent danger of losing a benefactor; Peder Sather was in a very poor way and declared that he did not have the strength to make any decisions. His partner Edward Church, on the other hand, was so inspired by William Parker's letter that he was all ready to set off for California right then and there. Eliza thought the man must have taken leave of his senses. Had his wife not just given birth to their first child, a frail little thing who did not look likely to see the summer out? No, Edward Church would do far better to stay at home.

Eliza, whose own husband was out west, could not understand how Edward Church could dream of leaving his family. But appalled though she was to start with, the speed with which he made up his mind to go seems to have impressed her. On May 12, 1850, she writes to Anthony:

Mr. Sather will write you with this letter, but I will tell you that Mr. Church leaves here for Cal, on or about the 1st of June! He comes out there with the intention of establishing a business similar to the one in which he is now engaged with Mr. Sather! And as a matter of course they will need assistance, and their thoughts naturally turn to you! As the mesmerists say Mr. Church is anxious to "put himself in communication" with you on his arrival, and when you come down to San Francisco call on Wells and Fargo, the bankers, who will tell you where you can find Mr. Church!

Over the spring and summer Eliza wrote letter after letter to Anthony, and was piqued that he did not reply quickly enough. He, for his part, was feeling very disheartened and thought she was being too demanding. Eliza was also worried sick that Peder Sather had too much to do at the bank with only Luther Lawrence to help him. All of her letters burn with concern for Peder, and a pattern emerges in which she rarely if ever mentions Sarah. This may have been because Peder was the person on whom their friendship hinged; nonetheless it strikes one simply because Eliza had something to say about everybody. Her remarks were often spiteful, sometimes gleeful, and occasionally so snobbish in tone that they tend to confirm that she had married beneath her. She filled each sheet of paper, margins included, while Anthony's replies were short and stoical. It could be days before he could get someone to take a letter to San Francisco for him, and the mail steamer only sailed once every two weeks. With so long between letters, Eliza began to think that he had forgotten her, or to fear that he would not contact Wells, Fargo & Co., to arrange a meeting with Edward Church and possibly secure himself a job in banking.

What Eliza did not know was that Peder Sather had decided to open a branch of his bank in San Francisco. The plan was to let Edward Church run it while he stayed on in the Nassau Street office. Sather informed Anthony of this in May 1850:

> I write at this time to you to inform you that my partner Mr. Church will leave this city next month for San Francisco, California, and it is our intention to establish a Banking House, either there or at Sacramento City; whichever may be considered the most favorable for us cannot be decided until Mr. Church is there.—We are of the opinion that it will be in San Francisco. I trust that you and Mr. Church will meet and perhaps this may happen when the present mining season is over.
>
> I hope that some method may be contrived by which an arrangement could be made between yourself and Mr. Church to commence some kind of trade between the mines and San Francisco or any other place where we may locate,

which would render it perhaps more agreeable for you than to be working in mining—and may be also more profitable. Of course we cannot tell how this may be and you will be able to judge wether [sic] such a plan could be adapted to mutual advantage.

When you shall have received this letter it would be well to meet Mr. Church (E. W. Church) and address it to the care of Messrs. Wells and Fargo at San Francisco—or perhaps it would be equally as well only to address it to E. W. Church, San Francisco, and Mr. C would probably receive it at the Post Office— as Messrs. Wells and Fargo are not yet acquainted with Mr. C individually, but they know us as Sather & Church and they know by this time that we intend to come there. You will state to Mr. C your particular address in case you should have left the place where we have hitherto heard from you.

Anthony followed his advice and wrote several letters to Edward Church, but received no reply. Not that it mattered anyway, he wrote bitterly to Eliza. Sather's suggestion was well-meaning, but utterly unrealistic. The prospectors in Tuolumne had all they needed and there was no point in trying to open any sort of trading establishment there. So he carried on as before in Tuolumne, toiling away with pick and shovel to no great profit; wading through mud in the winter; shivering under his blanket at night; munching dry crusts of bread; loath, sometimes, to write back to Eliza. She was always harping on about how many letters she had sent him, quoting the precise dates and keeping an exact account of how many he owed her in return.

In the summer he received a letter from Peder Sather which suggests that Anthony's gloomy frame of mind might be due to more than just the hard work and the loneliness: "Your friend Mr. Metcalf has been in a tight corner for some time, and I doubt wether [sic] he can hold out much longer. Mr. Townsend, his partner and formerly President of the Bowery Bank, resigned that situation some time since, being politely requested to do so, (as I have understood)." Sather does not expand upon this matter, but from an article in the *New York Times* on January 26, 1852, it is clear that it was some- thing of a sensation. Here it was reported that Daniel Townsend, the former director of the Bowery Bank, had been arrested on suspicion of fraud. Townsend had tricked a number of the bank's customers into buying stock in the New York Croton Steam Faucet Manufacturing Company, a bank- rupt concern owned by his friend William Metcalf. Townsend had meant to help Metcalf out of the mess he was in by drumming up fresh capital for him, with the result that the stockholders lost all their money.

So Anthony had ended up in Tuolumne because of Daniel Townsend's crooked financial transactions, conducted in order to rescue William Metcalf and his company. Just as I am sometimes taken aback by Eliza's snobbishness, which manifests itself in an obsession with money and social standing, so I find it hard to understand how a working man, an iron founder such as Anthony Lewis Tasheira, could have been friends with a businessman like William Metcalf. Social barriers were not porous enough for such connections to be a matter of course, and the same can be said of Anthony's relationship with Peder Sather. From the latter's side this seems primarily to have been of a paternal nature, not uncaring, but still maintaining a palpable distance, as is evident from a letter written to Anthony by Sather after the following events.

By June 1850 Anthony had seventy-five ounces—almost five pounds—of gold put by. A tidy amount, but not huge. There was a glut of gold and the market price was low. To Anthony though, this little nest egg represented a big milestone. The day had come when, for the first time, he was able to send gold home. In his cabin in Tuolumne he wrapped up the flakes of gold, placed them in a tin box, sealed it tightly, and dispatched it to the post office—addressed, for safety's sake, to Peder Sather. With the gold Anthony enclosed a letter in which he expressed the earnest wish that Eliza and the children have the chance to see the gold before Peder sold it for him and deposited the yield from it in his bank account. But things had not gone quite as he had hoped, so Eliza informed him, and Peder Sather explained why in the following letter, which says a lot about how a banker viewed gold and how easy it was to forget that there could be other ways of looking at it:

Brooklyn Sept 10th 1850

Mr. A. L. Tasheira

My Dear Sir

Your favor of June 17th is at hand, and was received last week. It had evidently been overlooked or mislaid in San Francisco, as I received the 75 oz of Gold Dust by the previous arrival 4 weeks before receiving your letter. I regret that I did not get it at the time when I received the Dust, on account of the direction contained in the same.

When I received the package of Adam's Express I endeavored to open the tin box, but could not do it—whereupon I took it to a Plummer in Spruce Street and got a person to heat an iron in order to melt the soldering—but it was so well done that after half an hour's labor I told him to give it up, which he did.

I could have had it cut open but thought I would not—but sent it to the Mint as it was; which I did, and wrote to the Treasurer Mr. Snowden to return me any letter or paper that might be inside, but there was none. You must pardon me for taking the course I did and will promise not to send another remittance to be coined before I have examined it, aswell [*sic*] as your family. I am not certain but that your wife was half inclined to think that I was in haste to send it to the Mint; and on reflection I acknowledge my error in so doing. But you will know that gold dust is no longer a curiosity, but an article of commerce aswell [*sic*] as a Medium of Exchange—myself unduly forgetting that the hand which had separated this from the Earth, was that of a particular friend and that there were those here also who would have been particularly interested to have seen it.

The 75 oz yielded according to the Mint certificate $ 1.377.40. One Thousand, Three Hundred and Seventy Seven 40/100 Dollars for which amount I have credited your account with Sather & Church and will pay interest at the rate of 6 percent per annum, until paid.—

... You perceive that I have dated my letter in Brooklyn. It is night, and I have no possible chance to write during the day time in New York.—I thank you for your kind wishes to myself and family. We are all thank God! well. My own health has been much better this summer than formerly. Receive the best wishes of myself and family.

Yours Truly P. Sather

Anthony was furious when he read this and did not feel that Peder Sather's apologies were good enough. On November 9 he wrote to Sather and told him exactly what a milestone it had been for him to send that gold. He had wrapped every single one of those fragile flakes in paper, to save them being crushed in transit. Sather had handled the box in "a typical business manner"; Anthony would have liked to have seen Peder Sather show a little more understanding. Having said his piece Anthony signs off humbly and appeasingly: "You, my Dear Sir, are the first kind Friend who has ever taken an interest for my pecuniary benefit and for your kind feelings towards myself and family, the trouble I have been to you and assistance you have rendered me, I shall be ever grateful."

Toward the end of the summer Eliza was begging Anthony to come home, even while rejoicing at the prospect of her husband becoming Edward Church's assistant. On the Fourth of July she and the children were guests of the Sathers in Brooklyn. Mrs. Church was there, too, with her baby. The infant was even more sickly than the last time she had seen it and it died a week later. Edward Church was still en route to California and would not hear of the baby's death until weeks later, when he reached San Francisco. Eliza did not dare think how he would react when he heard the news. She felt sorry for him, but—ignorant as yet of the arrangement between Church and

Peder Sather—she still thought it mean of him to have gone off, leaving his partner stuck with all the work. Not that she wasn't sure Peder Sather could cope, far from it, but what if he was forced to take to his bed again? Then there would be no one to manage the bank but Luther and Theodore, and that would never work, she complained.

This Theodore was a member of the Tasheira family and Eliza mentions him in almost every letter. Whose son he was we are never told, but he comes over as being a bright, if spoiled youth who—until offered a job by Peder Sather—had shown no inclination to work or to study. Theodore was a constant source of worry and Eliza writes, possibly thinking of Anthony's mother, "The best thing to happen is to take him away from home, where no one can control him." Theodore might in fact have been Anthony's brother or half-brother. If so, then, Peder Sather obviously treated the brothers very differently. "Mr. Sather has just given Theodore a new jacket, which cost $4, and also invited him to Brooklyn for Christmas dinner, together with your mother, my father, the children and myself. I cannot tell you half Mr. Sather's kindness to us; the slightest hint I make regards your mother's necessities, or Theodore's wants he immediately gets upon." One evening Sather called at Downing Street to make a surprising announcement. Eliza writes: "Again I said I thought your Mother would miss the help his money was in the family. Mr. Sather replied that he was not prepared to say what he would give Theodore or what he would be worth in addition to his expenses out west and other expenses here, but he should do for him as if he was his own child, in every respect, and of course would see your Mother should not miss him in that way, and should send her an order to draw some money occasionally." Everyone was completely bowled over by this proposal. Peder Sather had TB, he was overworked, and had four children of his own, including the chronically ill Caroline. What made him offer to do this? Such a promise gives the impression that Sather was more than just a kind and benevolent man. Did he know something about Theodore's birth; was that why he offered to be like a father to the boy? Here I succumb to the temptation to speculate, prompted by some lines in a letter from Anthony to Eliza. In these he mentions Theodore in one sentence and the Roosevelt name in the very next, something which inevitably leads me to surmise that Theodore might have been related to one or both of the future presidents.

"It really doesn't matter to me what James Roosevelt should think or not think," Anthony writes, adding: "and from William Roosevelt I never have heard a word." James and William Roosevelt were bankers on Wall Street, a

FIGURE 9. Anthony Lewis Tasheira, 1821–60. Iron founder in New York City and bookkeeper at Drexel, Sather & Church, San Francisco. Daguerreotype, ca. 1854–56. Photographer: Peter Welling, New York. Courtesy of the California History Room, California State Library, Sacramento, California.

small world where everyone knew everyone else. Since Peder Sather was by now acquainted with men like Henry Wells and William Fargo it seems not unlikely that he also knew James and William Roosevelt. Intrigued by the thought that Anthony Tasheira might somehow be connected to them, I decided to check the Roosevelt family tree. And sure enough: a Tasheira had married into the Roosevelt family. The tree shows that in 1856 a boy was born, and named Theodore Tasheira Roosevelt. Although it is clear from the date that this was not the Theodore from Downing Street, this discovery at least brings me closer to an explanation of why Anthony writes of James and William Roosevelt in such familiar terms. This link by marriage also may make us wonder whether it was through the Tasheiras that Peder Sather got to know the Roosevelts. But this was in fact not the case. The actual connection was made through the marriage in 1845 of Anthony's sister, Mercelena, to William Roosevelt, with whom she had a son, Theodore T. Roosevelt.

In the winter of 1849–50, Sather had only Luther Lawrence and occasionally Charles Farrar to assist him in the Nassau Street office, and on top of everything else he was trying to introduce Theodore to the banking business. He seldom left the office before eight, or even nine, in the evening and once again he became so ill that he was forced to stay at home. Edward Church was still in San Francisco, and he too tried to persuade Peder to come out to the West Coast. But Eliza reported that Sather had told her "that he is so completely exhausted in mind and body that he is not in a fit state to give Mr. Church's propositions a clear and calm consideration."

On Sundays he was too weak to go for his usual walk. On those rare occasions when he did, nonetheless, take a stroll he would have no one to accompany him but Theodore, Eliza wrote.

Then, one day just before Christmas 1850, Sather came to tell her that he would be leaving for San Francisco in January. And he suggested that he should take Theodore with him. Eliza was delighted: this was the best thing that could have happened as far as she was concerned. The neighborhood around Downing Street was not good for Theodore. And then there was Stanley, Anthony's brother—a drunk, just like his father, according to Eliza, and a bad influence on the young man. She goes on: "I feel sure if Theodore and Stanley are not separated, there will be murder in a few years' time between them, the temper of each is so violent and unyielding. I think Theodore going to Cal is the best thing that could happen, to take him away from the low neighborhood of Downing Street and place him with a gentleman like Mr. Sather where he will be properly provided for for life, if he conducts himself properly."

Sather called at the house in Downing Street again later, to take his leave of the whole family. He had bought Theodore everything he would need during his stay and he urged Eliza to tell him if there was anything she would like. "Don't be backward in speaking, just let me know," he says. Eliza took the liberty of asking if they could have a daguerreotype of Theodore, since it would be a while before they saw him again. "Very well," Sather replied, "I will have it done tomorrow."

If Peder Sather was really intending to open a bank in San Francisco he would have needed a considerable amount of initial capital, but this was not something he could drum up on his own. What had happened in the meantime, though, was that Francis Drexel had made Sather an offer that was hard to refuse. Eliza scribbles wildly and enthusiastically to Anthony about this suggestion, and with good reason. Francis Drexel had greatly expanded his banking activities and was now a well-known name in America—thanks, not least, to the massive loans he had made to the state to finance the war with Mexico in 1847. His sons had recently been brought in as partners, and of these, Anthony Drexel in particular seemed to have all the makings of a future bank chief, even though he was so different from his extrovert father. Anthony was a hard worker and a shrewd tactician, but in private he was a quiet, retiring man whose two great passions were music and literature. He was sixteen years younger than Peder Sather; nonetheless, in time he was to become one of Peder's closest friends. When Peder Sather's name crops up in any literature on Norwegian immigrants to America it always says that he was so wealthy by this time that he was able to put up all the money himself. This was not, however, the case. Only after Francis Drexel offered to invest thirty thousand dollars in his business was Sather in a position to consider whether there might be a future for a bank in San Francisco. One of the conditions made by Francis Drexel was that Edward Church and Peder Sather should both invest ten thousand dollars in the venture. If necessary, Francis Drexel would lend them this money. How could they turn down such an offer? The three men drew up a five-year cooperation contract, effective from 1851.

It is Anthony Tasheira who writes at a later date about this hitherto unknown agreement with Francis Drexel. Anthony was informed of it one day when Sather needed someone he could trust to whom he could dictate the wording of the agreement. Anthony was given strict instructions not to tell anyone what he thus learned. And yet he wrote of the agreement in some detail in a letter to Eliza. Confirmation of this agreement can be found in all literature on Francis Drexel. In these sources Drexel is usually credited with having established the bank in San Francisco, with Peder Sather as his agent.

The plan was for Peder Sather to go to San Francisco just to get the business up and running, and then hand over the reins to Edward Church. Peder would then return to New York and continue managing their banking activities in Nassau Street. He meant to stay in San Francisco for some months; Theodore and Edward's wife, Letitia Church, would be going with him. Sather had hired a black man, Nelson Cook from New York, as a messenger for the new bank. It appears from the passenger lists that they all traveled on the same boat.

Their departure was postponed twice, in January and March 1851. On March 26 Theodore had taken a few days off from the bank to say goodbye to his friends. A big farewell party had been held for him and "the house was in chaos," Eliza wrote. Everyone had thought they would not see him again for a long, long time. The reason for putting off the trip was a minor one, but of an exclusive nature: Sather had not been able to secure first-class tickets for everyone in the party. Soon afterward, however, they all boarded ship, Peder carrying with him the money from Francis Drexel in a safe. Eliza and the rest of the Tasheira family were on the quayside to wave them off. There, too, were the other members of the Sather family: Sarah, Caroline and Josephine, Mary Emma and little Peder.

EIGHT

Drexel, Sather & Church

It took Anthony Lewis Tasheira 165 days to travel to San Francisco via Cape Horn in 1849, but by the time Peder Sather and his party set sail from New York in the spring of 1851, the steamship companies had halved the time by offering a shortcut through Nicaragua or across the Isthmus of Panama. On the west coast of Panama a new ship waited to take passengers on the last stage of their journey, north to San Francisco. Something in the region of a thousand people were now arriving in this city every day, most of them men in their twenties and thirties. At close on forty, Peder Sather was one of the oldest.

The passage from the East Coast across Nicaragua to the West Coast could be a fascinating one. When Mark Twain took this same route in 1864 on his way to San Francisco to take up a job as a reporter, he jotted down lists of all the things he saw from the deck of the boat as it chugged through the jungle: "Dark grottos, fairy festoons, tunnels, temples, columns, pillars, towers, pilasters, terraces, pyramids, mounds, domes, walls, in endless confusion of vine work . . . no shape known to architecture unimitated—and all so webbed together that short distances within are only gained by glimpses. Monkeys here and there; birds warbling; gorgeous plumaged birds on the wing, Paradise itself, the imperial realms of beauty."

This was the world that met the eyes of Peder Sather, Letitia Church, and Theodore. We can just picture them, lounging in deckchairs, faces ruddy from the tropical sun, with fruit juice in their glasses, Panama hats on their heads, fanning themselves with palm leaves. The ship's paddles thresh the river surface as if it were a sodden field. The engine growls and grumbles, the water foams and froths, glittering droplets fly through the air to light on an eyelid or a hand resting on a chair arm of gleaming mahogany: these passengers are traveling first-class. Smoke and steam roll along the river like banks of mist before breaking up into gray-blue wisps and disappearing. Everything behind, everything ahead and here—midway between, on a pitching ship deck—Peder Sather, bound for San Francisco to open a bank; Letitia Church going to join her dearest Edward and wild child Theodore to . . . yes, what exactly was he going there for?

It took about two weeks to cross overland to the West Coast, and where lakes or rivers were too shallow passengers had to disembark and either walk or ride on donkeys led by Indians. The terrain was very hilly and hard to negotiate, there was always the risk of ambush, of being killed or attacked by wild animals. At night they slept in tents or in makeshift huts, and travelers did occasionally die of "Panama fever," a viral disease caused by insect bites. From Norwegian history we know that Ole Bull contracted this when crossing the Isthmus in 1854, on his way to San Francisco to give some concerts. He also had one of his violins stolen, along with jewelry and other valuables. Although he loved to exaggerate the things that happened to him, crossing the Isthmus of Panama really was a very hazardous exercise for him and all other travelers.

Peder Sather didn't come through it without a bit of a fright himself. A fierce fire broke out on his vessel, either on Lake Nicaragua or on the Chagres River—sources differ on this point. It was quite dramatic: a blazing boat in the middle of the jungle, full of panic-stricken New Yorkers surrounded by flames, screeching monkeys, snakes thick as ship's masts, snapping alligators, and fleeing parrots. The iron safe in which Peder Sather was carrying his money fell overboard and sank, but was, according to my sources, "miraculously" retrieved.

There can of course be all sorts of reasons—coincidences or unknown circumstances—why an episode such as this should have been remembered while so many other biographical details have been lost to oblivion. But if the fire could do so much damage that Sather's safe ended up in the water, it must have been so bad that those who survived it found the experience hard to forget and still talked about it long afterward. Disastrous events which end well can eventually become the stuff of fabulous tales of adventure.

So, once safely landed in San Francisco, Peder Sather may well have regaled rapt listeners with a colorful description of the incident, embroidering his account with spectacular details regarding the spread of the fire and their miraculous rescue. As night fell over the hills of the city so the suspense around the table would mount: one evening, two evenings, three evenings.

The flames shot up higher and higher from the boat, the snakes had the tongues burned out of their mouths, red-hot planks flew aloft as the smoke darkened the sky. In the first version of the story the passengers are put into lifeboats, in the second they throw themselves into the water while the captain holds the alligators at bay with his gun and the strong swimmers among the gentlemen drag terrified women up onto the riverbanks, and in the third they all grab hold of dangling lianas and swing themselves off the vessel like monkeys. First it's seven valiant sailors who dive for the safe, then nine Baptist ministers, and finally thirteen brawny Indians who haul the safe to the surface, dripping and scorched, but with the money inside unscathed—the money belonging to Francis Drexel, the great Philadelphian financier. Knock wood, gentlemen!

After the fire the passengers continued their journey west along the Chagres River to Panama on another boat, badly shaken and on the alert every time a sailor struck a match to light a lantern in the darkness. The ships that were to take them the rest of the way rarely ran to a fixed schedule and while they waited for one to arrive many travelers had to sleep in tents, in the open air or, if they were more fortunate, with local residents or in one of the few hotels. On March 15, 1851, Peder Sather, Letitia Church, and Theodore boarded the *SS Isthmus,* a combined sail and steamship of six hundred gross tons. The manifest presented by Captain Ottinger to the San Francisco Port Authority states that there were only eighty-six passengers on board the *Isthmus,* an unusually small number, even when we know that only first-class passengers were listed by name on such manifests. Theodore, for example, is registered only as a "boy" accompanying "P. Sather." The northward journey on the *Isthmus* took longer than expected because the ship had to call in at Acapulco to take on some passengers, then ran out of coal and only just made it to San Diego, where it could pick up a fresh supply.

From the deck the land looked desolate and hostile. Steep cliffs reared above the sea that rolled in and crashed against the shore, making progress slow and the work of the stokers even harder than usual. It took almost a month for the ship to reach the Golden Gate, a strait so narrow that it was hundreds of years before sailors out on the open sea actually spotted it. On April 10, 1851, the *SS Isthmus* paddled slowly between the plunging cliffs at whose feet sea lions snorted, while flocks of cranes swooped low over the waves. Up ahead the new arrivals saw a vast bay, ponderous and surging as an inland sea. On the starboard side, almost five hundred ships were anchored, in the roads below untold windswept heights bare of trees except for a few gnarled, stunted oaks: a seemingly uninhabitable spot. But this was in fact San Francisco, and from the deck, the whole of Montgomery Street could be seen: a long, straight line running the full width of the harbor.

On board the ships, anchored so close to each other that you could have walked dryshod from one end of the roadstead to the other, there was hardly a soul to be seen. The sailors had jumped ship and their captains whiled away their days in the town, waiting until they could gather together new crews to sail their boats south again. Here and there, though, there was some sign of life: shirts hung out to dry on a deck, the smell of food drifting across on a gust of wind, a man sitting on a box, shaving.

The water was too shallow for boats to sail right into dock, so the *SS Isthmus* had to wait at the mouth of the harbor for the tenders to row out and take its passengers ashore. While the prospectors often had no idea what sort of place they were coming to and knew no one there, Peder Sather was well prepared and fully informed on the situation in California from newspaper reports and letters. Edward Church had done some reconnaissance in San Francisco and the surrounding area and told his wife, Peder, and Theodore what they could expect there. Behind them they had left a cold, dreary, post-Christmas winter in New York; ashore here a springtime of warmth and poppies awaited them. And here, too, Edward Church was waiting to greet them all.

In 1851 the population of San Francisco was around twenty-five thousand, as opposed to a couple of hundred four years earlier. Topographically this spot, with its steep hills, was not the best location along the shoreline on which to build a city. That it had been chosen anyway was thanks to the great bay beyond the Golden Gate strait, which now formed the roadstead in which the ships anchored. The hills, at first thought to be solid rock, actually consisted of porous sandstone and sand dunes which, when the wind and rain blew in off the sea, would often cave in and come pouring down on to the heart of the city around the harbor. Down there on the waterfront, buildings were clustered close together, while on the hilltops habitation was sparse and of the poorest sort, consisting of tents and cabins.

Montgomery Street had been named after Commander John B. Montgomery of the United States sloop-of-war *Portsmouth,* who raised the American flag in the village of Yerba Buena in 1848 at the end of the war with Mexico. Due to its strategic location down by the harbor, by 1851 this street was already the finest in San Francisco, but it was as yet unpaved and in the winter months it was reduced to a noxious cattle track when the Mexican *vaqueros* drove their herds along it. The interminable showers of rain turned Montgomery Street into a quagmire in which horses and carts got stuck and into which more than once some poor mule had foundered and drowned. Nonetheless, Montgomery Street was the most popular street in town and real estate prices were, therefore, extortionate: as much as fifty thousand dollars a lot for anyone wanting to set up shop there.

It was the Americans who named the former fishing village San Francisco, after St. Francis of Assisi, as a tribute to the old Catholic province, symbolically represented by the Mission Dolores which now lay on the outskirts of the town and had already become a popular destination for Sunday strollers. The monks were still growing fruit and vegetables there, but part of the mission station had also been turned into a tavern.

In short, while San Francisco was not exactly Manhattan or Brooklyn, it was no longer a fishing village either. It was not the place it had been when Anthony Tasheira passed through it on his way to Tuolumne. Only a few days before Peder Sather landed there, gas lamps were turned on for the first time on Montgomery Street, one of several thoroughfares now furnished with street lighting. The city also boasted a number of playhouses and concert halls, including a theater named after the famous Swedish soprano Jenny Lind. San Francisco had also acquired its first mayor and city council, a chamber of commerce, a medical center, and a children's home, built to house the offspring of the cities "ladies"—prostitutes from the East Coast, many of them French.

After California became the thirty-first state in the Union in 1850, the city expanded by leaps and bounds, a development process which has prompted historians to dub San Francisco "the sudden city." Prefabricated buildings transported from the east in sections made it possible for homes and shops to be erected almost overnight, with the result that anyone who had been out of town for a few weeks would hardly recognize the place when they returned. Whole blocks shot up, with shops, offices, and workshops. The prefabs were cheap, but the lots on which they stood were not, and it was not unusual to see people pulling their homes along the street on carts, out searching for patches of ground on which to set them down temporarily.

Peder Sather was not planning on being there any longer than necessary. Nonetheless, he joined the local Baptist church, the first place of worship in San Francisco, established the previous year. The Baptist church looked more like a tent than a house of God; due to a lack of building materials its roof and walls were of canvas. Preachers and ministers of every sort traveled west during the Gold Rush, intent on offering riches other than the gold that glinted in the American River and could almost be picked up with the bare hands at the foot of the Sierra Nevada.

Every Sunday Peder Sather sat in a pew in the First Baptist Church, along with a few score others, safely arrived and with a wife and four children on the other side of the continent. On Sundays the bells pealed from more than twenty churches in the town, while saloon owners wiped the whisky slops off their tables and swept up the broken glass.

Men of every profession flocked to the city: liquor merchants and craftsmen, journalists and engineers, shop assistants and hairdressers, coachmen, smiths, and bankers. There was a state to be built and everything was in short supply, not least the money necessary to finance both public and private ventures. Francis Drexel was well aware of this, and with an initial capital of fifty thousand dollars Peder Sather and Edward Church had a golden opportunity to make their mark in a loan market that knew almost no bounds.

It was not only the banks who spied the possibility of making a quick killing, especially in those first years. Instead of taking his cows to the slaughterhouse and paying for them to be killed and quartered, one Ohio rancher drove his cattle to San Francisco, where he sold them as "beef on the hoof," for astronomical prices. And then there was the doctor who bought a bulk load of timber in Boston and rather than pay for it to be cut into planks in a sawmill there, he sailed the undressed timber to San Francisco and sold it at a fabulous profit. But not everyone found it so easy. Anthony Lewis Tasheira thought he might be able to make a little extra cash by selling a consignment of axes, but he was not quick enough off the mark. Someone else got there before him with a whole shipload of tools and equipment, leaving him stuck with the axes. And as time went on he was having to delve deeper and deeper with his crowbar and shovel to bring up the tiniest slivers of gold.

During their visit, Peder, Theodore, Edward, and Letitia probably stayed at the St. Francis Hotel, owned as it was by their friends from New York, the Parkers. Most saloons and hotels in San Francisco were frequented by prostitutes, but the St. Francis placed advertisements in the newspaper in which the proprietors assured prospective patrons that their hotel offered "civilization and comfort." Women were in the minority in the city, but those who would attend the Saturday night dances arranged by the hotel were, it said, refined. This may have been why the excellent profits which William Parker had written about to Peder Sather soon dried up. The main reason, though, was probably that the makeshift hotel could not stand up to the competition

FIGURE 10. A check from Drexel, Sather & Church, June 15, 1854, one of the few San Francisco banks that survived the rest of the century. Courtesy of the Bancroft Library, University of California, Berkeley.

from more elegant establishments. Before it collapsed during an earthquake in 1853, the hotel was used as a polling station for the elections to the first state senate.

The bank which Peder Sather had come to San Francisco to open was named Drexel, Sather & Church, Bankers. The offices which Edward Church had taken for the company were on Washington Street, and when Peder Sather left the St. Francis Hotel on an April day in 1851 and strolled over to Washington Street for his first day at the bank, what awaited him there was a wooden shack with a corrugated iron roof. But Edward Church had been fortunate in the spot he had chosen: the lot on Washington Street was almost right on the quayside, a location which helped to ensure the bank of customers. Prospectors in the Sacramento Valley were in the habit of taking the overnight boat down to San Francisco, either to sell or deposit their gold the next morning. When they arrived they were very happy to be able to walk straight into a bank with their gold: if they had it on them when they went to have breakfast up in the town they ran the risk of being robbed. Things were no better out in the goldfields. True, the prospectors left guards on watch while they were out prospecting, but these weren't to be trusted, either; many of them ran off with the valuables they were paid to watch over.

In the newspaper *Alta California,* advertisements could now be found for Drexel, Sather & Church, a bank that tempted clients with loans, depositing facilities, currency exchange, and the best prices in town for gold: fourteen dollars an ounce. Sather needed a cashier so he hired James Sloan Hutchison, a New Yorker, born in Philadelphia in 1826, who had tried his hand at prospecting but with no great success. Now he was being given his big chance, and he set to work with a will, even going so far as to sleep in the bank, primarily to guard the safe, but also so that he would be the first person to greet the prospectors when they came ashore early in the morning with their gold. Long before other bankers were out of bed, Sather's cashier had completed his business and could present the results to his boss the minute he walked through the door.

Nelson Cook had settled into his job as bank messenger, and the sight of a black man striding in and out of the bank made more than a few heads turn. The state senate in California might have abolished slavery, but prejudice against black people was still very strong, there as elsewhere. Under the 1850 constitution of California negroes were, for instance, denied the right to give evidence in court or to hold public office. Which makes it all the more interesting to note that Peder Sather and Nelson Cook formed a lasting friendship. This fact is cited in a book entitled *Blacks in Gold Rush California*, published in 1977, as proof that good relationships between black and white did occur.

Peder Sather knew that California lay in a seismically unstable area, and he must have thanked his lucky stars that he had not brought Sarah and the children with him, when, on May 1, 1851, San Francisco was hit by a severe earthquake that reduced scores of buildings to matchwood. As if that wasn't enough, only four days later one of the worst fires in the city's history broke out. Discovered just before midnight, over the next ten hours the fire burned more than a thousand buildings to the ground, leaving eighteen blocks in ruins. Strong winds swept the flames from house to house, and the wooden sidewalks led it from street to street. Firefighters could only stand by helplessly and watch the fire's progress: the city had only a limited water supply, and the small amount available to the fire brigade evaporated before it reached the flames.

The smell and the sounds were terrifying. The city's inhabitants had to flee up into the hills—among them the Churches, Peder Sather, Theodore, James Hutchinson, and Nelson Cook. From the heights they watched the flames rise into the sky like one monstrous fiery tongue, as the entire center of the city collapsed. Three-quarters of San Francisco was devastated that night. The glow from the fire was visible for miles around the Bay Area, and all the way down in Monterey, over a hundred miles away. During the night the suspicion arose that the fire had been started deliberately by a notorious gang that was running amok in the town, and this caused people to fear that there might be more fires to come.

To guard against such disasters some citizens had opted for iron as a building material—a fateful decision. The flames caused the metal to expand, with the result that doors and windows jammed and several merchants were burned to death in their stores. Drexel, Sather & Church's wooden shack was also destroyed by the fire; the bank safe crashed through the wooden floor and plunged into the harbor. For the second time in a very short period the bank's initial capital had fallen prey to fire and water. But a few days later, when it was possible to negotiate a way through the smoldering ruins around the waterfront, some fishermen managed to haul the safe out of the sea and its contents were found to be intact.

Within a matter of weeks a fifth of the city center had been rebuilt. But even though as little timber as possible was used in the new buildings, in the middle of July another fire broke out and this time three hundred buildings were destroyed. Peder Sather and Edward Church had to look for new offices. At auction they bought an empty lot on the corner of Montgomery Street and Commercial Street. There they set about building a bank that would be as fireproof as possible.

Millions of dollars had been lost in the fires and very few householders were insured. Gangs of criminals were behind a number of arson attacks; they robbed and beat up people in broad daylight, broke into stores and homes, and committed a string of murders. All of this greatly alarmed the city's residents and made it difficult for business to continue as normal. And yet the city council merely sat back and did nothing: many county officials were, in any case, thoroughly corrupt. By June people had had enough and set up a committee of vigilance. Over seven hundred citizens promptly added their names to the committee's manifesto, and during the summer many more followed suit, including Peder Sather.

Immediately after its inaugural meeting the committee set up armed militias, which proceeded to patrol the streets day and night, in the mining camps too, where the gangs made life unsafe for everyone. The committee took the law into its own hands. It made arrests, deposed judges, and expelled troublemakers from the city and the state. The campaign took a dramatic turn when the committee carried out four public lynchings, cheered on by thousand-strong crowds of furious citizens. Corrupt politicians were kicked out of their offices, new ones appointed, and law and order restored. In due course the committee also dissolved itself and for a while at least the people of the city could sleep safe in their beds.

According to Peder Sather's plan he should long since have been on his way back to Brooklyn and his family, but he stayed on in San Francisco through the summer and fall. The climate was good for his health, it was a long time since he had felt so fit and well. At midsummer he and Theodore set out on horseback to visit Anthony Lewis Tasheira in Tuolumne. Although Anthony had not managed to make a go of his axe-selling venture, he was doing quite well. Peder was given a bag containing several ounces of gold to be deposited in the bank. Once back in San Francisco he wrote to Eliza to assure her that a prospector's life also had its charms and that things were soon going to be looking up for Anthony. With this letter, Theodore enclosed one of his own in which he said that he was having a wonderful time and that he was much happier in San Francisco than in New York. For one thing he could go riding almost every day, and on the Fourth of July Peder Sather had bought him four skyrockets.

Eliza was pleased to receive their news, but disappointed that Anthony had not taken the opportunity to send a letter to her through Sather, who could have mailed it for him in town. She had, moreover, heard of several fresh cases of cholera in the camps and begged Anthony to come home as soon as possible. Eliza also wrote that Anthony's mother was afraid Theodore would become even more spoiled and pick up bad habits.

For Anthony, slogging away in the gold fields, everyday existence contrasted sharply with the life which Theodore was obviously leading. Anthony was ashamed of the latter's indolent lifestyle and felt that Theodore was given far too much money by Peder Sather without having done anything to deserve it. If Anthony and Theodore were brothers, the difference in the way they were treated certainly does seem hard to understand. If Sather really meant to lick Theodore into shape then lavishing money on the boy and allowing him to shirk his work was hardly the best way to go about it. Whatever the case, it appears that Peder Sather, the man who had taken it upon himself to be like a father to Theodore, was afraid to put his foot down.

By late summer the new bank building was almost finished, and in September 1851 Drexel, Sather & Church placed an advertisement in the *Californian Gazette* announcing that the bank was now open for business in a solid brick building on Montgomery Street. Situated right next door to Wells, Fargo & Co., owned and run by two of Sather's acquaintances from New York, Drexel, Sather & Church was one of the first banks to open on Montgomery, a street which was gradually establishing itself as the financial hub of the city.

Leaving Edward Church in charge of the daily running of the bank Peder Sather sailed from San Francisco at the end of October. Theodore did not accompany him; Edward Church was now going to be responsible for him.

FIGURE 11. Banking House of Drexel, Sather & Church, northeast corner of Montgomery Street and Commercial, San Francisco, 1854. Established May 1851. Courtesy of the California Historical Society, San Francisco, MS CHS2013.1125.

Sather made it clear to his partner that he was to send Theodore back to New York if he became too homesick or if he and Church did not get along.

On December 1 Peder Sather arrived in New York on the steamship *Prometheus,* after a voyage that had taken him via Nicaragua and Havana. Eliza and the children were invited to Christmas dinner in Brooklyn, as usual. The weather was terribly cold, but Eliza informs Anthony: "Mr. Sather seems very content, and it encourages me so much that he, though his health generally is or was poor, continues in perfect health and has not suffered the slightest inconvenience, or unpleasant feeling on account of the weather." And she concludes by saying: "William Roosevelt has enough to do, but finds it hard to collect money enough for family expenses." Eliza may have considered William's and Mercelena's circumstances to be somewhat straitened, but in the census of 1850 the couple were recorded as employing two domestic servants.

But Anthony was having a far harder time of it. In Tuolumne it rained for weeks on end and the mud made digging impossible. Edward Church and Anthony had not been able to set up any sort of trading venture together. Peder Sather had said that Anthony was doing well, but this was not in fact the case. Anthony froze at night, and in the daytime he could not set foot outside the cabin without sinking up to his knees in mud. And so 1851 drew to a close.

NINE

Congratulating Himself on Freedom

Only months later, Peder Sather was back in San Francisco. He kept the office in Nassau Street, as planned, but left Luther Lawrence to run it when he was away. Luther was still a bachelor and and still living with his uncle, Charles Farrar, on Willoughby Street in Brooklyn. Farrar occasionally assisted Luther in the bank, but I have not come across the names of any other employees.

All the sources would have it that Sather actually moved to San Francisco at this point, and if this is so then 1851 saw the start of years of commuting back and forth. I did, though, come across a check which might cast some doubt on this theory. It is dated July 3, 1856. I was so excited to be looking at an original document from Drexel, Sather & Church that only later did I notice the legend on the bank's logo, an ornamental oval in the bottom left-hand corner: "F. M. Drexel, Philadelphia. P. Sather, New York. E. W. Church, San Francisco." This can only mean, surely, that in 1856 Francis Drexel was living in Philadelphia, Peder Sather in New York, and Edward Church in San Francisco. On the other hand, the information on the logo may only refer to the locations of the bank's three offices and not necessarily to where the three partners were permanently residing.

According to the employment register for New York, as late as 1858 Peder Sather still had his office in Nassau Street in Manhattan and his home address was still given as 82 Willoughby Street. Which is not to say, of course, that he was actually living in Brooklyn; this may only have been his official address. And two notices in the *New York Times* that same year provide clear proof that Peder Sather's time in New York was indeed at an end. One states that he had sold the house in Brooklyn to John Falconer, a famous artist, the other that Luther Lawrence had taken over the business at 164 Nassau Street, but that he would also continue to act as agent for Peder Sather who had now settled permanently in San Francisco.

From this we can conclude that the Sather family was not reunited before 1858, and that for seven long years Peder Sather traveled back and forth between New York and San Francisco. At one point, Eliza wrote to Anthony that on her last visit to Sarah she found that "Mrs. Myers had moved in with Mrs. Sather." This Mrs. Myers was not a servant or a nanny, but a childless friend of the Sathers, and, as far as I can gather, the wife of a parson. If she was living in the house in Brooklyn while Peder was away, Sarah must have been in need of help, support, and company. And what of Mrs. Myers? From a census taken some time later it looks as though her husband had gone to California to preach the gospel. Thus a picture begins to emerge which fits very well with what is known of the San Francisco demographic at that time. The city was populated by men, generally living alone, either because they were bachelors or because their spouses had agreed to them coming out there to try their luck. The climate on the West Coast soon proved to have a beneficial effect on Peder Sather's health—assuming, that is, that it was the tuberculosis that had tipped the scales in favor of his returning to San Francisco. But seven years of living apart must have been tough, not least for Sarah and the four children, including Caroline who still required regular medical treatment.

Eliza writes screeds and screeds, but never says much about Sarah. As always, her talk is mainly of Peder and rarely, if ever, of the other members of the Sather family, even though one would have thought that Eliza would have had more in common with Sarah—since they were both women and mothers, had known each other since Eliza was married in Bridgeport, and both had husbands on the other side of the continent. In spite of this, in Eliza's letters Sarah's name is often mentioned only in passing, even when Peder is at home and Eliza and the children are invited out to Brooklyn. Other letters containing more on Sarah may, of course, have been lost, but going by the correspondence we have, Eliza appears to have idolized Peder and thought Sarah hardly worth mentioning.

According to an article in the *San Francisco Chronicle,* Sarah was a delicate, high-strung woman. Such a description may simply be a reflection of contemporary chauvinistic attitudes toward women, but the piece makes reference to certain specific examples which give the impression that Sarah was not the most stable of characters. And that would have put Peder Sather in something of a dilemma when advised by his doctors to move to California.

Address records show that, in 1856, Sarah and the children had moved in with banker John Thompson. He lived in Union Street, Brooklyn, with his wife and children and five Irish servants. This change of address supports my theory that Sarah and John Thompson were closely related. This would have given Peder a great deal to live up to in terms of his professional and social standing, and the Californian gold could have presented him with a—quite literally—golden opportunity to put himself on an equal footing with his in-laws.

In the spring of 1852 Sather returned to San Francisco earlier than planned. This time he stayed at 129 Montgomery Street, not far from the bank at number 134. By now Drexel, Sather & Church was making great strides. In mid-May, for example, the bank was able to send gold to the tune of seventeen thousand dollars to New York. The New York papers always reported on the worth of individual shipments from San Francisco: the largest, carried on the same boat, amounted to $445,000. This does not, however, tell us the whole story about the strength of Drexel, Sather & Church relative to other banks, because on other occasions Drexel, Sather & Church came much higher up on the list. However, the New York *Weekly Herald* refers to Drexel, Sather & Church as Drexel & Co., an indication that Francis Drexel was regarded as sole owner of the bank on Montgomery Street.

Drexel, Sather & Church placed weekly advertisements in the local press in which it listed its main collaborative partners: banks in New York and Boston, Baltimore and New Orleans, St Louis and, of course, Philadelphia, where Francis Drexel and his son Anthony now managed one of the biggest financial institutions in the country. The advertisements make it clear that right from the start Drexel, Sather & Church had had firm agreements with banks in all the major cities of America. These collaborative partners were proof that the bank was part of a network, something which was absolutely essential since there was, as yet, no national banking system. A check issued in San Francisco could not, for example, be redeemed in just any bank in America, or at any rate, not without the risk of a drop in its face value. Consequently, wherever possible, checks were cashed in a bank with which the issuer had an agreement.

Drexel, Sather & Church's offices in Montgomery Street were on the ground floor; the third floor was rented out to an instrument maker who produced navigational equipment for ships and the second floor to Edwin B. Mastick, a lawyer who had come to San Francisco in 1849 and was now the bank's attorney. On the ground floor rows of tall, narrow windows looked out onto Montgomery Street and Commercial Street, and although the building was not large it had a fine, elegantly wrought facade. So far, apart from Peder Sather and Edward Church there were by all accounts only two full-time employees, Nelson Cook and James Hutchinson, while Theodore came and went as he pleased.

In the early 1850s Wells, Fargo & Co. was already the biggest bank in San Francisco. It too had its offices on Montgomery, as did a score of other small or medium-sized banks. None of these was on a par with Wells, Fargo & Co., but Drexel, Sather & Church soon showed itself to be a thriving concern, and the newspapers described Peder Sather and Edward Church as bankers one could trust. The same could not be said of all, at a time when you did not need a government license in order to open a bank; when, indeed, it seemed that all you really needed was a safe.

One crucial reason for Henry Wells's and William Fargo's rapid rise to the top was the introduction of their Express Service, the forerunner to American Express. By using horses and wagons as a means of carrying mail and passengers to the east, Wells, Fargo & Co. set out to compete with the steamship companies. It was not long before they were running the biggest mail and passenger service in America. Elegant stagecoaches painted red and green and drawn by six horses carried passengers, gold, letters, and parcels across wild mountain passes and barren deserts to the cities of the East Coast.

Drexel, Sather & Church was notable more for its good service and careful calculations than for bold investments. Francis Drexel, who was famous for his ability to analyze the needs of the market, pulled the strings. Nonetheless, Peder Sather was in charge in San Francisco, and hand-picked his own employees. Francis Drexel only visited San Francisco once, for the opening of the bank in 1851.

Peder Sather had intimated to Eliza that things would gradually pick up for Anthony, but on the prospecting front things were steadily going downhill. Nor did it make him feel any better to have Eliza constantly expressing her disappointment over how little money he was making. She had read in the papers how much gold was being shipped to New York, and kept asking after a "piece of Californian gold jewelry" which Anthony had promised to send her. But she never received anything in the mail. On the one hand she wanted Anthony to earn as much as possible, on the other she made him feel guilty by telling him that the children were wondering where "Papa" was.

While Eliza had a large circle of friends in New York, Anthony was struggling to cope with the loneliness of life in his cabin in Tuolumne. And the more difficult it became to satisfy her expectations, the greater his self-loathing grew. Even Nelson Cook the bank messenger was better off than Anthony, and Theodore lived like a little prince. But it would not be long before Peder Sather's hints of brighter prospects for Anthony took a more concrete form. He suggested that Tasheira should try working in the bank. Glad though he was of the offer, Anthony was not sure whether he would be able to keep accounts and deal with paperwork; nonetheless he decided to give it a go.

On the day he left the cabin in Tuolumne he took nothing with him but a blanket slung over his shoulders and some crusts of bread tucked into his pocket. Once again he had to thank Peder Sather for giving him a chance, and this time in a way that could take his life in a better direction. Some days later, when Anthony rode into San Francisco and, for the first time in years, laid eyes on the sea and the Golden Gate, he thought to himself: This is where I mean to live, this is where I mean to stay, I'm never going to leave California.

Peder Sather now had two former prospectors in his employ, a black man from New York and a teenage boy. Anthony Lewis Tasheira had not had a steady wage and regular working hours since leaving New York in 1849. He regained his strength, he had his evenings to himself, and when the Mercantile Library opened in 1852 he started visiting it, to sit in the reading room browsing through newspapers and magazines and to borrow books, among them the novels of Charles Dickens. What pleasure these gave him, he told Eliza, but she was suspicious of this news. "You never read a book when here and now you mention Oliver Twist! You obviously appreciate (being) on your own, and Mr. Sather congratulates himself on (his) freedom as he now has a place where he can pass his evenings alone, he is something like you."

The source of a comment such as this can only have been Sarah, and from Eliza's wry tone it sounds as though Eliza was not happy about the rumors she had heard. Sather does not seem to have missed New York for a moment; he was very happy in San Francisco and his health had never been better. He noted with satisfaction that Anthony was conscientious in his duties as bookkeeper, and he popped in to his office one day to give him a pat on the back. Anthony told Eliza about this, and of how much better he was feeling. He was no longer exhausted in the evenings as he had been in Tuolumne, where often when he eventually got to bed he was unable to sleep.

Once Anthony had shown what he could do, Peder Sather informed him that he would like to make him a permanent member of staff. This was the best news Anthony could have had, and he immediately wrote to tell Eliza about this fresh turn of events. In this letter there is a hint from Anthony of some conflict between him and William Roosevelt: "I don't care at all what Bill Roosevelt would think," he says. This animosity related presumably to the idea of the whole Tasheira family moving to San Francisco for good.

Rents in the city were still astronomical, so Anthony opted to live in the bank, partly to guard it, partly in order to save money for a future home. Peder Sather had hired a second bookkeeper, Speer Riddell, a young man from Allegheny City—now a part of Philadelphia, Pennsylvania—where he had brothers who were either businessmen, bank employees, or lawyers.

Speer too camped out behind the counter. Anthony found Riddell a pleasant, sensible person of "high personal morality," but he also thought him an odd character and one who took too many liberties. He was a sloppy dresser, did not give a hoot what people thought of him, and was so absent-minded that he had been known to wear his right shoe on his left foot and vice-versa. The other men in the bank kidded Riddell about this and on one occasion, when he had put a pair of boots in for soling and Nelson Cook went to collect them, the latter chalked the words "right" and "left" on the soles—just to be on the safe side.

Although there is no mention of this in the letters, the man with whom Anthony was camping out in the bank was the nephew of James Buchanan, former secretary of state under President James K. Polk. In 1856 Buchanan was elected fifteenth president of the United States. He was unmarried, had no children of his own, and word has it that he was very good to his nephew. It may just be coincidence that Peder Sather should have taken on a young man with a relative in top political circles, but since the position was not advertised it seems likely that Sather knew Speer Riddell from before, and that the same went for his uncle James Buchanan. Buchanan was born in Pennsylvania and served several terms as a Democratic senator of that state, so the odds are that Sather knew him through Francis Drexel. The latter worked very closely with President Polk during the war with Mexico from 1846 to 1848, and raised a lot of money for the federal coffers through the widespread sale of government bonds.

The link between Peder Sather, Speer Riddell, and James Buchanan provided me with a lead that may shed some light on our Norwegian immigrant and help to explain how he came into contact with such people. The key figure here is James Buchanan, a boy from a poor home who studied to become a lawyer and who, like most American presidents, was a Freemason.

FIGURE 12. Tammany Hall, during the presidential campaign of 1856. Peder Sather's bank is to the right, from this year managed by Luther S. Lawrence. Courtesy of the New York Public Library.

The Masonic Order has always been a powerful organization in the United States, so much so that an attempt in the nineteenth century to form an Anti-Masonic Party was doomed to failure.

That this Masonic lead is not without substance is also evident from a number of Eliza's letters. At one point she writes that she has nothing new to report regarding "the mason," at another that "the mason" had helped friends of hers by giving them food, clothing, and work. As a Norwegian, and not so familiar with the Freemasons, I at first thought she was referring to some poor relief organization or charitable body, but "the mason" turned out, in fact, to be short for the "Masonic Chapter 21" in Manhattan. This was a local branch of the Washington Lodge, named after George Washington, the most famous Masonic president of a bunch that includes Abraham Lincoln, Theodore Roosevelt, and Franklin D. Roosevelt.

In one lodge register I found the proof that Luther Lawrence, Peder Sather's right-hand man and latterly his agent in Nassau Street, was also a Freemason. Lawrence was a lawyer, so the fact that he was a mason did not really surprise me; not as much as the discovery that so too was iron founder Anthony Lewis Tasheira, who became a member of the Washington Lodge on April 4, 1843, in the presence of his father, cabinetmaker James Tasheira. In 1854 Anthony was still a member; in a letter to Eliza from May of that year he told her that he had been to a meeting at the Lodge. At this, the lodge brothers had had the pleasure of inspecting the Lodge's new regalia which had just arrived by ship from New York. This included "crapes," that is, mourning bands or something of the sort, and other ceremonial paraphernalia and insignia.

So two of Peder Sather's friends and employees were Freemasons, which makes it reasonable to suppose that he was too. This, in turn, might explain why, in the letter to Anthony in which Sather apologizes for sending the tin box containing the gold to the Mint, he says: "myself unduly forgetting that the hand which had separated this from the Earth was that of a particular friend."

At any rate, there is clear proof that in San Francisco Peder Sather made at least one new friend through the Lodge: Democratic senator Charles F. Lott. The two would later work together in the insurance business. But Lott was not just an ordinary member of the Lodge, he was the grand commander of the Grand Lodge of San Francisco.

So the bookkeepers who slept on mattresses on the floor in Montgomery Street were both Freemasons, and a third "particular friend" was pleased with his two nightwatchmen and with the bank's financial situation. In January 1854 the *Public Ledger* in Philadelphia printed a long article on banks on the West Coast. This rated Wells, Fargo & Co. and Drexel, Sather & Church as being two of the strongest financially and the most reputable, along with Davidson & Co., the West Coast representatives of the Rothschild banking dynasty.

All the banks in San Francisco were privately owned and independent, and, as the *Public Ledger's* reporter remarked laconically, anyone was free to set up their own bank, provided they had enough capital, a safe, and a fireproof building. The main sources of income for any bank were the depositing and sale of gold, currency exchange, and the issuing of loans, never at less than 3 percent interest per month, usually much more. There was no public control of banks, but those that gambled on loans went under very quickly anyway.

Paper money was not in general use, only coins. The fifty-dollar gold piece was particularly popular; ideal when large sums of money were involved because it was quickly and easily counted. Two million dollars' worth of gold was shipped out of the city every month. From dawn to dusk hordes of messengers could be seen tramping up and down Montgomery Street, bent double under the weight of sacks bulging with precious metal. The sun itself seemed to scatter gold dust over the street, and in the bank windows the light sparkled and danced off the fifty-dollar gold pieces set out on display as soon as the doors were opened in the morning.

Many of the banks were built of granite imported from China, but Drexel, Sather & Church's had a fine facade of mastic, a rare and fireproof wood. Montgomery Street was paved with wooden boards and when horses clattered along it pulling grand carriages or loads of vegetables, flour and sugar, hardware or building materials the sound reverberated from the buildings on either side. In the evening the gas lamps were lit and the "French ladies," the prostitutes from Paris, wandered down to the center of town to entertain the gamblers around the tables in the saloons, where the air was thick with tobacco fumes and the smoke from flickering candelabra, liquor glasses chinked, and the road to riches or ruin was short.

San Francisco was already the undisputed metropolis of the West Coast; in 1850, Los Angeles had, for example, a population of only about fifteen hundred. Terms such as *work* and *capital* were freely bandied about during these years, but did not create the clear social divides that one might have expected. In the early 1850s a craftsman could, for instance, earn so much that a judge might have been tempted to swap his courthouse for a carpenter's workshop.

Here the work controls the capital. So said harbormaster James Collier, referring to the fact that a workman could often demand as much as he liked in wages from a wealthy employer. This state of affairs was, however, purely temporary. The influx of workmen and craftsmen was so great that it soon led to growing unemployment. And in no other state did the gap between rich and poor widen as rapidly as it did in California. A great many people ended up in poorhouses run by the county or by charitable organizations. Often the rates of pay varied so widely that there was no point in workers attempting to organize themselves. Instead, the first priority was to get people to identify socially with one another. Unless they could do that there was no hope of waging any sort of class struggle. Not only that, but among the working class, affiliations with the countless ethnic groups in the city were so strong that it was difficult to form a common political front. Last, but not least, San Francisco was a city of men who had no plans to stay there, and thoughts of home made the idea of a workers' movement seem rather meaningless.

Among those who were hardest hit by all this were the prospectors. Three to five dollars a day was as much as they could expect to earn, and for men like James Hutchinson and Anthony Tasheira their jobs in the bank were a world away from what they had been used to. On one occasion Anthony was able to send Eliza a hundred dollars and still put a little money aside. But he found the life in San Francisco offensive: the gambling saloons and promiscuity, the poverty, and the sad, lonely faces he saw on the streets.

Although Anthony was enjoying his work as bookkeeper he still complained to Eliza. He felt he might as well be sleeping in a dungeon; the bank was bolted and barred and there was no ventilation. He had slept better in the cabin in Tuolumne, he wrote. At least there he had had fresh air. Each evening Anthony and Speer Riddell made up their beds behind the counter and each morning they cleared them away again. But they soon discovered that at night the place was crawling with rats and neither man could get any sleep. Riddell shooed them away like chickens, but, said Anthony, it did no good. Tasheira himself eventually decided to sleep on top of the counter. One Sunday morning he went off on his usual walk up Telegraph Hill to look at the view, and while he was away Peder Sather looked into the bank. His eye immediately fell on the bedclothes still lying on the countertop. Speer Riddell explained why they were there, and Sather asked him to tell Anthony to be sure to push another desk up against the counter, to save him from falling off it in his sleep.

Bearing in mind how few people worked in the bank and how close the relationship between Anthony and Peder Sather had otherwise been, this episode is an interesting illustration of how little contact they appeared to have had with one another at this time. It was a lonely and downhearted Anthony who sat up there on Telegraph Hill, brooding and gazing out to sea while the church bells chimed from thirty-odd churches, calling Christians of all denominations to worship. Peder Sather answered the call while Anthony thought his thoughts.

There seemed no end to the influx of newcomers to the city. Anthony followed a ship with his eyes. It passed through the Golden Gate and dropped

anchor offshore. He knew from personal experience how impatient its passengers would be to go ashore, and the deck was swarming with people. The
ship on which he had come had brought eight hundred men to San Francisco,
but the ship lying down there was carrying more than two thousand. The
sight of the crowds gathered on its deck brought up gloomy thoughts in
Anthony Tasheira. He knew how full of anticipation they were, and how
disappointed they were soon going to be. There was nothing for them here
but pain, want, and hardship, he thought bitterly. The prospectors sacrificed
everything, and all for nothing. They ought at least to have been awarded a
small pension for all their hard work, but, he wrote, they could forget that
idea. Peder Sather had helped him to get out of Tuolumne, but Anthony was
miserable; all he wanted now was for Eliza and the children to come out and
join him.

———

TEN

Cigars, Wine, and Other Evils

Compared to prospecting for gold in Tuolumne, keeping the books for Drexel, Sather & Church was as good as a vacation for Anthony. Nor had he forgotten the din and dust and steam of William Metcalf's foundry. Back then he had rarely had the strength to answer Eliza when she wanted to chat in the evenings, and he would often fall asleep in his chair. Now he wrote to her and said that he must have been an awfully boring man to have in the house, always exhausted and no fun at all. Had he stayed in that job he was afraid that his mother would not have been the only widow in the family.

So life was good now, as far as he was concerned, although he missed his family, missed having someone with whom to spend his free time. He consoled himself with the thought of all the fresh fruit and vegetables to be had here, even in winter: radishes and cauliflower, green beans, carrots, and good potatoes. In the evenings he went for walks in town, then read for a while and fell asleep as soon as his head hit the pillow.

Theodore's name comes up again and again in Anthony's letters. The latter felt that the youth was given far too long a leash and he was ashamed of Theodore's idle ways. The only person capable of making him toe the line was Peder, but he didn't and it did no good to ask him either, Anthony wrote.

After 1854, however, there is no mention of Theodore in Anthony's letters—apart from the words "since Theodore left" written later in that year, which seem to imply that he had left San Francisco early in 1854. So Peder had obviously abandoned any attempt to knock Theodore into shape. His days of acting the surrogate father and giving a helping hand were over.

Theodore had left San Francisco for good and all and embarked on what was to be a somewhat rootless existence. According to census reports, newspaper items, and employment records, he initially lived for some years with

Mercelena Tasheira and William Roosevelt in Jersey City. But in 1858 Mercelena died of tuberculosis and not long afterward Roosevelt remarried. When the Civil War broke out he joined the Union Army and so did Theodore. On May 21, 1861, the latter enlisted as a volunteer in the First New Jersey Infantry Regiment, First Company. He started off as a corporal, but in September 1862 he was reduced to the ranks. In January 1863 he was wounded and admitted to the military hospital in Washington, DC. After being released from hospital he received a disability discharge from the regiment and returned to Jersey City.

After the war William Roosevelt and his family moved to Cedar Rapids in Franklin County, Iowa. That he and his offspring took great pride in being related to President Theodore Roosevelt is clear from the obituary in the *Cedar Rapids Evening Gazette* of Theodore Tasheira Roosevelt, who died in 1909 at the age of fifty. This says that he "is said to be a distant relative to the former president Theodore Roosevelt."

The disabled, demoted corporal Theodore Tasheira could not boast such exalted kinship. He seems, by all accounts, to have lived in Jersey City until 1877. Throughout his years there he was a member of and secretary of the local Masonic Lodge. He tried working as a clerk in a savings bank and as a real estate agent, but did not do particularly well in either job.

Theodore then left Jersey City and went to work as a farmhand with Anton Bradley in Canaan, Columbia County, New York. The two men were the same age and had served in the same regiment during the Civil War. After the war Bradley had gone back to the family farm. He stayed there, running the farm with his widowed mother, and remained a bachelor all his days. In 1883 Theodore left the Bradleys and worked for a while as a night porter at a hotel in Providence before gaining a place in the National Home for Disabled Volunteer Soldiers in Woodstock, Connecticut. He died there in 1904, leaving neither wife nor children behind him.

And so the Theodore Tasheira who left San Francisco in 1854 and was the object of many an indignant tirade in Anthony's letters also makes his exit once and for all from this story. But while Anthony had ceased to report on Theodore's activities he was still keeping a close eye on his employer. In the spring of 1854 Anthony noticed a change in Peder Sather. In the old days, when he was working in Nassau Street, Peder had been distant, drained of energy, and depressed. Now, though, he was bright and cheery and fitter than ever. Anthony hoped that Peder's health would remain good, but as the weeks went on he became aware of other, hitherto unknown, sides to Peder

Sather which he found very hard to accept. Among other things Sather no longer went to church as regularly as he used to, and Anthony wondered whether he would soon have to be considered a lost sheep.

Peder Sather was not the only one to have his faith put to the test during the Gold Rush. So many souls separated from family and old friends, surrounded by multitudes of strangers; with no stable environments or established institutions; with the gold, which made everything else of value look dull and gray. This was a society with no sense of community. In such a world the churches were like ghost houses or castles in the air, all spirits and nothingness. Not everyone felt this way, but a great many did.

But Tasheira the bookkeeper's mind was much more taken up by other things; things that he carefully recorded, like a guard, indignantly more often than not, always in the lonely office where he filled the emptiness of his life with the stories told him by the people who came by, bringing with them anecdotes and news. One day James Hutchinson came into Anthony's office and confided to him that Peder Sather had also become a first-class card player. Apparently he visited the home of a Scottish banker by the name of William Turnbull every evening to play whist. The cashier knew this for a fact because he lodged with the Turnbulls. Anthony himself had noticed that Peder had taken to smoking cigars; he was not happy about this and thought his benefactor looked most awkward.

William Turnbull was also a merchant, and he became very successful very quickly before leaving San Francisco with a huge fortune, which he then lost by making some bad investments in New York. In that city he became a dear friend of entrepreneur Cornelius "Commodore" Vanderbilt, who helped Turnbull to get back on his feet and included him in his inner circle for the rest of his life.

It certainly seemed as though some change had taken place in Peder Sather's life since he came to San Francisco, something similar to the transformation he had undergone after arriving in New York at the age of twenty-two. Back then he had become a Baptist and had himself baptized; now he no longer saw any point in going to church. The journey to California had been as long as that from Norway to New York, so leaving his family in Brooklyn had been like emigrating for a second time. And this time he was enjoying his freedom. He did not stay in the office until late at night: instead he spent his evenings engaging in the worldliest of pursuits at the home of the Turnbulls. All of this is in stark contrast to the anxious Peder Sather who wrote to Anthony in 1849 and urged him to trust in God when he left New York and ventured out into a dangerous and unknown world.

On the other hand Peder Sather was no moody skeptic, unlike Anthony Tasheira in that regard. In the early 1840s Søren Bache had described Peder Sather as gregarious and approachable, a linchpin of the Norwegian community, keeping open house in Brooklyn. But Anthony Tasheira gives the impression that Sather took pleasure in other things in life besides the bank, his family in Brooklyn, and the Baptist Church. A person's character is not like a different coat that can be slipped on in every new port; it develops, rather, in different ways under different skies. If Anthony was right, and a new side of Peder Sather's nature had begun to emerge, this suggests that Peder was following a less strict regime than before. Anthony was a keen observer, always out and about, the iron founder and the prospector in him constantly assessing his surroundings and in many cases finding them wanting—he rejected most of what he saw going on around him in San Francisco. He sat at his desk, kept careful account of everything he got wind of, and wrote about it all to Eliza. It was, of course, easier for him to keep in touch here than it had been in Tuolumne. Back then he had had to rely on others to take his letters to San Francisco for dispatch on the mail steamer, and sometimes they did not even make it that far. Now he could write as many letters as he liked and deliver them to the harbor personally.

According to Anthony, Peder Sather was doing more than just playing cards and smoking cigars. He had been most sympathetic when the bank's black messenger and porter, Nelson Cook, learned that his wife, Sara, and their little daughter Ann would be arriving from New York sooner than expected. Nelson was thrilled to bits when he told this news to his fellow workers at the bank, but he was also at his wit's end because right then he could not afford to buy even the most basic necessities for his family. When Peder Sather heard this he immediately offered to help Nelson by giving him one hundred dollars and arranging a loan for him.

In San Francisco it was still not the normal way of things for blacks and whites to have dealings with one another, and certainly not for a wealthy white man to employ a poor black man or to help him financially. This was long before Abraham Lincoln staked his presidency on the abolition of slavery, and a very long time indeed before equal rights for black and white became an issue. The number of black people in San Francisco was small, and those who had come there during the Gold Rush kept to themselves. The ethnic ghettoes in the city and along the West Coast did nothing to help shape the new state into a unified society; instead they delayed the process or prevented it from happening. Peder Sather's relationship with Nelson Cook was a special case—not the only one, it's true, but their friendship stands as a good example of exceptions to the rule.

Peder's stays in San Francisco became more frequent and lasted longer than he had originally intended. Two things seem to have made him change his plan of only staying in San Francisco until the bank was up and running. The first was the climate and the beneficial effect this had on his health, the other was Sather's feeling that Edward Church was somewhat lacking in initiative. He even said as much to Anthony one day. Sather had not been long in San Francisco before he realized that this was where he wanted to spend most of his time. He made up his mind, therefore, to buy a house in the town, a decision he can hardly have made without consulting Sarah. She for her part could see how much fitter he was, and the thought that his financial prospects were looking better than ever must also have been an appealing one. Like most other people, Peder Sather had gone to California in the belief that he could make money there, and this was, of course, what all the grass widows in the east expected, including Sarah.

That Sather was looking for a house in San Francisco suggests that Sarah and Peder had already agreed that eventually the whole family would move to San Francisco. Peder Sather purchased a lot on Rincon Hill, an almost unpopulated hill within walking distance of Montgomery Street. From it one had a marvelous view of the roadsteads and the bay, and the air up there was clean and fresh, not like it was down in the center of town, where smoke from the chimneys stung the nostrils and the most appalling stench rose up from the open sewers. Dung from the horses and the herds of cattle that were driven through the streets was another serious problem, especially on hot, still days.

Peder Sather was one of the first to build on this hill, but he would not be the last. From the mid-1850s onward Rincon Hill became the most popular spot for the upper-middle classes, an area that has been described at length by historians and architects and captured for posterity in a wealth of old drawings, daguerreotypes, and photographs. Sather's house features in a number of books, alongside elegant villas and the most stylish residences, built on several floors, complete with turrets and oriel windows, broad staircases, marble pillars, terraces, and porches. These last were very much in vogue, although pretty useless in a city where it rained all winter and the summers were cool, with fog and wind blowing in off the sea, sweeping

FIGURE 13. Sather house at Rincon Hill, northeast corner of Second Street and Harrison, San Francisco. Courtesy of the Bancroft Library, University of California, Berkeley.

through the streets and sending up clouds of sand that got into every nook and cranny.

Compared to the sumptuous mansions built later, Peder Sather's house was really quite a modest affair. Architects think it may have been a prefab, sent over from the east and erected in double-quick time. It had two floors to it, with the bedrooms upstairs and the public rooms and the kitchen downstairs. It had tall narrow windows, a high pitched gable with brick dentils, and, to the right of the front door, a small porch.

From one of Anthony's letters, it would appear that Peder Sather moved in to the new house in the late spring of 1854. One Saturday night not long afterward, Peder was asleep in his room on the second floor when he was rudely awoken by a jingling, jangling sound. He opened his eyes and down by the foot of the bed he saw the shadowy figure of a man. This person was in the midst of slipping his hand into Sather's trousers, which were draped over a chair. At first Sather thought it was William Turnbull playing a trick on him, but it very quickly dawned on him that this stranger was in fact a burglar. Peder Sather started shouting and yelling for all he was worth in hopes of alerting the neighbors and calling someone to his aid. When this did not work he jumped out of bed and chased after the man, who flew down the stairs, dashed across the hall, out through the front door and off toward the town.

The thief had got into the house by boring a hole in the door big enough to stick his hand through and turn the key in the lock. He had dropped a glove on the floor and left behind a lantern; he left no other trace of himself. He had got away with a pewter soup tureen, a pair of theater glasses, some antimacassars, the keys to Sather's desk, and his gold-rimmed spectacles. It could have been much worse: the thief had probably been looking for the keys to the bank's safe. The police had been warning citizens for some time of a gang that was on the rampage in the city and was rumored to be planning to rob bank after bank.

Peder Sather told Anthony about this incident the following Monday. It does not only provide some insight into the level of lawlessness in San Francisco, but also into the contrast between Peder's world and Anthony's. While the bookkeeper slept on the counter and guarded the safe, Peder Sather resided in a house on Rincon Hill, enjoyed himself with William Turnbull, and was a keen theatergoer. Sather and Turnbull must have been great ones for pranks and practical jokes, if one of them was capable of sneaking into the other's house in the middle of the night just for a laugh. Downstairs in the public rooms empty furniture was covered in sheets, white in the moonlight: a reminder of a time that was gone and of times to come.

Peder told Anthony that it would not be long before the rest of the family came out to San Francisco. He had, he said: "no intention of trying the experiment unless circumstances render it necessary." What circumstances could have rendered it so necessary for them to come to San Francisco, and why would it be an experiment? Was it Caroline—would the move be too much for her? Or was it Sarah who was too delicate? Did none of them want to move? The antimacassars could have lain where they were until they turned gray with dust, waiting for the couple to agree on what they should do.

The contract with Francis Drexel ran out in 1856, and it may be that Peder Sather wanted to delay making a final decision on the family's living arrangements until then. In the meantime he concentrated on running the bank, which was now going through a rough patch. In addition, he had been elected a member of the San Francisco Grand Jury—a clear sign, surely, that he had no immediate plans to leave San Francisco for good.

By 1854 gold production had fallen drastically, with the result that prices rose and so did unemployment. This in turn led to a drop in the demand for loans, and Anthony noted that there was a lot of money in the bank vault—a bad sign. Peder Sather was not happy—he felt the bank was too small to support two directors—but at the same time he did not believe his partner capable of managing it alone if he moved back to New York.

Anthony had also observed that Edward Church was not quite up to the mark; he seemed lazy, distant, and incapable of acting independently. And, Anthony added: "He seems to shirk from all responsibility. I'll wager a cow he is not of sound mind." Strong words. In other letters, though, Tasheira remarks on how exhausted Edward Church was every time Sather went back to New York, leaving the rest of them with all the work.

But Church agreed with Sather that he would stay on at the bank and began, therefore, to build a house on Rincon Hill, right next door to Peder Sather. Letitia Church had come to San Francisco to see her husband in 1851, but she was still living in Brooklyn with the child they had had after their first baby died. In the spring of 1854 Edward Church was at last able to go back to New York to collect them and bring them to San Francisco to stay. The three were expected at the end of May, but they arrived earlier than supposed. William Turnbull and James Hutchinson spotted the ship at six in the morning when they were out riding in the hills. They went straight to Peder Sather's house to tell him the news, and when he walked into the bank later he was in great good humor, Anthony wrote. Sather had just popped in to give some orders about work before hurrying down to the harbor to welcome the Church family. Then they all took a carriage up to Rincon Hill, where the Turnbulls had a big welcome breakfast waiting for them.

A few days later yet another big fire broke out in the city. Overnight, in just a matter of hours it destroyed forty homes in one of the poorest districts in town. It was here that Nelson Cook had found lodgings for himself, his wife, and his daughter; now they had nothing. The fire had spread so fast that Nelson had no time to save any of their possessions. When Peder Sather learned what had happened he told Edward Church that they simply had to give Nelson a leg-up. Anthony overheard this and mentioned it in a letter to Eliza: "As to Mr. Sather," he says, "it was as usual a very kind and characteristic proposal, but Mr. Church just hawked and would obviously not give our porter any kind of support."

In the late summer Peder Sather received a letter informing him that Caroline had been admitted to hospital again. Anthony was present when

Sather opened it and remarked that this news left him "totally discouraged." The only explanation, as far as Tasheira could see, for Peder's shocked response had to be that Sarah had said nothing to him beforehand about what had been going on at home. This suggests that husband and wife might not have been on the best of terms.

So Peder Sather had his worries, and his evenings with the Turnbulls, his next-door neighbors on Rincon Hill, were possibly a way of escaping from these. Anthony knew what they got up to there because Sather gave him a bundle of receipts to enter in the books. To his horror the bookkeeper discovered that these receipts were for the purchase of large quantities of wine and champagne, as much as six gallons at a time. Anthony didn't know who attended these parties or how often they were held, but he had his suspicions. Again he picked up his pen to tell Eliza about the goings-on at the Turnbull residence:

> They have card parties nearly every evening and I suppose (as they play for refreshments) he gets (as the saying is) stuck pretty often, though I am told he has learnt to play an excellent game of Euchre and smokes a cigar too, quite up to the stump! which is a decided improvement on the few whiffs that used to satisfy him, the performance always suggests an inward smile from its extreme awkwardness, which you can readily imagine. Sitting in the Bank on Sunday he asked me if I could accommodate him with a cigar! Since then a supply has been kept on hand.

Bearing in mind that Eliza was in touch with Sarah in Brooklyn, one has to wonder whether Eliza told her what was said in this letter.

Anthony himself felt very much on the sidelines as far as Sather's circle of friends on Rincon Hill was concerned, and the picture he paints of certain of its members is not the most flattering. When Letitia Church called in at the bank, for example, she scarcely deigned to nod in his direction. Edward Church noticed that Anthony was looking rather lost and asked him whether he was feeling homesick. Because if so, why didn't he just buy a house? Then he'd have no problem persuading his family to come out and join him! Peder Sather was of this same opinion, but Anthony had no money and no idea what to do. All he knew was that he wanted to go home to Eliza at the earliest opportunity, preferably together with Peder Sather.

The Churches had moved in to their new house on Rincon Hill and Letitia Church dutifully invited Anthony to dinner. But he could not bring himself to go, feeling as he did that she looked down on him and regarded him as an idiot who could barely spell. But Letitia's sister, who lived with the Churches, was, to his mind, even worse: "Coralie has the most insincere expression I ever saw in a woman's face, and then such airs, out with them. I like to see a woman act and look natural, like Mrs. Turnbull, no affections, no false pride, plain," he wrote. "Nevertheless, Mr. Hutchinson is too stoical to fall in raptures with anything or anybody, not excepting his lady love." According to Anthony, James Hutchinson tried to act nonchalant when this lady popped into the bank, as she frequently did—although without ever so much as saying hello to Tasheira himself.

In the end Anthony reluctantly had to admit that there was no way round it, he would have to pay the Churches a visit. He almost made it to their front door too, but then he began to feel sick and could go no further. He could not stand such formal gatherings, he said, and his dislike of them was steadily growing. Anthony wished he could take pleasure in the same things as other people, but he didn't have it in him; he wasn't like that, he wrote.

The next day Edward Church wanted to know why he had not turned up. Anthony excused himself by saying that he had had a headache, but all this got him was a fresh invitation. This time he forced himself to go. He had dinner, his stomach aching as he did his best to make conversation. Letitia Church did nothing but complain about the dust that blew in through the cracks in the walls and made it impossible to keep the furniture really clean, not unless she got the maid to take a duster to it two or three times a day. "They have everything money can buy, and yet Mrs. Church always manages to find fault with something," Anthony wrote.

On the Fourth of July Sather went on an outing to the Santa Clara Valley, south of San Francisco. In the carriage with him were Letitia Church, Mrs. Turnbull. and a "Mr Johnson"—a name that does not crop up anywhere else in the correspondence. This may have been George Johnson, originally from Bergen in Norway; he was a steel merchant, president of the Scandinavian Society in San Francisco and latterly the Norwegian-Swedish consul general.

When the gentry returned a few days later, Anthony was told that they had had a very interesting outing. Anthony knew that the Santa Clara Valley was exceptionally lush and fertile, so much so that it was called "the garden of California." He, on the other hand, had spent the Fourth of July at the bank, going out only to watch the parade go by. The only part of it that had made any sort of an impression on him was the two hundred Chinese clad in strange Oriental uniforms, all of them carrying shields and spears. The firework display later in the evening had been pathetic, smothered as it was in clouds of smoke and fog.

In the late summer Ole Bull had made his eventful crossing of the Isthmus of Panama, the one in which he had been robbed and had contracted Panama fever. Now he was in San Francisco to give a series of concerts, something which, in an article from August 24, the *New York Times* hailed as a sign that Californians were becoming more civilized. People turned out in droves to hear Ole Bull play at the Metropolitan Theatre in Montgomery Street, and in a letter dated July 30, Anthony says that Peder Sather bought tickets for all of the bank's employees, and "the women folks" too.

Sather and Bull had become friends in New York, "very close friends" according to the editor of *the Daily Alta California* in a memorial article written in 1884. In this article the writer described an extremely lively dinner party at the Turnbulls' home, attended by Ole Bull. Bull had accepted the invitation simply because the party was Peder Sather's idea. A more informal dinner would have been hard to imagine, the editor recalled. Ole Bull had entertained them with vivid, animated descriptions of his tours of Europe and Russia, including an account of a meeting with the mighty and much dreaded Tsar Nicholas, whom Bull had totally won over with his playing, his charm, and his dauntless personality.

Peder Sather and Ole Bull later left San Francisco on the same ship for New York, but Anthony says nothing of the concert or of all the socializing. He would probably have refused to accept the ticket had he known that during his stay the violinist called on the legendary Lola Montes. Anthony had heard rumors about this lady, whom, as he said in a letter to Eliza, he regarded as nothing but a scandalous chorus girl. And he added: "But at present the veritable Lola has made a retreat to Grass Valley. There she is living together with her pets, among others a grizzly bear."

Lola Montes was the stage name of Eliza Gilbert, born in Limerick in Ireland, around 1820, and possibly less well known for her musical talent than for her Bohemian lifestyle and amorous adventures. Before coming to California she had been a member of the most eccentric artists' colonies in Europe, and not least in Paris. In that city Montes had had an affair with Franz Liszt—a mutual friend of hers and of Ole Bull. Through Liszt, Montes met another friend of his, the writer George Sand, and for a while she was also the mistress of Alexandre Dumas the elder. In San Francisco she had married a newspaperman with whom she lived in Grass Valley. But the marriage only lasted a year before she divorced him and went on living out there on her own.

Ole Bull visited Lola Montes in Grass Valley and was by all accounts quite besotted with her. In 1854 she performed with a group of Spanish dancers in San Francisco and the surrounding area—these were men-only affairs, Anthony remarked meaningfully. But there must have been more to this woman than the bookkeeper supposed. A year later, when crossing the Isthmus of Panama, she gave up her mule to a young soldier suffering from Panama fever while she made her way on foot through the dense jungle.

On October 10, 1854, the New York *Sun* reported that the steamship *Northern Light* had sailed into port in the city the previous day, and that Ole Bull had been among its passengers. So too was Peder Sather, and having spent almost a month on board the same boat I'm sure these two Norwegians must have made good use of the opportunity to cement their friendship.

Anthony Lewis Tasheira did not get to travel back to New York with Sather, but the latter dropped him a line from San Juan to tell him that all was well with him and that the journey home was going as planned. Before leaving he had doubled Anthony's salary, thus giving him two hundred dollars a month, which was a pretty decent income. He took this raise as a sign that Peder Sather was happy with his work and, he wrote: "It is very satisfying, because when Mr. Sather offered me an employment it was more of an experiment, as I had no knowledge of such business."

Peder Sather would definitely be back in San Francisco within a year, Edward Church declared. This seemed an awfully long time to Anthony, but he comforted himself with something which Peder Sather had told him in confidence before he left and which was to remain a secret for the time being, namely that he had decided to close down the office in Nassau Street. At the same time he had urged Anthony to stay on in San Francisco and to start making all the necessary preparations for bringing Eliza and the children out to the West Coast in the spring.

Anthony was afraid that they would not be happy, so far away from their family and friends. He wrote to his son Lewis and explained to him that a new state like California did not have all the wonderful things that New York had to offer. There were no trolley cars there, no picnic spots to match Hoboken and Washington Heights, there wasn't even a park or a square where children could play. In California there were sand dunes and mountains everywhere, dotted with small, gnarled, and windswept trees. But there would be one very special treat in store for his dear son Lewis, because in San Francisco little boys could fish in the streets! He explained how the center of the city spread all around the harbor and how the streets were not paved with stones, like the ones Lewis knew, but with planks; and that much of the city was built directly over the water. In some houses you could actually fish from the doors or windows!

While Peder Sather was away Anthony continued to live at the bank. Speer Riddell had succumbed to a serious bout of dysentery and was in hospital. In the evenings Anthony would sit alone, gazing out at the street and the hurdy-gurdy man who played outside the saloon next door. Every time he heard him Anthony was reminded of his father, who had always had a coin to spare for the street musicians who used to play outside their window at home.

And so the days and the weeks passed, and when the ships from New York came gliding into the roadstead, and, soon afterward, Montgomery Street rang with the voices of the newsboys crying out the news from the East Coast, it was sweet music to every Californian's ears, so Anthony wrote, because one of these ships might carry a longed-for letter. And eventually his ship, too, came in: one day the mail steamer brought word that Peder Sather would only be staying in Brooklyn for a couple of months and that he would not be returning to San Francisco alone.

ELEVEN

The Turning Point

Eliza and the Tasheira children, sixteen-year-old Harriet, ten-year-old Lewis, and eight-year-old George, left New York with Peder Sather and set sail for San Francisco at the end of February 1855.

I have the younger of the two boys, George, to thank for the insight I have been given into Peder Sather's life at this time. George kept all of his parents' correspondence, and as an old man he presented it to the California State Library in Sacramento. In the last letter sent by Anthony before his family made the move west he expresses a hope that the children will be able to receive an education and not have to toil and struggle as he had done. It upset him to see young lads fishing down by the canals around the harbor in the middle of the day when they ought to have been in school.

It was a large party that set out for San Francisco on that cold February day in 1855. First they took the boat to Aspinwall in Panama. From there they had, of course, to cross the Isthmus, but now they no longer needed to do this on foot, by boat, and on donkeys: only a month earlier the new Panama Railroad had been opened, and Peder Sather and his traveling companions were among the first to travel from the East Coast westward by train. A locomotive hooked up to a handful of yellow coaches now chugged along a narrow track through the jungle. Together with speedier steamships the new railroad link cut two weeks off the traveling time from New York to San Francisco, a trip which now rarely took more than twenty days.

On March 17 the steamship *John L. Stephens* headed through the Golden Gate. Peder Sather's party had left an icy white New York City and arrived in San Francisco when spring was at its greenest and the meadows were aglow with poppies. Anthony Lewis Tasheira was on the quayside to welcome them, although for some time he had been unwell, with stomach pains so severe that he could neither sit nor stand.

On Rincon Hill a house was all ready and waiting for the Tasheira family. The address was 420 Second Street. Peder Sather lived at number 436, so the Tasheiras and Sather were now neighbors in one of the most exclusive residential areas in the city. Even though Anthony had set aside a little money every month he cannot possibly have had enough to buy a house, let alone a residence on Rincon Hill. It seems more likely that he received some help from Peder Sather, either in the form of a loan or the chance to rent the property relatively cheaply. To safeguard the bank against financial slumps, Sather had already started to buy up property in San Francisco and elsewhere around the bay.

As women, Eliza and Harriet were soon to discover that they were in the minority, as were the children. Of the approximately sixty thousand inhabitants of San Francisco in 1855, only three hundred were minors and about eight thousand women. Of the women, a large proportion were prostitutes who hung around the bars, hotels, and gambling saloons, and it was this group on which the first public and philanthropic initiatives focused. Children's homes and homes for unwed mothers were, in reality, institutions set up to care for prostitutes and the fruits of their profession.

Respectable women were in short supply, the papers said—by which they meant wives and mothers. Without them this society would never become civilized, it was said. And without them, the male population of the city might have added, there would be no one to cook their meals or wash their clothes. Before the men were able to bring their wives out to California, all such odd jobs were done by black people and the Chinese. In the social pecking order no group came lower than the Chinese, who were despised by everyone. In an attempt to get rid of them the state legislature in Sacramento cunningly introduced the Foreign Miner Tax, whereby all foreign—that is, Chinese—prospectors had to pay an extra monthly tax so high that it drove them into San Francisco, where they were, quite literally, spat on in the ghettoes if they were unable to secure a passage on a boat back to China.

For the Tasheira family this was the start of a new life in a world that could not been more different from the slums of the Lower East Side. Around them, from day one, they had a whole clan of relatives and friends. They had never lived as well or as comfortably as they did on Second Street, in a neighborhood that had grown and was now home to the cultural and financial elite: pastors and booksellers, merchants and bankers, artists and foreign envoys. Eliza's and Anthony's children were immediately enrolled in Rincon School, a private school reserved for the residents of the Hill. Although the fact that it was a private school did not really mean all that much: with the population growing so fast and the county unable to meet the demand for schools, a whole host of private establishments had sprung up.

In 1855 the Tasheiras, Mr. Lee (a book-keeper in the bank), the Church family, and Peder Sather were all near-neighbors on Rincon Hill. Sather himself must have had some contact with Odalen, because in the summer of this year his nephew Bernt Dysterud came to visit him and stayed with him for almost a whole year. Bernt was the son of Ole Dysterud and Sather's sister Anne, and the brother of Peder Olsen Dysterud who had died at Red Cedar Lake in 1837. The fact that Bernt stayed with Peder for the whole of that year suggests that Sarah did not see much of her husband. But if he could afford to pay Bernt's fare from Norway, it cannot have been lack of money that stopped Sarah and the children from taking a trip to San Francisco, and there was room for all of them in the house on Rincon Hill. It could be that neither the children nor Sarah wanted to go out west; it could be that she and Peder were not getting on; it could be that their daughter Caroline, now nineteen, was the problem. It's possible that she was not fit to travel or that she was reliant on the care of medical specialists in New York. In any case, none of this had any influence on Peder's decision to remain in California. As can be seen from the aforementioned notice, posted in the *New York Times* by Luther Lawrence on July 4, 1856, which announces: "Luther Lawrence & Co—bankers. No 164 Nassau Street New York. Successors to P. Sather, his agents. Dealers in bills of exchange, bank notes and specie. Signs drafts on Messrs. Drexel, Sather & Church, San Francisco."

Peder Sather confirmed the truth of this announcement in the same newspaper on July 7, in a notice penned in San Francisco on May 12:

The Banking and Exchange Business hitherto conducted in this City by my Attorney, Luther S. Lawrence, Esq., on my account, will be discontinued from this day. L. S. Lawrence is authorized to receive any outstanding collections, as well as to collect other claims arising from the above business. Persons having claims on me will please present the same for payment previous to June 1, 1856.

Luther S. Lawrence has associated himself with Mr. Charles Farrar, and will continue the Banking and Exchange Business, under the name of L. S. Lawrence & Co. I take pleasure in stating that during my absence for the last five years Mr. Lawrence has conducted my business with prudence and faithfulness and I cheerfully recommend him as implicitly reliable in any business that may be entrusted to him. Yours Truly, P. Sather

Here, Sather refers to the bank in Nassau Street as *his,* thus implying that Edward Church was not in fact an equal partner. Sather closed down the bank on Nassau Street in the same year that the five-year contract with Francis Drexel expired, and from 1856 the bank in San Francisco operated under the name of "Sather & Church."

In works on the history of American finance Francis Drexel is usually said to have "withdrawn," a choice of words which gives the impression that he was dissatisfied with the business in San Francisco, and there's no doubt that he could have extended the agreement had he so desired. But since we now know that the collaboration was never meant to last longer than five years, it rather looks as though Drexel's main aim was to help Sather and Church get started. Both Francis and Anthony Drexel were well known for presenting colleagues with opportunities. This did no harm for their reputations, obviously, but it also ensured them of a wide and loyal network of associates. Likewise, when Francis Drexel put up such a large slice of the initial capital for Drexel, Sather & Church he wasn't just doing it out of the goodness of his heart. He was not blind to the lucrative business to be made from gold, and the contract contained detailed provisions regarding his share of the profit.

All of this Anthony the bookkeeper had been made privy to when a very mysterious Peder Sather popped his head round his door and asked him to come to his office to transcribe some papers. This was normally one of Speer Riddell's duties, and Anthony could not understand why he was suddenly being called upon. Transcribing documents was a dreadfully boring task, but when Sather whispered to him that the document in question was the contract with Francis Drexel, Anthony felt honored to have been given the job, and at the end of the day he left the office feeling proud to be the only person in San Francisco in whom Peder Sather had shown such enormous trust.

Trust was a key word in the world of finance, and when Peder Sather concluded his notice in the *New York Times* by declaring that Luther Lawrence was a reliable man this was much more than a pleasantry in a testimonial for a colleague. The banks were privately owned; their business was totally dependent on the trust which their clients showed in the owners. And for this trust to be maintained there had to be a balance between loans and liquidity, so a bank could not gamble by lending out money which it had borrowed itself, possibly in a speculative manner. This sort of gambling was fairly common and led to the collapse of bank after bank, or to bank owners professing their innocence and occasionally even absconding, leaving their customers cleaned out. Then as now this is how banking crises are created, although there is a tendency to describe them as natural disasters.

Peder Sather had built up the necessary trust, but—just as importantly— he also *showed* trust. A new friend of his, Samuel Merritt, a San Francisco doctor and businessman, said later that Sather could often be a little too naïve where clients were concerned, and could be charmed into mistaking a swindler for a man of honor. The bank had already loaned ten thousand dollars to just such a crook. The worst of it, Anthony writes, was that it was Sather himself who had been taken in by him. The man's name was Henry Meiggs, an entrepreneur who owned boatyards, sawmills, and planing mills, and was also involved in a large-scale development of piers and warehouses on the harborfront. Meiggs had got himself into very deep water; he reneged on his creditors and fled to Peru before he was brought to book.

In 1856, however, there are no signs of Peder Sather's days being clouded by swindlers or crooks. His nephew from Odalen was still living with him; I can almost hear the way they lapse into their native dialect as they stroll along Montgomery Street, chat over dinner at the house on Rincon Hill—fresh fish and plenty of vegetables to keep illness at bay—or poke fun at Turnbull on buggy rides out to the Mission Dolores or outings to the Santa Clara Valley. And on the Fourth of July, too, nudging each other in the ribs and passing comments in their own private language. They were good, solid Odal men, and who knows, maybe Peder even cracked open a bottle of his best champagne.

The bank was doing so well that it could now stand on its own two feet. Even though the office in New York had been handed over to Luther Lawrence and the contract with Francis Drexel had expired it kept the name Drexel, Sather & Church until the summer of 1857. By then the partnership was over, but Sather's friendship with both Francis and Anthony Drexel was not.

The fact that Bernt Dysterud had come over to visit him suggests that Peder was now on good terms with the family in Odalen. In the summer of 1856, when Bernt was preparing to go home to Norway, his uncle gave him a gold hunter watch. This elegant watch, inscribed with a dedication to Bernt from his Uncle Peder, is the only memento of Sather to be found in Norway. I have seen it with my own eyes on a dusky-green day in Odalen. Time stopped long ago for that watch, but I wind it up and set it turning again as I write. Or at least, that's how it feels. Turning it back to the day of Bernt's departure. On that occasion, for the first time since leaving Norway, Peder Sather wrote a letter to his brother Christoffer on the farm of his childhood:

> Dear Brother,
> It ought not to be so very difficult to write a few words to a Brother, and yet for me this is close to being the Case. The reason, I suppose, is partly that we have never Corresponded, since this is the First Time I have written to you and till now I have received nothing from Your Hand.
>   But having such a good Opportunity to send something with our Nephew B.D., who is now returning home I feel bound to write a few Lines, even though I really I have nothing to tell.

By 1856 Peder Sather had been living in America for twenty-four years, and in all that time he had never heard from or got in touch with his brother. After such a long while Sather must have had a great deal to tell, and yet he refrains. This letter was the first sign of life from him, so one can understand if he was a little reserved, and it's clear from those first words that it had cost him a lot to put pen to paper. That he did so anyway shows just how much he must have missed his brother. This is also there between the lines when Peder Sather goes on to say:

> When he (Bernt—K.S.) arrived here from Norway last Summer he told me that You visited his Father at Hoel to say goodbye to Him and that you asked him to give Me your Greetings, which proves that you have not forgotten me, and for that you have, hereby, my Appreciation.

It was a wary and humble Peder who wrote this letter, a man who had received a greeting from his brother a whole year earlier, through Bernt, and was now citing this as reason to get in touch. That the family in Odalen was in Sather's thoughts, and that he longed for news from home, is particularly evident in a couple of later passages relating to his friend Hans Rees, the tanner and leather goods merchant, husband of Lucinda Krom and brother-in-law to Jane, Peder Sather's future wife.

> Some Years ago I also had the Pleasure of hearing of You from my Friend Hans Rees in New York, who was visiting Christiania at that time, and I asked him to go to Odalen to see my old acquaintances . . . On that occasion Mr Rees also called on You.

Peder Sather had not yet been back to Norway and he was so keen to know how things were at home that he dispatched Hans Rees to his birthplace:

> On his Return to New York he told me that the House where I was born was the one in which You were now living and it warmed my Heart to hear that it was still standing and in good Shape, also when Bernt left, and I hope it will stand for a long Time yet, that you will continue to live in Peace and free of Care and live to a good Age. God alone knows if I will ever see You or Your Dwelling again, though it would do my heart good to see my Father's House once more before my Time here on Earth is over.

And that is how he closes the letter, as if it were up to some higher power to decide whether he would ever see Nordstun Nedre Sæter and his native soil again. Wistful words, and puzzling too. After all, it was not as if he couldn't afford to go back to Norway for a visit; he had done better for himself than he could ever have dreamed of as a young trainee in the bank in Trondhjem or a shop assistant in Christiania. For Peder's daughter, Petrine, back in that same town, 1856 also proved to be a crucial year. She bore a child out of wedlock to Encke the stonemason.

Did Peder know that he had become a grandfather? He had obviously thought long and hard before writing to Christoffer, but those first hesitant words marked the end of the brothers' estrangement. They were permanently reconciled and kept in touch for the rest of their lives, with Peder eventually signing his letters "Your devoted Brother."

By 1855 Drexel, Sather & Church had expanded. The bank had moved for a while to premises on Battery Street, on the corner of Clay Street. Francis Drexel and his sons were its principal collaborative partners—they had just opened their first office on Wall Street. Sather and Church were now part of an extensive banking network that encompassed Boston, Baltimore, Pittsburg, Cincinnati, Richmond, Louisville, and New Orleans, as well as London, Frankfurt, and Stuttgart. As part of this expansion, in 1855 Drexel, Sather & Church also opened a branch on Third Street in Sacramento. Counting their new bookkeeper, Henry C. Lee, Peder Sather and Edward Church now employed five people at the bank. They had also had a wagon sent over from New York for Nelson Cook's use. Every now and again Drexel, Sather & Church moved to a new address, but always on or near Montgomery Street, where the Tontine, one of the city's most notorious gambling saloons, had once lain. That was Montgomery Street then. Montgomery Street now was high finance, newspapers, concert halls, and theaters. Montgomery

Street now was processions and parades, oyster bars and dinner music. Montgomery Street now was ladies in muslin and brocade, lawyers and bankers in top hats, gentlemen with big beards and mustaches, sideburns and monocles.

Every day on his way to the office Peder Sather passed a peculiar figure standing on the street corner outside the bank. He sold the *Alta California* newspaper and he always wore a broad-brimmed hat pulled so far down over his face that his eyes were completely hidden. He stood so still that he might have been fast asleep, but every now and again he would utter a long-drawn: "Mornin' pa-pu-z, mornin' pa-pu-z!" For some reason he always put most stress on those last syllables and every time he was handed a coin he took it with a series of actions as protracted as his cry. First he closed his left hand around the coin, then he brought his right hand up ever so slowly, slipped the coin from the left hand to the right, and dropped it into a huge purse that he kept in the inside pocket of his thick and very heavy jacket. Hour after hour, like one of the cranes down on the docks, he repeated these actions, never raising his bowed head, never letting anyone see his eyes. No one knew him but everyone knew him, as one of the town's familiar but enigmatic figures.

Money changed hands on the sidewalks, stocks and bonds inside the buildings, and gold: gold flakes, gold dust, gold nuggets. The quality of the gold was tested beforehand by an assayer and if it was good enough it was melted down and turned into coins at the Mint before being sold or deposited in the bank. The assayer, the Mint, and the bank were three links in the chain, but before the gold got this far it had already had to pass through several checks at the gold fields, for all of which the prospectors were charged extra, and all before the gold could even be sold. During the first years the large production of gold was the biggest problem. With so much gold in circulation prices plummeted, inflation rose, and it was only a matter of time before the market would collapse. Later, when gold became harder to come by—when prospectors were having to dig down as much as twenty feet before finding even the merest sliver—the prospectors closed up their cabins and drifted in to San Francisco. There, with no money to pay for a ticket home, they wandered the streets, unemployed, filthy, drunk, waiting for something to happen, hoping for a miracle. There was no point in going back out to the fields. So much special equipment was now needed to get the gold out of the ground that only the big contractors could make any profit from it.

Drexel, Sather & Church made sure very early on that they had several strings to their bow: foreign currency, real estate, lending facilities. They took the long view, they worked hard and they managed to keep their doors open. Drexel, Sather & Church was never a big bank, but it was big enough. And it was one of the two which would, in the long run, survive. The other was Wells, Fargo & Co.

Privately, too, Sather had begun to invest in property. In 1855 the *Sacramento Daily Union* notes that Pastor Abraham Myers, the husband of Sarah's friend in Brooklyn, and Peder Sather owned large orchards in Alameda. The farmer's son would not be denied, nor would the businessman! In Alameda he grew vegetables and peaches, but was outdone by Myers, who produced abundant crops of apples, nectarines, cherries, pears, plums, and apricots.

Antony Lewis Tasheira worked alongside Speer Riddell, entering transactions large and small in the ledgers. Tall, narrow, close-set windows ran the length of the facade, and when the sun was high in the sky and its rays beat down on Montgomery Street the office became like an oven and the staff had to work with the windows open. "We might as well have been sitting on the sidewalk," Anthony wrote, "and strangely enough, no one tried to rob us." The city did not yet have a sanitation department and the streets were strewn with garbage. Peder Sather was insistent that the stretch of sidewalk outside the bank be kept neat and tidy, and was forever checking on it. Whenever he went to the front door and looked out onto the street, the other men knew exactly what was wanted and without a word being said Nelson Cook would hurry off to fetch the broom from its closet.

Sather usually kept the door of his office open, but one day he had it rehinged. Anthony and Speer Riddell had no idea why, they did not dare ask, no explanation was forthcoming, and the door stood open as before. Tasheira and Riddell were ordinary members of staff, they noticed the little, ordinary, everyday things; they heard the click of the safe, saw a rat scurrying across the floor, jumped when a ledger was closed with a bang, rolled their eyes when Letitia Church swanned past without vouchsafing them so much as a nod, pricked up their ears when a dubious customer approached the counter and tried to talk his way to a favorable loan.

At midday, when they stopped for lunch, the men went out to eat. It's said that so much liquor was drunk in the town and establishments made so much on the sale of alcohol that they did not charge for food. This meant that simply by ordering a glass of water teetotalers like Anthony and Speer could enjoy a free lunch—all the oysters, lobsters, crab, and asparagus they could eat. So too could Peder Sather. At any rate, Anthony's waspish reports of evenings of wine drinking and card playing at the Turnbulls' had gradually ceased. There is no more mention of bottles and glasses, and there could be a good explanation for this. Within just a few years Peder Sather would be an ardent teetotaler, or so the newspapers tell us. The city was awash with liquor and full of people who drank either because they were doing well or because everything was going to hell in a handbasket—life was full of ups and downs. The Temperance Movement had a strong following in America and an even stronger one in San Francisco where homesickness wore down the spirit and drove washed-up sailors, bankrupt traders and lonesome, hard-up prospectors to knock back all the booze they could lay their hands on.

The gold left California, transported on an armada of ships to the East Coast and from there to Europe, until the last grain had been scraped up from the bottom of the Sacramento and American Rivers and hacked out of the rock at the foot of the Sierra Nevada. Some called it a downright draining of the state; others compared California to Ireland, a backyard devoid of raw materials and natural resources.

Peder Sather struggled with his God, he struggled with his homesickness, he struggled with thoughts of his family, in Brooklyn, in Odalen, and, perhaps, in Christiania, but he stayed in San Francisco. And before too long he had a coachman whom he could order to hitch up the horses and bring the carriage round to drive him at a gentle trot from Second Street down to Montgomery—a street paved with gold. When Ole Bull and Peder Sather sailed to New York together on the *Northern Light* in October 1854, the ship was carrying precious metals to the tune of $960,000. The largest single consignment came from Wells, Fargo & Co., of the rest half belonged to Drexel, Sather & Church, and that half was far more than any of the smaller banks could muster. Shipping the gold was not without its risks, though: the coastlines were wild and rugged, bandits lay in wait on the Isthmus of Panama, and on the train you could never be sure when a gunman might take a notion for gold, start shooting, fill his bags, and vanish into the night. What could you do? Peder Sather did not spend much time in his office wondering about this. Between 1851 and 1855 Drexel, Sather & Church had paid $200,000 in transport insurance.

Many of their competitors gambled and suffered big losses, but Sather never put all of his eggs in one basket and he planned all of his operations very carefully. Consequently, he never had to think twice. According to Anthony Tasheira, Edward Church was the one who always seemed at a loss and could never make a decision. On one occasion Sather confided to

Anthony that Church had a tendency to be too cautious and was unable to act on his own initiative.

But no matter how clever a strategist and how dedicated a banker Peder Sather might have been, these qualities did not gain him entry to the ranks of high finance. Drexel, Sather & Church ran on diligence and trust; and, during the financial crisis of 1855, when a string of banks were forced to close, this one carried on, seemingly unaffected.

TWELVE

Law in a Lawless City

In the letter which Peder Sather sent to Christoffer at Nordstun Nedre Sæter through Bernt Dysterud he says that his nephew had "experienced a little of the life here and can probably tell you more about it than I can say here." This may seem a pretty harmless remark, but behind it lie events which shook the whole city and embroiled Sather in a series of violent events that belong to one of the darkest chapters in the history of San Francisco. When Bernt Dysterud returned to Odalen just before Christmas 1856 he must have had plenty to tell the family, and not just about good times with a generous uncle in America, dinners, walks and buggy rides, the gold watch he was given as a present and which, on a dark evening during Advent, was passed from hand to hand amid the glow and reek of the paraffin lamps while Bernt told his stories.

During Bernt Dysterud's stay the number of house break-ins in the city increased dramatically; the situation became so bad that people were almost as loath to bide at home as they were to go out and leave their houses unattended. Shops were also being plundered, storehouses emptied and set alight, and on the streets no one could feel sure that they would not be beaten up, robbed, stabbed, or shot. The police seemed to be more or less powerless to do anything but stand by and watch. The fire brigades were sabotaged, their wagons destroyed, their water tanks drained and smashed up. In the space of a few months about a hundred people were murdered by gangs of criminals.

A great many of the local politicians were corrupt and had been offered huge bribes to stand for election. The more prosperous inhabitants took no interest in politics, with the result that the running of the city was left in the hands of rogues big and small.

One of the main topics in the press in May 1856 was the bitter, long-standing feud between James King of William, the editor of the *San Francisco*

Bulletin, and James Casey, a corrupt district supervisor. When the *Bulletin* finally refused to accept any more of Casey's articles he started his own paper, the *Sunday Times,* thus giving himself a mouthpiece through which he could respond to his critics. Casey launched a searing attack on James King of William for having revealed that Casey—far from being the honorable supervisor he made himself out to be—had a criminal past and had indeed spent eighteen months in the notorious Sing Sing prison in New York. When James King of William proved the truth of this statement by printing a fac-simile of a document from the prison, James Casey got out his revolver and headed straight for the *Bulletin*'s offices.

Peder Sather was appalled by what was happening in the city, and followed the newspaper feud closely. On one particular day, when James Casey had writ-ten a highly critical piece on the banks, an indignant Sather marched over to the office of his colleague William Tecumseh Sherman with his copy of the *Sunday Times* to show him the article. Sherman was to become a legendary general in the Union army during the Civil War, and a staunch supporter of Abraham Lincoln. Before coming to San Francisco he had served as an officer in the war against Mexico, but he was now working at the bank of Lucas, Turner & Co. Sherman too was a neighbor of Sather's on Rincon Hill. He would later write his memoirs, in which he described Peder Sather's visit to his office that day: "Mr Sather ... called my attention to an article in Casey's paper so full of falsehood and malice, that we construed it as an effort to black-mail the banks generally. At that time we were all laboring to restore confidence, which had been so rudely shaken by the panic." What he and Sather were so upset about was that Casey was castigating honest bankers for the mess created by financial speculators. With no one to monitor their activities a lot of banks went to the wall, including some that had played by the rules. Neither Sherman nor Sather had been affected by the wave of speculation in the financial markets, but they were furious with Casey for tarring all bankers with the same brush.

It so happened that Casey had rented an office from Lucas & Turner on the floor above, but he had not said that he would be printing his pamphlets there. Sherman took strong exception to this: "I went upstairs," he writes, "found Casey, and pointed out to him the objectionable nature of his article, told him plainly that I could not tolerate his attempt to print and circulate slanders in our building, and, if he repeated it, I would cause him and his press to be thrown out of the windows."

By the time the news got out that James Casey was a former inmate of Sing Sing he was already standing outside the offices of the *San Francisco Bulletin* on Montgomery Street. He hid round a corner and waited for the paper's editor, James King of William, to leave the building after work. When he finally appeared Casey took two steps toward him and shot the editor at close range. James King of William fell to the ground and Casey took to his heels. His victim was taken to a hospital where he died some days later of his injuries.

From the moment it became known that the editor of the *San Francisco Bulletin* had been killed, until the day of his funeral, tens of thousands of citizens gathered for meetings and demonstrations in the streets. The decision was immediately taken to set up a vigilance committee like that formed in 1851. Within just two days over six thousand men rallied to the committee's flag and many more would join in the course of the spring. Private individuals, businesses, and societies all wrote letters of support to the newspapers, among them Anthony Lewis Tasheira and Drexel, Sather & Church.

Volunteers were armed and formed into militias which patrolled the streets, and an endless procession of people followed James King of William's coffin through the city to Lone Mountain Cemetery. Casey was then arrested by the vigilantes and locked up in the city jail by Sheriff David Scannell, who was notoriously corrupt and well known for turning a blind eye to the activities of criminal gangs in the city. After James King of William had been laid to rest, the funeral procession, with the vigilance committee at its head, made its way to the jail, kicked the sheriff out of his office, and took Casey to a newly erected gallows in the center of the city. A large proportion of the city's population was present at the lynching of James Casey, and if Peder Sather and Bent Dysterud had been in town that day, if they had not driven out to look at the floral delights of the Santa Clara Valley, they too must surely have witnessed what happened to the district supervisor. For when we know that around twenty thousand people, women and children among them, witnessed the execution, it seems unlikely that Uncle Peder was off riding somewhere or enjoying a healthy, appetizing meal with his nephew.

Bernt Dysterud must have had lots of shocking tales to tell when he got back to Odalen, because during 1856 four more men were to suffer the same fate as James Casey. The vigilance committee had stated in its manifesto that it would dissolve as soon as law and order had been restored, as it was six months later—a move by which punishment was replaced by politics. An election was called and a new and more trustworthy city council was chosen.

The first thing that struck me when I read about these events was that this was a case of reactionary citizens taking the law into their own hands. But historians maintain that it has never been possible to plot the supporters and the opponents of the vigilance committee on a particular social or conservative-liberal axis. William T. Sherman, for example, did not support the committee; instead he felt it would be better to leave it to the state militia to tackle corruption and crime, although this would hardly have been a better solution. Above all, the vigilantes are an indication of how drastic the situation in the city was, how insecure people felt, and how dangerous it was to ignore politics in an effort to build a society.

The latter half of the 1850s was marked by financial crises and fierce political clashes, not only in San Francisco, but throughout the country. The rift between north and south was great and growing ever wider, particularly over the issue of slavery. Speer Riddell's uncle, James Buchanan, who became president in 1857, seemed completely powerless to do anything. While the representatives of the northern states were in favor of a national law which would abolish slavery in all the states of the Union, Buchanan sought a compromise whereby it would be up to the legislature of each individual state to discuss the issue and decide where it stood on it. However much one might argue that in this, as in other matters, Buchanan was only trying to please everyone, he merely helped to maintain the status quo and thus to heighten the conflict.

The people of California were split on the question of slavery: 40 percent of them were from the southern states and were against any suggestion of a national ban. When Abraham Lincoln was elected president in November 1860, it was with the backing of only seven out of fifty-three Californian newspapers. The governor was a Democrat, there was a Democratic majority in the state legislature, but the Democrats supported the southern states, as did the Democratic senators and congressmen from California.

I have been able to find little or nothing that would give me clear proof as to which party Peder Sather supported. But he had been an American citizen since 1847, and according to the lists of foreign-born voters in San Francisco, he certainly did vote in elections. It may be that because of his position as a banker he felt it best to keep a low profile, but he took an interest in current affairs and he had a social conscience. He seems primarily to have been a man of action, a problem solver who was open to compromise.

I found an illustration of this last hypothesis in a newspaper announcement from 1857, at the time of the nominations for election to the state senate in Sacramento. This announcement had appeared in the local paper at the end of February and was later reproduced in the New York *Daily Globe*. In it, a number of businesses and private individuals urged politician Frederick A. Woodward to stand for the senate on behalf of what was termed "our local reform movement." Among the signatories we find Drexel, Sather & Church, and although it was the bank that put its name to this, it shows nonetheless that Peder Sather numbered among those in favor of getting Republicans and Democrats to agree on a common policy and commit themselves to making it as concrete and practical as possible. This desire to form a cross-party collaboration derived also from the feeling among Californians that their interests were being ignored at national level. A lot of people believed, therefore, that they ought to form a common Californian front, rather than waste their energies on internal political strife.

While Peder Sather may have been a man of compromise where political matters were concerned, there was one point on which he would not budge. This concerned the rights of black people and the slavery question; on these two issues I think it is fair to say that he was an active advocate of social change. In December 1867, two years after the end of the Civil War and the national abolition of slavery, a group of men were working on the preparations for the celebration of the annual Emancipation Day, to be held on January 1, 1868. The purpose of this day was not just to mark the end of slavery, but also to campaign for equal rights for blacks and whites, a struggle which was still only in its infancy, even in the northern states and in California.

The group in San Francisco were part of a national organization entitled the American Freedmen's Aid and Union Commission, the word "freedmen" here referring to those black people who had been given their freedom with the abolition of slavery by Congress in 1862. Top of the commission's agenda was the right to and the possibility of education, financial aid, and housing. Peder Sather was one of the moving spirits of the organization on the West Coast, and before Christmas 1867 it issued an appeal to all the people of San Francisco in which its secretary, Dr. D.C. Haynes, "most respectfully and earnestly ask[ed] of all a donation on Emancipation day" to help provide "the necessaries of life and school . . . and particularly to help the poor Freedmen through the winter and spring." Dr. Haynes emphasized that the situation was urgent and begged citizens to: "Please forward your donation to Peder Sather, Treasurer of the Commission." This appeal was published in the *Elevator,* a San Francisco newspaper founded in 1865, the year of Abraham

Lincoln's assassination. The aim of this publication was to elucidate and promote the rights of black people.

The year 1857 began with a series of powerful earthquakes, ominous forewarnings of what was to come. The papers said that at Drexel, Sather & Church all the clocks stopped and that two were stolen. It was also reported, in the *Daily Alta California* on January 4, that the bank had imported three puncheons of rum. Were they planning some big celebration, or did they simply desire to drown their sorrows? Whatever the case, time truly did seem to stand still for a moment, before the entire American financial sector ground to a halt. A new and far more serious financial crisis was brewing, engendered by speculative overinvestment within the country, especially in railroads and canals. This was exacerbated by the huge drop in exports following the end of the Crimean War.

A piece in the *New York Herald* on January 16, 1857, testifies to the fact that Peder Sather took an active part in the debate on the national economy. Presented in this was a reply to a letter sent to the governor of California by Drexel, Sather & Church, in which the bank expressed its concern regarding the state's growing debt. This petition was dismissed with assurances that public finances were in excellent shape—which was by no means the case, in California or elsewhere: 1857 was to lead to another financial slump, the worst to hit the country since 1837.

With Francis Drexel's time as a co-owner of Drexel, Sather & Church now over, in the summer of 1857 the bank moved out of the premises on Montgomery Street, which was already regarded as the Wall Street of the West Coast. In the first instance, Sather & Church found new offices on the corner of Battery and Clay Streets, but later the bank also operated from a couple of other addresses for brief periods before returning to Montgomery Street, this time for good.

On September 12 of that same year Sather & Church itself was struck by a disaster which everyone felt sure would spell the end for the bank. It had just dispatched a shipment of gold to the east on the *SS Central America,* but a storm blew up as the ship was on the way from Aspinwall via Havana to New York. There were around seven hundred passengers on board, and gold and securities from several different San Francisco banks, worth something in the region of two million dollars all told. Off the South Carolina coast the storm increased to a hurricane and on the evening of September 11 the ship sprang a leak. The pumps had been damaged and could not be used, and due to the volume of water now flooding into the vessel the steam engine also stopped working. The brig *Marine of Boston* came to the *Central America's* aid and managed to rescue women, children, and about fifty men. But when darkness fell the rescue operation had to be called off and the ship began to sink. Around one in the morning the *Ellen,* a Norwegian barque, reached the scene and succeeded in rescuing another forty-nine people, "among them a man on his wedding tour with his wife whom he had married in San Francisco the day before the steamer sailed." The *SS Central America* went down, taking with her the captain and crew, 439 passengers, and all of its precious cargo.

This still stands as one of the worst shipwrecks in American history, the shock of which was also felt on Montgomery Street and on Wall Street. Only half of the treasure on board had been insured, and losses were so great that it was feared the insurance companies would not be able to cover them. Many banks on both the West Coast and the East Coast were suspended from trading, including Sather & Church, due to persistent rumors that the bank had lost everything—as much as four hundred thousand dollars it was said. According to the newspapers, though, Peder Sather did not have to worry. On October 22, 1857, the *San Francisco Bulletin* published the following letter from the vice-president of the American Exchange Bank in New York:

> The American Exchange Bank, New York, 18th September 1857
> Messrs. Sather & Church, San Francisco, California
>
> Dear Sirs,
>
> By this steamer you will receive the painful intelligence of the loss of the steamer Central America, with most of her passengers and all her mails and treasure. Our Insurance Companies have, with the most admirable promptness, already held a meeting and agreed to cash the amount covered by their respective policies, immediately on presentation of Bills of Lading, which will doubtless come forward by the next steamer, together with duplicate drafts and advices, which will enable you to prosecute your business without inconvenience.
>
> *Yours truly,*
> *Geo S. Coe, Vice President.*

It was some months, however, before the bank on Montgomery Street and the branch in Sacramento could open for business again. Unforeseen problems arose with the payment of the insurance money and a substantial proportion of the loss was never covered. As a result, partner banks in New York refused to pay out on checks, bills of exchange, and notes issued by Sather &

Church. This in turn led to a run on the bank. By midnight on November 2 a large crowd had gathered on the sidewalk outside Sather & Church and refused to leave until they got their money.

Peder Sather and Edward Church were both present in the bank and promised to open the doors as soon as they possibly could. More and more worried and impatient customers showed up, and police were posted outside the doors to prevent anyone from trying to storm the bank. Inside, Peder Sather was frantically trying to ascertain how much cash they actually had in the vault. In this emergency he received both practical assistance and financial support from one of his loyal friends, the plump and jovial Samuel Merritt. Merritt was a popular figure in town, a confirmed bachelor, businessman, and doctor, known for doing his rounds of the harbor area, going out onto the boats and into the slums, offering free medical examinations and medicine.

When Samuel Merritt came to Sather's rescue on the night of November 3, 1857, the trust between the bank and its customers was being put to the ultimate test. Merritt advised Sather to pile up all of his cash reserves on the counter; that way people could see with their own eyes that he was not bankrupt. So at two in the morning, Peder Sather opened one of the bank's doors. He asked all of those who had money in the bank to come in and collect it, and urged the rest of the sensation-hungry crowd to go home to bed. By four o'clock in the morning a large number of customers had withdrawn the balance of their accounts and the three men could go home. The Sacramento branch was closed as of that date.

Early the same morning new queues formed outside the bank and this time, according to the newspapers: "Many women were among the crowd, and anxiety and excitement were to be seen on every side." When the doors were opened a little after nine o'clock the crowd pressed forward and had to be held back by the Sheriff's officers as "the packed masses swayed backward and forward in front of an opening about two feet wide, through which now and then one battered creditor could squeeze into the building." This went on for half an hour and then the bank closed again. Immediately after the doors were closed the bank's attorney, Edwin B. Mastick, appeared at a window on the second floor. He opened it and shouted to the throng below that all the money in the bank had been paid out. Further "bills receivable" had, he said, "been assigned over to J. B. Roberts, Samuel Merritt and Thomas H. Selby, for the benefit of the creditors of the house." The last-named was later to become mayor of San Francisco, and Roberts was a friend of Sather's from the Baptist Church.

The following day the New York *Daily Globe* announced that the American Exchange Bank had resumed payment on bonds issued by Sather & Church. According to a memorandum received by the paper: "On the 6th inst. the drafts of Messrs. Sather & Church on the American Exchange Bank of New York were refused payment by them and were protested. Arrangements were, however, speedily made by the friends of Messrs. Sather & Church and on the 7th inst., at 11 o'clock a.m. payment was resumed again." The *Daily Globe's* reporting of these "'arrangements" is laced with a not entirely unwarranted irony. Peder Sather appeared to be surrounded by keen supporters and it may be that much of his financial skill lay in his knack for procuring solid backing.

In order to inform his customers and the general public of the bank's financial situation following the sinking of the *SS Central America,* Peder Sather had a full statement of the bank's accounts published in the *San Francisco Bulletin.* A list of the bank's remaining creditors was also made public. The smallest of these was owed seventy dollars, the largest, ten thousand dollars. Two days later the newspaper was showering Sather & Church with compliments. The bankers were commended for not having reneged on their obligations, were congratulated on not having gone bankrupt, and were praised to the skies for resolutely having sought financial help, "and that from the gentlemen Mr Merritt, Mr Roberts and Mr Selby."

With the help of their friends, Peder Sather and Church soon regained the confidence of their customers—a vital asset. It also has to be said, though, that it was not so easy to topple a bank that never put all its eggs in one basket, but was careful to diversify. In a city ravaged by earthquakes and fires, Peder Sather had gone into the insurance business, and in an area where the population doubled every five years he had for some time been aware of the money to be made from the real estate market. In this way he seems to have been a banker of the old school, not one for gambling or taking uncalculated risks.

Every now and again he returned to Brooklyn and maintained his contacts on the East Coast: bankers on Wall Street, foremost among them Anthony Drexel. In 1857 Sather had been living apart from his family for six years, and when Sarah and the children came out to join him later they would find a well-kept house waiting for them on Rincon Hill, with its own stables and coach house. Bordering on the street was a low brick wall with an arched gateway in the middle. The gateway was topped by an arrow-shaped tower, more bizarre-looking than elegant. In the garden was a greenhouse which at this time of year was brimming with dahlias, plants that were no strangers to windowsills in Norway. Around the margins of the property cypress trees were growing nicely and the lawn was dotted with neatly trimmed box trees and flower beds full of exotic blooms, interspersed with small fountains and sculptures—a garden unlike anything ever seen in Odalen. A collection of antique clocks ticked and tocked in the reception rooms downstairs; time passed and still Sarah and the children did not come. Caroline was twenty-one now, Peder junior was twelve, and the older the children became the more difficult it must have been for them to move. All their friends were in Brooklyn, they went to school there.

Peder Sather who, in a letter to his brother Christoffer, expresses his regret that he had not received an education when he was young, was living in a city in the grip of a depression. The schools were also affected by this and many were forced to close. Teachers were now being paid less than store clerks, and no new schools were being built. Those that did exist were in some cases very basic and the classes were overcrowded, often with one teacher to seventy or even ninety pupils. In 1856 there were around twenty-six thousand children of school age in California, but only six thousand were attending school. Even so, the children of San Francisco were better off than those in the rest of the state, since most of the elementary schools were in the city.

For a man with no education who was eager to make up for lost time by broadening his mind and keeping up with current affairs, the Mercantile Library was the place to go. Speer Riddell was the library's treasurer, Henry Lee a member of the board, and Anthony Tasheira a regular visitor to the reading room, so no one bank or other workplace could have been better represented here than Sather & Church. In the early 1850s the Mercantile Library contained five thousand volumes and was a renowned cultural institution. The library provided an intellectual forum and a venue for evening talks and discussions on a wide range of literary and general topics, among them advances in public education and a ban on corporal punishment in schools.

Peder Sather was also a member of the California Academy of Natural Sciences, so the minutes of the academy's meetings tell us. The Academy of Natural Sciences was founded in 1853 at 129 Montgomery Street, at which address Peder Sather had been registered as living the year before, although I cannot see any particular connection here. But 129 Montgomery Street was later to become a neighbor to a historic address in San Francisco, when it became the site of the legendary Montgomery Block, a massive building containing apartments, offices, and salons which became a gathering point for the city's cultural elite: actors and painters, journalists, writers, and artistes of all sorts. Lola Montes lived here for a while, for example; Mark Twain was a resident in the 1860s; and much later Jack London also stayed there.

The California Academy of Natural Sciences was the first academic institution on the West Coast and was notable, not just for the fact that it accepted women as members, but because it also encouraged them to become involved in the academy's activities, something which caused quite a stir back then. Initially the academy concentrated mainly on the natural sciences and held discussion groups on Charles Darwin's expeditions and works. Interest in Darwin was great, and in recognition of his achievements the academy made him an honorary member.

It wasn't long, though, before the academy widened its range to include all of the sciences, holding lectures and discussions on all manner of topics. Peder Sather, who was by nature a practical man, distinguished himself as a member and some years later the academy acknowledged his efforts by honoring him with a life membership. Details like this show that Sather's life did not revolve solely around banking and finance; he also strove to become an enlightened individual. And we can draw a line from his involvement with the academy right back to Odalen and the parents who arranged private tuition for their children. This line suggests that his break with Norway was not a break in a cultural sense, and that the dream of knowledge and learning had survived intact.

By 1857 Peder Sather had become a well-known figure in the city, a man with a wide range of interests and contacts in many different camps. In the not too distant future, when Sarah and the children arrived, they would find a husband and father who, while he could certainly introduce his family to his friends and acquaintances, also had a head start on them socially. But he could offer them a home in the smartest district in the city, a neighborhood full of familiar faces: Eliza and Anthony Tasheira, Letitia and Edward Church. A school stood ready to receive the children: Shepherd's School, a private school in the traditional sense of the word. The school of choice for well-to-do families, it lay only a stone's throw from Montgomery Street.

Horse-drawn omnibuses now ran up to Rincon Hill from the center of the city, and ferries darted this way and that across the bay, serving the small townships around its shores, among them the quiet village of Oakland and the even more pastoral Alameda peninsula—a favorite spot for outings due to its balmy, sheltered location, its idyllic oak groves, and the fact that it was so sparsely populated. Edward Church and Peder Sather often went for

Sunday picnics there, only an hour away on the ferry. But Sather's days of congratulating himself on his freedom—as Eliza had put it, not without a hint of sarcasm, some years earlier—would soon be over. Just before Christmas 1857, with the storm at the bank ridden out, Peder Sather sailed for Brooklyn and New York: the last occasion on which he would have to cross the continent to see his family.

THIRTEEN

———

Gold, Pigs, and a Summer Residence

The insurance company in New York and Sather's friend Samuel Merritt had not been alone in helping Sather & Church out of a tight spot. Francis Drexel, too, had pulled a few strings in order to get the bank back onto an even keel again, or, as the newspapers wrote: "It is also believed that Mr Drexel of the old firm Drexel, Sather & Church, has taken Sather & Church's affairs on his own shoulders." Meanwhile, Peder Sather and Edward Church were doing everything in their power to pay their creditors. According to the *Daily Missouri Republican,* Sather & Church even went so far as to cover the balance owed to their customers by purchasing a consignment of hides, pelts, and tallow and shipping it to New York to be sold there through the agency of Letitia Church's brother Peter Naylor. Hides, pelts, and tallow? Apparently sent care of Hans Rees. Newspaper reporters could be very sycophantic, given to filling column after column with phrases such as "the highly respected" and "impressively strong-minded" when writing of bankers or businessmen. Such qualities were also attributed to Peder Sather and Edward Church, but during the financial crisis of 1857 there seems to have been good reason to construe such words as more than hot air. At the annual general meeting of the chamber of commerce in May 1858, Henry Wells, William Fargo, Peder Sather, and Edward Church were singled out for special mention for having put their affairs in order in a resolute and honorable fashion. Such conduct was not necessarily a given; the banking world was crawling with swindlers who loaned out money that they themselves had borrowed then left their customers in the lurch, having failed to pay either the interest or the principal.

In the spring of 1858 the suspension on Sather & Church's operations was lifted and the bank carried on trading, undaunted. So too did many of the crooks in the city; reports regularly appeared in the press of people who had tried to con the banks. Henry Lee and Speer Riddell were completely taken in by one bearded gentleman who came into the bank one morning to cash a check, which, it transpired, he had stolen. When the two clerks discovered this later in the day they set off into town to look for the man. They managed to track him down, but in the meantime the crook had removed his beard, and when they tried to have a word with him he pretended not to understand English. On another occasion a hefty leather bag full of gold wrapped in gray paper had to be sent by boat from Sacramento to Sather & Church in San Francisco. But when the delivery men set the bag on the bank's counter the package was found to contain not gold but chunks of iron.

Things returned to normal in Montgomery Street, with a contented Peder Sather working with his office door open and Edward Church ensconced behind a closed door, wondering what to think about a loan application from an import company; with James Hutchinson hunched over lists of creditors and debtors; with bookkeepers Anthony Tasheira, Henry Lee, and Speer Riddell sitting side by side at their high desks, all clad in black waistcoats and white shirts; and with Nelson Cook coming in, lugging a bag of brand-new gold pieces from the Mint.

One day the peaceful routine of the bank was disturbed by a dreadful squealing sound from outside. James Hutchinson had pricked up his ears at the screams, and as they grew louder he ran from his office to the front door to see what was going on. Out on the street he saw some Mexican vaqueros driving a herd of pigs before them. As they drew closer he also saw that the men were beating the animals: blood was flying, the pigs stumbled and fell, and were whipped back onto their feet only to keel over again and lie as if dead. It was a shocking sight: the hurt, panic-stricken creatures, shrieking and howling. Crowded in the bank doorway the bank clerks shouted and yelled at the swineherds and ran after them, but it was no use. The pigs limped and stumbled onward—those that could. Others were left lying in the road, bleeding and lifeless.

This was the street of gold, where freshly minted coins glittered behind gleaming glass, Parisian creations were displayed in the drapers' windows, and the city's notables promenaded up and down. Now it was littered with dying pigs, sprawled in pools of blood, writhing in agony, while the vaqueros went on their way, still wielding their whips over the remainder of the battered herd. James Hutchinson was so outraged by what he had seen that he decided right there and then to set up a society to fight such ill treatment of dumb creatures. He persuaded Peder Sather to join what was to become the city's chapter of the Society for the Prevention of Cruelty to Animals.

Brutality and bullion, battered pigs and bright, shining gold—the precious metal was no longer the only mainstay of the Californian economy, but was beginning to lose its hegemony to other industries: livestock breeding and agriculture, manufacturing and trade. A lot of people had also done very well for themselves out of real estate, having bought property for next to nothing in the early 1850s and sold it later at enormous profit. Peder Sather, too, had purchased real estate in San Francisco, Oakland, and Alameda. Although by all accounts he and Edward Church did a lot more than just lounge on the grass under the oak trees and snooze among the poppies, occasionally stretching out a lazy hand for an apple from the picnic basket. They explored the surrounding area, bought up plots of land of which no one else at that time could see the value: stretches of brush and scrubland far from a city in which so many were struggling simply to find a corner in which to lay their heads, never mind the sort of lots that only the very wealthiest could afford. So great was the influx of newcomers to California that for those with foresight real estate had the potential to be as fabulous a source of income as the gold had been.

In addition to investing the bank's profits in real estate, Sather had come up with some new business ideas, prompted by the loss of the *SS Central America* off the South Carolina coast in 1857. In the wake of this disaster the bank started selling transport insurance. For Peder Sather this was to be the start of a long career in the insurance business, often in collaboration with Samuel Merritt, but occasionally also with Senator Charles Lott or contacts from the Baptist Church.

In the fall of 1858 Sarah and the children finally moved to San Francisco. Sarah was fifty-one by this time, Caroline was twenty-two, Josephine was seventeen, and Peder Jr., thirteen. And while it's true that they had a fine house waiting for them on Rincon Hill, it cannot have been easy for any of them to uproot like that, leaving behind everything they were used to. Nor were they migrating to the other side of the country for the same reason as Anthony and Eliza Tasheira: in hopes of being better off financially. Sarah and the children came to California primarily on account of Peder, his health and the bank.

On the subject of Caroline the sources I have consulted are silent, except to say that she was suffering from a chronic illness, by Eliza once described as "some curvation of the spine." But her sisters were strong and healthy. They both started straight away at the Young Ladies Seminary in Benicia, while their brother Peder was sent to the Classic School in San Francisco, along with the sons of men such as Mayor Thomas Selby.

Established in 1852, the Young Ladies Seminary was the first women's college on the West Coast, and it received Peder Sather's support and commendation in an announcement in the *Sacramento Daily Union* on December 29, 1856. Josephine graduated from the seminary in September 1859, Mary Emma in June 1861. The sisters receive a mention in the *California Farmer and Journal of Useful Sciences,* which reports that at her graduation ceremony Josephine read an essay she had written, while at hers Mary Emma played the *William Tell Overture.* Another student is said to have given a talk entitled "Is the Mind of Woman Inferior to the Mind of Man?"

The college was known for its commitment to the cause of women's rights, and both Peder and Sarah were liberal in their view on this question. But if their daughters were to go on to higher education they would have to move back east because there were no universities on the West Coast yet.

In March 1859 the family's belongings arrived from Brooklyn, nineteen crates in all. Sather had by this time taken over a property which he thought would make a good country house for the family. Situated in a secluded spot in Alameda, this was a large, white wooden building on two stories. It had an odd-looking tower on the roof and broad front steps leading up to a grand porticoed entrance. This Southern-style building had originally housed a small boarding school with just eighteen pupils. A Christian school run by Methodist brethren, it had had to close due to lack of funds. Well, that and the fact that one of the brethren fell for one of the young schoolmistresses, incurred the wrath of his wife, and scandalized his fellow Methodists. It was Peder Sather who had originally granted the brethren a loan in order to build the school and under the terms of their agreement if they defaulted on the payments the property reverted to him. Sather also owned the land on which the school was built, a large stretch of open countryside with no other houses for miles around. The schoolhouse was totally unsuitable for use as a family home, but since Peder Sather could find no one to rent it and did not want to sell it, he decided to use it himself.

Every ten years a national census was conducted; during the summer, government officials went from door to door, registering the number of people in each household, thus providing a record of exactly who was living where and who their neighbors were. In the census of 1860, all the members of the Sather family were registered as living in Alameda, as were the Church family, bank cashier James Hutchinson, now a married man, and Abraham and Sarah Myers. Abraham's profession is given as "pastor," so it seems reasonable to assume that his wife Sarah was the same Mrs. Myers who had stayed with Sarah Sather in Brooklyn. If this is correct, then there appears to have been a real little New Yorker coterie out in Alameda. The only ones missing were the Tasheiras.

The fact that they were recorded as living in Alameda does not necessarily mean, however, that any members of this coterie had moved to Alameda, only that they were staying at their summer houses when the census was conducted. On the other hand, the census taker would normally make a note of any other home address which a family might have. In this particular case, though, there is no such note. This tends to suggest that the Sathers, while still having the house on Rincon Hill, were spending so much time in Alameda that they were recorded as residing there more or less permanently. And if that is so, then the move from busy, bustling, urban Brooklyn with its hundred thousand inhabitants to the oak woods an hour's ferry ride from San Francisco must have entailed something of a readjustment. That said, it was usually so windy and cool in the city, even in summer, that as time went on Alameda became a popular spot in which to build cottages and, eventually, to move to.

In 1860 the Sather's oldest daughter, Caroline, was twenty-four and unmarried, and Peder Jr. must just have finished elementary school. It was his father's great dream that his son should take over from him at the bank when the time was right, and he must now have been about to start his training. This calls to mind Francis Drexel's ambitions for Anthony when he took him on at the bank at the age of just thirteen.

Ferries sailed from San Francisco every half-hour: little paddle steamers, sometimes with a Norwegian captain. In my mind this conjures up a picture of Josephine and Mary Emma speaking Norwegian to this gentleman on their way across the bay, but I've found no evidence that Peder Sather ever taught them his mother tongue.

Sarah had three servants to help her in the house in Alameda: thirty-year-old Mary Ann Fowler and the Irish couple Jeremiah and Kate Morisse, both in their twenties. Why she needed three servants when at least two of her daughters were fit and strong enough to lend a hand and fourteen-year-old Peder was old enough to start working in the bank is hard to say. But Caroline must have needed help with just about everything, and it may be that Mary Ann Fowler also functioned as a nurse. Jeremiah would have been the handyman and Kate probably helped Sarah with the cooking and housework. That, at any rate, is how I envisage the work being divided up in the big house in Alameda.

There were nine people living in that house, which is a lot, but not enough to fill premises that had once served as classrooms and dormitories. Very few would have considered using this building as a private dwelling or country home. And nothing was done to remodel the place and make it more homelike. A couple of sources state that Peder Sather moved into the building to save it from falling into disrepair while he was looking for someone to rent it, and if that is the case then the decision to live here must have been based on a strict financial calculation. This does not, however, tally with other sources which point out that he did not give the house so much as a lick of paint. That the family did, nonetheless, spend a lot of time there may have been for health reasons. In the country the air was fresh and, unlike in San Francisco, you didn't have to worry so much about becoming infected should an epidemic break out.

With Sarah on the little Alameda peninsula, the house on Rincon Hill provided a bolt hole for Peder on those occasions when he did not go straight home from the office but worked late or attended meetings or dinners. Although the rest of the family did live for spells at Rincon Hill, it does look rather as if Sather also had a life separate from his wife and children. Not that he was alone in this; it was quite normal for the family to be "in the country" while the man of the house was at work in the city.

Anthony and Eliza Tasheira had been living on Rincon Hill since she and the children came out from New York in 1855. Because Anthony had a steady job as bookkeeper with Sather & Church they did not have to worry about money. Their children were in school and doing well in arithmetic, grammar, and writing. In the fall of 1859 Eliza's daughter married Henry Lee the bookkeeper, who was thirteen years her senior. She later trained as a teacher.

The future looked bright, but as it turned out there were dark clouds on the horizon for the Tasheiras, and this may explain why Peder and Sarah were in Alameda in the summer of 1860.

Eliza was not to have many years in San Francisco before the one thing that she had dreaded for so long in New York actually happened. Anthony had previously been troubled by severe stomach pains, and in the spring of 1860 these returned. This time, however, his body was soon covered in suppurating boils and eventually he could only lie in bed, debilitated and delirious. The doctors could only say that he had contracted typhus, a disease for which there was no cure.

Anthony died on April 3, 1860, only thirty-nine years old. The following day a note in the *San Francisco Bulletin* said that all friends of the Tasheira family were invited to their home on Second Street for the funeral service. Afterward, all those who wished could follow the coffin to Lone Mountain Cemetery. Printed in the same newspaper was another announcement from the Freemasons' California Council No. 38. Anthony had been treasurer of the lodge; now the lodge masters urged all "the members of Californian Council N. 38 of the Royal and Select Masters to be present at their Hall on Thursday 5th at 1½ o'clock p.m. for the purpose of attending the funeral of Companion A. L. Tasheira deceased, late treasurer of the Council." So ended the life of the hardworking iron founder and lonesome prospector who had left Tuolumne with a blanket over his shoulders and some crusts of bread in his pocket. When Anthony died Eliza was left high and dry. She and her sons were forced to leave the house they had called home for the past four or five years and move in with Harriet and Henry Lee. And there Eliza stayed until her sons were able to support her.

It is not known whether Peder Sather attended the funeral. From one of his own letters it is clear that he was doing a lot of traveling around this time. But if he did attend the funeral it seems fair to ask whether he did so as a "brother" or a friend, or possibly as both. This last seems likely, particularly when one remembers how he styled himself, in the letter regarding the tin box full of gold, as Anthony's "particular friend." If Peder Sather was indeed a Freemason then the silence with which in many cases he surrounded himself in life and that he left behind him when he died may not be purely coincidental.

Three weeks after the funeral Peder Sather returned home to San Francisco. In his mailbox he found a letter from a group of men who were trying to establish a university in California. Sather already knew at least two of these men, possibly more, but here I have to stick to what my sources tell me. One of these acquaintances was the scholar and theologian William Kip, bishop of California. Kip, a graduate of Harvard and Yale, was Sather's next-door neighbor on Rincon Hill. The other was Pastor Samuel Willey, the secretary of the group, who had written the letter. Willey wished to know whether Peder Sather would be willing to become a member of the Board of Trustees for a prospective university. At a recently held meeting the trustees had voted unanimously to extend this invitation to him, they hoped that he would agree to join them and that he had the time and the opportunity to do so.

The meeting referred to here was an historic one, held on April 16, 1860, at what is now known as Founders' Rock, a rocky outcrop on the campus of the University of California, Berkeley. The event was reported in the *Daily Alta California* on April 23, and the article concludes with a note that Peder Sather had been unanimously elected to the Board of Trustees. The letter from Willey was dated April 24, and on May 1 Sather replied, accepting the invitation, but saying that he had been surprised by it and uncertain whether to accept it.

This man, who had always regretted his own lack of education, ought to have had the best of incentives for taking on this task. But there can be many reasons for his hesitancy, both family related and otherwise. For one thing, he was not an academic; for another, he already held posts with a variety of bodies—the Baptist Church, the San Francisco Orphan Asylum Society, the Society for the Prevention of Cruelty to Animals, the banking and insurance businesses. He also supported the Sisters of Mercy and was involved with the Mercantile Library and the Academy of Sciences. Most recently, just before New Year 1859, he had again been elected to the San Francisco Grand Jury, a public committee with a wide mandate. The Grand Jury's main remit was, however, to decide whether a case could be brought to court, whether enough evidence had been gathered and whether it was in accordance with the law. The commitments I have mentioned here are the ones that I have been able to confirm, but it is not necessarily a complete list.

Nine years earlier Peder Sather had been living the high life, with wine and champagne and cigars that he smoked right down to the stump, and which, according to Anthony Tasheira, he could not do without. The Peder Sather of 1860 was a very different person. He was regarded as a pillar of the community and a "public-minded man," intent on contributing to society and providing financial aid to people and local institutions in need. Although he was just one of many private individuals and "voluntary associations" who sponsored public ventures, this won him a lot of respect. That this was the way in which vital social undertakings were funded was largely due the fact that California was a new state, its public bodies poorly developed and its public finances weak. In addition, a lot of newcomers were not sure whether they would stay here, and did not therefore see any point in committing themselves to long-term projects.

Not many citizens were interested in building a society; most felt that they had more than enough to do just finding their feet and seeing to themselves and their families. The gold had been behind the mass emigration to

California, and the gold was behind the climate of individualism that evolved there. Visiting Europeans were immediately struck by this and wrote of it in their letters home. Anthony Tasheira, too, had used the word in a letter in which he aired his thoughts on all of the people who hurried by him on the street, wrapped up in themselves and their own concerns. You could not depend on help and support from the county, and why should you support local authorities that often proved to be corrupt—especially if you were so homesick that all you really wanted to do was get on the first boat out of there? In a state whose inhabitants entertained no deep sense of belonging, private enterprise was both a cause and a consequence of official neglect.

Californians also resented the fact that the federal government still seemed to be treating the state as a national province. One result of this was that "politics" was often construed simply as meaning local politics, which in turn led to local politics becoming a partly practical, partly private affair. The first decades after the discovery of gold were the era of practicality and men of action. This turned Californians into "doers"; deeds and enterprise ranked above artistic and intellectual pursuits. It had got to the stage, the clergy complained, where their flocks spent most of their time and energy on building churches that were meant, first and foremost, to impress. Faith and worship had given way to financial and practical considerations. And it was in such times that a self-elected group of men set out to found a university, to discuss which subjects should be given priority and who would be best qualified to teach them.

Eighteen-sixty was a year of great turmoil in America, for while the country was slowly recovering from the economic crisis of 1857, it was also inexorably moving toward civil war. The conflict between North and South over the question of slavery appeared to be insoluble, and that fall a new president would have to be elected to replace the outgoing incumbent, James Buchanan, a man who had proved totally ineffectual. The election campaign was well under way when Peder Sather received the letter from Samuel Willey, and between then and the time when he replied to it events occurred that would be on everyone's lips.

In the middle of February Abraham Lincoln checked into the Fifth Avenue Hotel, where he would write the most important speech of his life. The hotel was one of the most elegant in the city, with a marble facade looking onto Madison Square, a magnificent dining room, the best chefs, costly Oriental rugs, a library offering the latest newspapers from home and abroad, copies of Greek statues and original sculptures of figures from American and

European history, drapes of the finest brocade, lounges furnished with sofas and armchairs in exclusive woods … but no guests. Apart from Abraham Lincoln.

People felt that the hotel was too far away from the city center, so no one went there. The Fifth Avenue Hotel had been built in an out-of-the-way spot, on the site of Madison Cottage, the old stagecoach stop. It sat there in splendid isolation, apart from a few scattered farms and the odd secluded villa. But for Abraham Lincoln the location was perfect. Here, he had all the peace and quiet he needed. The address was due to be given on February 27; in it, he would state the conditions whereby he would accept the nomination as presidential candidate. Lincoln had two weeks in which to write it and he spent all fourteen days in his hotel room. At the end of that time he left the hotel and went straight to the Cooper Union, a school in the East Village, where he had long since arranged to make his address.

The first thing he did when he stepped up to the lectern was to declare his opposition to slavery. The second was to ask the people for their confidence. The order here was important and had been carefully thought out: if he was to become the nation's next president it would be on condition that slavery was abolished throughout the whole country—the individual states would not be free to decide for themselves on this issue.

When the news of Lincoln's address made the headlines the following day it was not only its content that was hotly discussed. In the public debate, great symbolic significance was ascribed to the place in which he had chosen to make the address. The Cooper Union had opened its doors the year before; it had been founded and financed by businessman Peter Cooper. Shock and dismay had greeted Cooper's announcement that his aim in building the school was to provide free education for blacks, Indians, and young working-class people of both sexes. Cooper himself had had only one year of schooling and had not learned to read or write as a boy, but thanks to his technical skills he had become one of the country's most gifted engineers. He built, for example, America's first locomotive and played a vital part in the laying of the transatlantic telegraph cable to Europe. The wealth this brought him did not, however, leave his memory any the poorer. He never forgot the hardship of the world in which he had grown up, and was determined to do everything he could to eradicate poverty. Poverty was unworthy of the country, Peter Cooper declared, and the only way to fight want was to ensure everyone of the right to education, regardless of race or creed, gender or financial situation.

In Dan Rosenberg's biography of Anthony Drexel, *The Man Who Made Wall Street,* he says that Peter Cooper was a good friend of both Drexel and George Childs, and that later Drexel was following Cooper's example when he founded the Drexel Institute, a famous Philadelphia college which subsequently became Drexel University.

Anthony Drexel and George Childs were Peder Sather's "most intimate friends"—so writes Hans Rees's sister-in-law, Jane Krom, in a letter to the then secretary of the Treasury, Lyman Gage, in 1898. Jane was a friend of the Sathers and would later become Peder's second wife. Her reason for writing the letter is a personal one, and in it she reminds Gage—by the way, almost— of the circles in which her husband moved. As sources go, Jane surely must be considered reliable, and this information shows Sather to be more than a skillful but otherwise anonymous banker from Montgomery Street.

Drexel and Childs both lived in Philadelphia, and both became extremely famous and successful, Drexel as a financier and Childs as a doyen of the arts and editor of the *Public Ledger,* which he turned into one of the leading newspapers in the country. These two wealthy and influential men were also unparalleled philanthropists. Unlike Anthony Drexel, George Childs started with nothing. They met in 1853—the beginning of a legendary friendship— and shortly afterward Drexel gave Childs the money to purchase the *Ledger,* which was then a failing newspaper. Both men were married, but they became so close as to be almost inseparable. They went to and from work together, had lunch together, traveled together, and mixed together with the cultural and political elite of the day, up to and including the U.S. president, Ulysses S. Grant, himself. George Childs never had any children, but Anthony Drexel gave one of his own sons his friend's full name. Shortly after Anthony passed away, George, too, fell ill and died, and was laid to rest in his best friend's grave.

I'm a little shocked by my own temerity in linking Abraham Lincoln and Peter Cooper with Anthony Drexel, George Childs—and Peder Sather. But the close friendship between Sather, Drexel, and Childs is a fact, and Jane's letter speaks of a network that has Peder rubbing shoulders with some of the leading figures of his day. Do I dare? Yes, I dare.

Sather's intimate relationship with Drexel and Childs appears, in all likelihood, to have been forged out of strong mutual interests and values, and it serves to present a picture of a very complex character: Peder Sather, between a poor Anthony Tasheira and a rich Anthony Drexel; between the extravagant violinist Ole Bull and the straitlaced brethren in the Baptist Church;

between a troubled family life and carefree days as a grass widower on Rincon Hill: and, in 1860, between the bank directors on Montgomery Street and the champions of education.

Heaven forbid, though, that I should present Peder Sather's agreement to become a trustee of the proposed University of California as a slavish response to Peter Cooper's philosophy, Lincoln's speech, and the influence of his friends in Philadelphia. But all of this does form a backdrop to the ideas that were circulating at that time and that were dear to the heart of those closest to him. Sather would hardly have been offered the post of chairman at the meeting at Founders' Rock if those present had not known of his interest in education. But when set against the great names of the age, Peder Sather from Odalen was just a little man. And compared to the founders of the university—or at least, going by his hesitant reply to Samuel Willey, *that* seems to have been how *he* saw it.

FOURTEEN

The Foundation of Man's Future Circumstances

The majority of American universities, large or small, were private institutions, run by different denominations—Presbyterian, Methodist, Baptist, Roman Catholic, Lutheran, or Congregationalist. This had been the way ever since the founding of the country's first university, Harvard, in 1636, and the custom had continued with the establishment of Yale in 1701, Princeton in 1746, and Columbia in 1754. The idea was that study should not only impart knowledge and culminate in an exam, it should also ennoble the spirit and turn students into good and pious citizens. Education had to serve a higher purpose and help to imbue society with faith, knowledge, and cultivation. These were the classic ideals, carried over from Europe and particularly from the English universities of Oxford and Cambridge.

All of the old, established universities were on the East Coast; in 1860 California had several college but no universities. This does not mean that no one was interested in changing this state of affairs. When gold was discovered at the end of the 1840s, California became a magnet, not only for fortune hunters and workhorses like Anthony Tasheira, but learned theologians, missionaries, and ministers of one church and another, all of them educated at eastern universities, also headed west. These men were concerned that the lust for gold would warp the souls of the people out there, and they intended to do whatever they could to save them. To these men of the cloth this vocation did not merely mean preaching the gospel and giving the sacrament to the newcomers; they also saw to it that children and young people received schooling.

The Methodist brothers who had run the boarding school in the house in Alameda are one case in point; other groups provided higher levels of education and offered university preparation courses. Had it not been for such faith-based educational establishments only very few children would have learned to read and write at all. There was an acute shortage of both teachers and schools, and it was difficult to scrape together the tax dollars necessary to pay for these, not necessarily because people were reluctant to pay taxes and were only moderately interested in enlightening their minds and ennobling their spirits, but more because the majority had no intention of staying in California for any length of time. This does not, however, explain why the craving for gold should have been stronger than the thirst for knowledge. Particularly in the first years after the yellow metal was discovered scarcely anyone heeded anything but the chinking of gold, and those few citizens who worked their way up to public office found the forging of a new state hard going. The state constitution of 1850 contains articles concerning the establishment of a public school system with a school year of at least three months, but even such a modest goal as this proved difficult to put into practice, and higher education was nothing but a pipe dream.

The Reverend Samuel Willey, who had invited Sather to join the Board of Trustees of the College of California, a precursor to the university, was a graduate of Dartmouth College in New Hampshire. He had campaigned for years for the new state to put education on its agenda but had encountered resistance, even from those he had expected to agree with him.

An incident related in his memoirs provides a good illustration of the situation at that time. One day in the late 1850s he was on Montgomery Street when a long procession of young people came marching down the street, shouting and chanting that they wanted to go to school, to school, to school! They were carrying small, homemade placards which they waved aloft, then from side to side, then up in the air again, before disappearing from view. Willey's heart sank at this sight; he glanced around the crowd that had gathered and his eye fell on another man who looked as dejected as he felt. Willey went over to speak to him. It turned out that this gentleman was a judge, and he too believed that the situation regarding schools was quite untenable. Willey told him that he was thinking of inviting a number of businessmen to a meeting to discuss plans for a Californian university and possibly asking them to help fund it. He had already hired a room in Oakland and was hoping that that pathetic procession would have made these men think and move them to give up part of their evening and take the ferry across the bay. But the judge had sighed and advised him to cancel the meeting right away. "You won't get a single one of them to come, not if you hired the restaurant right across the way and lured then with the finest of dinners."

Willey knew that many of these men had been educated at universities on the East Coast, so he was all the more disappointed when the judge was proved right. No one was prepared to give so much as a dollar, and the general opinion seemed to be that anyone wishing to pursue higher education should simply go back east, since that was where all the good universities were anyway. This sort of attitude did its part to consolidate California's reputation as an outpost in the country, where the last things people were interested in were culture and education. Nevertheless, in a state which, in 1860, had a population of almost half a million, as opposed to only ninety thousand ten years earlier, a university was an absolute necessity. But time went on, things dragged out, and not until almost twenty years after the founding of the state did the university open its door to students.

But, one might ask, surely California—the gold state—could afford all the schools and universities it needed? And were teachers really that hard to come by? To take the second question first: an academic moving from the eastern seaboard to California might as well have been emigrating to a foreign country, and a very far-off one at that.

As to the question of money: well, the fact was that the general public did not really benefit from the gold, for one thing because it was discovered before the state became a member of the Union. In California at that time, large tracts of land were in private hands. In the old days these ranchos had often been given as a reward to certain individuals for services rendered. Some rancheros used the land only for hunting and fishing, others farmed it or raised cattle or sheep on it. So when gold was discovered this too fell into private hands. The fact that it took so long to establish a university had more to do with individualism and materialism than with availability of funds. There were historical reasons too for the sharp divide that emerged between public poverty and private wealth. In a region which was a state in political terms, but not in terms of social welfare, the economic pressure on ordinary people was so great that few were willing or able to assume public office or make any financial contribution to the common weal.

One of the most thought-provoking facts is that the religious organizations seem almost to have been the only ones to look beyond the pursuit of property and gold, to stand up for things of more lasting value. This brings us back to what Alexis de Tocqueville said in the 1830s about churches in America, that they could be good breeding grounds for a democratic frame of mind. As a Baptist, Peder Sather fits this picture very well. In his church he was used to sharing what he had with those who were less well-off and giving money to the church. He had also learned how to negotiate in order to make compromises and reach agreements that benefited the individual within the framework of the community.

From the thoughts on education which Sather expressed in his letter to his brother Christoffer it looks, though, as if he might also have had personal reasons for being involved in the setting up of a new university. For one thing, he regretted his own lack of schooling; and for another, he took a great interest in education generally: "What are the schools like in Odalen now?" he asks, "I hope they are better than when I was there."

Thirdly, it is quite possible that he dreamed of studying as an adult; he may even have done so, although, as he writes: "Youth is the right time for this." In that letter, though, he also goes on to say: "Later it is difficult to make Progress with this and then there are other Things to be tackled and thought about than study, this I have learned in my Life and I believe I am not the only one for whom this is the case."

The Peder Sather who left New York to go to California at the age of forty did not do so in order to study; he went there for his health and, not least, because of the tempting offer from Francis Drexel that enabled him to open a bank there. As a banker he counted among those "practical men of affairs" whom historians believe did so much to form those times. In one of his letters Anthony Tasheira remarks on how hard Sather worked and how proud he was when he succeeded in something. But this era has been described as "practical," not only because these men were preoccupied with themselves and their own concerns, but also because of a mentality that manifested itself in a utilitarian spirit and entrepreneurship in all fields, from the laying of streetcar tracks to the building of a children's home. Higher education was not included on the list of useful and necessary undertakings.

Speaking in support of the establishment of the College of California, the Rev. H. W. Bellows advocated "Minds over mines" as an expression of the wish that priority be given to culture, education, and intellectual pursuits. This sentiment perfectly encapsulated the lines of conflict in the young state, and with literature and philosophy, language, and rhetoric as its projected core subjects, higher education clearly needed to be very much on the offensive in the California of the Gold Rush.

It would have been easier if the college's curriculum had also featured technical subjects. But with their predilection for the classic subjects—which were supposed to instill character as well as knowledge, the founders found it an uphill struggle when they started knocking on doors and asking for donations. Samuel Willey and the rest were eventually forced to go back east, hoping to drum up funding there, but everywhere they went they were met by shaking heads and raised eyebrows. No one could understand why California could not afford to finance its own university.

The prioritization of the classic subjects was strongly opposed, regarded as they were by the practical men of affairs as both useless and unprofitable. Nonetheless, these were not removed from the curriculum; instead it was expanded to provide future students with a complete range of subjects to choose from. Professors and leaders of the university thought the criticism would die down when the university was finally completed in 1868. But not so. On one particular day a local notable who had been publicly singing the praises of the new university had been invited to give the students a lecture on the importance of education. To everyone's horror, this gentleman proceeded to hold forth on future careers and possible sources of income, and warned the students about wasting precious years of their youth on subjects that were of no use to society and would not put money in their pockets either. When he was done he happily surveyed the auditorium, waiting for the applause to erupt, but no one clapped and the professor who had organized the event was left bewailing the fact that he had been so wrong about this man.

But the curriculum and lack of funds were not the only reasons for the plans for the university getting bogged down. There may have been plenty of pious and idealistic men on the Board of Trustees, but this did not stop destructive disputes breaking out between members of different religious persuasions, with many of them keen to make the university a subsidiary of their own denominations. As a result, internal strife regarding religious influence almost put paid to the whole project.

One trustee after another threatened to break away and set up his own university. Rumors flourished in the press about certain individuals trying to initiate a coup and gain control of the board, but in the end they all decided to ease up on their own demands and join together to form a common front. The university's job was to educate and conduct research, while the gospel should be preached in churches designed for this purpose. The board finally agreed that religious sectarianism was incompatible with the sort of free-thinking on which a university ought to be based—a conclusion which was, for them, a major step forward. They were also agreed that the university should be open to everyone, regardless of their religion, their beliefs, or their sex. This last point had not in fact been resolved when the university opened, but women students were admitted the following year.

The next task was to decide whether the university should be a private or a public institution. Principle and national regulations dictated that it should be the latter. A university could best safeguard its freedom by being a public responsibility, or so the founders maintained, believing that this was the only way to avoid private control of the institution's activities. Meanwhile, the state government promised to help with funding if practical subjects such as agriculture and engineering were added to the curriculum. In 1860 the religious disputes were settled, and the College of California Board of Trustees to which Peder Sather was elected is regarded as the first to enter into concrete negotiations regarding the planned university. But it was to be many years before the university could open its doors. Work was delayed because of the Civil War, the necessary capital was not immediately forthcoming, and it took years to decide where the university should be situated.

If unearthing biographical material on Peder Sather was hard work, digging up information on the part he played as a cofounder of the university certainly wasn't any easier. Most of the existing documents on these educational pioneers are kept in the archive of the Bancroft Library at Berkeley, and the details on Peder Sather furnished by these were so scant that I began to wonder whether there had been any reason at all to raise those many monuments and memorials to his name—one that is known throughout the academic world.

I arrived at the Bancroft Library full of anticipation, imagining that I would find plenty of information there. I had brought a big fat notebook with me and was expecting to be there for ages. But all I found in the archive were two letters, the one shorter than the other and both extremely formal. The first of these was the one that Sather had sent to Samuel Willey, accepting a seat on the Board of Trustees, the other was a letter written three years later in which he resigned from the board.

It was wonderful, though, to be at the Bancroft, which specializes in the history of California. The library is named after the historian and ethnologist Hubert Howe Bancroft, who, in Peder Sather's day, had a bookstore and publishing business in San Francisco. He was also a book collector whose collections—which also included manuscripts, pamphlets, newspapers, periodicals, and maps relating to the whole of western America—were acquired by the university in 1905. For me, though, it was just as interesting to discover that Bancroft had been a neighbor of Sather's on Rincon Hill. This thought made me feel as if both of them were, in a way, there with me in the reading room, waiting for the letters to be brought to my desk. I was so sure that I was about to learn why those monuments had been erected. I never imagined for one moment that I would be leaving there with more questions than I'd brought.

Peder Sather's letters were in a folder along with piles of others written by the founders of the university. A lot of these were just quick notes, off-the-cuff and unceremonious in both form and content, dealing with matters great and small: "I am in Boston at the moment, I will be here for four days and had just returned to the hotel after having dinner with a friend when I opened your letter." Judging by the writing, the ink splotches, and words scored out, these missives appear to have been written with no particular thought for how personal or impersonal they might seem to their esteemed recipient, the Reverend Samuel Willey.

I had, of course, already seen examples of how formal Sather could be in his letters. Even when writing to his brother Christoffer he was liable to sign himself "P. Sather." He is reputed to have been of a reticent nature, and if so then his letters certainly reflect this trait. Be that as it may, the contrast between the way in which he and the other trustees formulated themselves was great, and there was absolutely no explanation for the memorials to be found here.

San Francisco, May 1st, 1860
Reverend S. H. Willey, Esq.,
Secretary

Dear Sir,

On the 25th ultimo April I received your favor of the 20th, informing me that I had been elected a member of the Board of Trustees of the College of Cal at a meeting held on the 16th of last month.

My absence from the city as well as the entire occupation of time since your letter was received has prohibited an earlier reply, and I have also entertained a hesitancy about accepting the office. I have however decided to accept, at least for a time—and beg to return my acknowledgement for the unexpected honor upon me by the action of your board.

I am most truly yours,
P. Sather.

Reading between the lines, I have to say that I was quite taken aback by Sather's reservations and uncertainty. This letter gave the impression that Sather was so occupied with other things that he was having to weigh up whether he had the time to be part of the board. Memorials to a man like this?

He was honored by the confidence shown in him and found the invitation unexpected, he says. Was he being pompous? And why had the letter from Willey come as such a surprise? Or was this a case of an unschooled man, daunted by the prospect of joining a group of academics and scholars and resorting, therefore, to stiff standard phrases? He hesitated, he was uncertain, he had so much to do, and the job might be too much for him. By 1860 he also had Sarah by his side; what did she think of her husband taking on still more commitments?

As the letter shows, Sather was elected to the Board of Trustees of what was at that time called the College of California, a name which was used until the University of California, Berkeley, was opened eight years later. The College of California was housed in a classic white-brick building set among the leafy groves of Oakland; it boasted a handful of professors and a modest number of students. This was never meant to be the university's permanent home, though. When it expanded it was going to need a big campus and Oakland did not have the space for this.

Quite a number of books have been written about the beginnings of the university, one of the most comprehensive of these being historian William Warren Ferrier's *Origin and Development of the University of California*. Published in 1930, this has a full-page illustration of Sather Tower on the first page together with a poem, an ode to the campanile. This poem was presented at the dedication of the bell tower in 1917 and after the last verse had been read out, the bells began to peal and an extract from Beethoven's *Destiny Symphony* rang out across the campus and the buildings scattered round about. All of this Ferrier describes, but is there any mention of the man who had lent his name to the tower?

Ferrier does make one point that might provide a clue to the mystery: "It is worthy of note that Peder Sather, in whose memory some of these gifts were made, was a trustee of the College of California and a generous supporter of that pioneer institution." Considering that Ferrier was a historian one might have expected him to cite sources to substantiate this statement— but no. He maintains, however, that Peder Sather made large donations to the university, and if a man like Ferrier has had trouble documenting this fact then perhaps it's not so surprising that I also had difficulty. In the days of the pioneers it was often quite simply the case that official documents and other papers were not systematically filed and preserved.

It is reasonable to be curious as to how much money Peder Sather donated, but as far as I am concerned the financial aspect pales in comparison with the wide vista that unfolds at the thought that a young man from Nordstun Nedre Sæter should have wound up as cofounder of the university at Berkeley. Nonetheless, I have tried to find sources that would support Ferrier's statement. Here are five that I have discovered.

In a book on historic places in California, published in 1932, historian Mildred Brook says: "Sather gave much money towards the establishment and building of the university."

My second source is Ernst D. Wichels, author of articles on historical subjects for the *Sunday Times Herald,* published in Vallejo, a town not far from San Francisco that for some unknown reason is twinned with Trondheim in Norway. On March 14, 1874, Wichels writes: "It was in 1868 that the University of California in Oakland decided to accept the offer of land and money from Peter Sather, born in Trondheim, Vallejo's sister city, and move to a site to become Berkeley."

The third source, Barbara Jaffe Aronson, corroborates the previous one. As a young woman she went to college with Kenneth Hamilton Sather Bruguiere, brother of Kathleen Bruguiere Anderson, and hence Peder Sather's great-great-grandson. In an undated article in which no sources are cited Aronson writes that "Ken's great-great-grandmother [. . . on his father's side] was Josephine Sather, the daughter of Peter Sather who gave the land which came to be the UC Berkeley campus."

The fourth source is somewhat different and more interesting—an announcement in the *Oakland Tribune* on November 16, 1905, regarding two hundred acres of land bought by Peder Sather in 1862: "A mortgage which has run since 1862 was released by trust deed from the estate of the late Pedar Sather for $7000. The mortgage was executed by Elanthan B. Goddard on July 30 1862 and has only been paid off within the last day or two. It covers 200 acres of land in North Berkeley near Peralta Hall and has drawn several times the amount of the principal in interest."

Of these four sources the last is the oldest and the most concrete. It proves that Sather owned a large parcel of land in what was to become Berkeley. The announcement does not say anything, though, about him presenting this to the university.

Last but not least there is the fifth source: *Redlands: Biography of a College.* This book, published in 1958, was written by historian Lawrence Emerson Nelson. In it he claims that Peder Sather wanted to donate his property in

FIGURE 14. Campus of the University of California, Berkeley, 1874. North Hall and South Hall, viewed from the west. Courtesy of the Bancroft Library, University of California, Berkeley.

Alameda to the new university, but that, for various reasons, the Board of Trustees turned down his offer. Nelson says that Sather was offended and upset and that Jane Krom found out later how badly he had been treated. The accuracy of this account is questionable. But the fact that he mentions Jane Krom is interesting

So, including Ferrier I have come up with six sources, all of which state that Peder Sather's contribution to the university went far beyond sitting on the Board of Trustees. There is also a seventh source, which, though it provides no documented proof, claims that Sather was active on, or possibly chaired, the board of the foundation set up to raise money for the establishment and management of the university.

If Peder Sather's involvement with the board of trustees lasted for so many years and was as extensive as these sources would have it, then there may have been other reasons—ones he preferred not to name—for his hesitant response to Samuel Willey's invitation. Since these sources also serve to support the suggestion that Sather donated the land on which the campus now stands, Sather Gate, the main entrance to it, could be construed as a historic allusion to this gift. And if the gate was indeed erected to mark Sather's generosity then it looks as though someone wanted to do him the honor that was not paid to him during his lifetime. Monuments are not generally raised by random individuals to commemorate unmemorable people—not unless said individuals are either crazy or extremely conceited.

My research has entailed reading a good deal about the university's history, particularly its early history. And one could be forgiven for thinking that the oldest works would be the most reliable sources, but I am not so sure about this. Many of the authors seem rather to have been competing to see who was the greatest pioneer. In some cases we are dealing with memoirs which are more like verbal gateways, enveloped in clouds of pathos and semi-mythical, self-congratulatory recollections. This is certainly true of the writings of the Reverend S. H. Willey, Esq., while William Warren Ferrier succumbs to the temptation to let his account unfurl like a flag to be waved in celebration of the year 1868.

Peder Sather resigned from the Board of Trustees after three years, but he remained a patron of the university. And an article in the *Daily Alta California* on February 19, 1864, testifies to his enduring commitment to the cause of public education. The newspaper reported that a group of men in San Francisco had submitted a petition to the state legislature in Sacramento in which they earnestly requested that something be done to provide schools and educational opportunities for the children of California:

> To the Hon. the Legislature of the State of California: The Undersigned tax-payers of the City of San Francisco would respectfully ask that your Honorable Body will, by favorable legislation, enable the Board of Education to supply increased school accommodations. The fact that so many children are deprived of all means of education, not being able to obtain seats in the too crowded schools, and the further fact that many of these children are thus left to grow up in ignorance, and to become prey to every vice and crime, induce us to make this petition, even though the granting of it should render an increase in taxation necessary.

This was a very clear and controversial message in a world in which no one paid taxes if they could avoid it, and the have-nots were left to stew in their own juice. Here, Peder Sather was in the vanguard of the philosophy which forms the basis of a modern welfare state, in which everyone has a duty to everyone else. The petition's signatories were few in number, but it is worth noting who they were. Some were representatives of finance companies such as Wells, Fargo & Co. and Donohoe & Ralston. Others, ten in all, were private individuals, like Hubert Howe Bancroft, Samuel Soulé, and Peder Sather. He was in good company and all of these men were his friends.

In his letter of resignation to Samuel Willey Sather apologized for having had to make this decision. "Various circumstances" had made it impossible for him to attend the Board's meetings and he was afraid that this would continue to be the case. What these circumstances were, the letter does not say, but this remark put me on the trail of a serious problem in the Sather family.

FIFTEEN

Morals, Money, and War

In 1860 Peder Sather was on the Board of Officers of the First Baptist Church in San Francisco. The old wooden church had burned down and a new one had been built in Washington Street, right round the corner from the bank on Montgomery Street. This church was constructed out of fireproof brick, the newspapers said, and a second-hand organ had been sent over from the East Coast for it. The congregation was growing, it now had two hundred members. Prayer meetings were held every Wednesday evening, services and Sunday school on Sundays.

This was Peder's religious arena, two hundred souls with the board at its head. Sarah was a member of the Reformed Dutch Church, and thus excluded from a society that meant a great deal to her husband. What did Sarah think about Peder attending prayer meetings and board meetings and always out traveling? After all, here she was, fifty-three years old and only recently moved away from all her family and friends on the East Coast.

As to the children: well, the Baptist Church does not seem to have held any attraction for Peder Jr. On the contrary, in his father's eyes he had developed intolerably extravagant tastes and freely indulged in all the pleasures that the family's improved financial situation allowed. It was not all that long since Sather himself had shown similar tendencies, but the family had been living in Brooklyn then and by 1860 the intemperate days on Rincon Hill were behind him. Peder Jr. proved to have little interest in working in the bank either and was thus a constant source of worry to his father, who had been expecting his son to inherit the business. Sather's daughter Mary Emma, the apple of his eye, had also incurred his disapproval. She had fallen in love with a man whom her father felt was not good enough for her and he did all he could to end this relationship.

All of this information is drawn from the biographical notes given to me by Kathleen Bruguiere Anderson, and if it is correct then the newly reunited family was already deeply divided. On the other hand we also have the testimony of an elderly lady who told the *San Francisco Chronicle* that in the 1860s the Sather family home was renowned for its hospitality and for parties and gatherings of all sorts. This is confirmed by a number of sources, but corresponding reports are, of course, not necessarily reliable—if they all stem from the same original source then there is as much chance that they are untrue as true, so all of this should be taken with a pinch of salt. The aforementioned elderly lady had been interviewed about life on Rincon Hill in the old days, and the *Chronicle* had devoted two full pages to the article. She had been a member of San Francisco's high society herself and had moved in these circles. She does not say much about the Sathers, but does mention that the daughters were very beautiful and popular and had lots of admirers. I am prepared to believe this source, since her account ties in with descriptions of the family's life in Brooklyn in the 1840s, when the house in Willoughby Street was always full of visitors and dinner guests. If there were problems with the children these did not get in the way of the Sathers' social life; they were not cut off from the world up on Rincon Hill.

While mother and son did not attend the Baptist church, Caroline, Josephine and Mary Emma were members there. In December 1862 the *San Francisco Bulletin* wrote that "the Orphan Asylum tenders special thanks to the Misses Cheney, Sather and Baldwin of the First Baptist Church for the sum of $589.50 collected by them for the benefit of the orphans." All of these young women were, it appears, daughters of the church officers, and while their fathers attended board meetings they were going round the doors with collecting boxes and holding bazaars to raise money for orphaned children.

The members of the church board did not just encourage their daughters to do good works; according to the press they were also dedicated to upholding public morals. Speaking at one annual general meeting the pastor of the church, the Reverend David B. Cheney, said that something would have to be done soon to ensure that the Sabbath day was kept holy in the city. Visitors from the East Coast must be shocked, Cheney felt, when they saw the immorality that prevailed in the city's streets. What got his back up more than anything else were the brass bands that marched down Washington Street in the middle of church services. They were a dreadful nuisance and often made it impossible for him to "worship without molestation" during Sunday services. At the annual general meeting it was therefore agreed that a Sabbath

Observance Committee should be set up to note down all breaches of the Sabbath peace and report these to the city council.

One of the members of this committee was Stephen A. Bemis, a bag and suitcase merchant. Bemis mentions Sather in his memoirs and describes what a big help Sather was to him at a time when he was down on his luck. Bemis had come to California to prospect for gold, but he had no success and soon found himself flat broke. To his great surprise, Peder Sather had given him some money to tide him over, even though the two men barely knew one another. "I have often wondered since," Bemis writes, "how it was that he came to my rescue with so few words and no security forthcoming to him in the undertaking. We were members of the same church and no doubt he came to that conclusion that the outcome would justify the risk."

That Peder Sather was a generous man is not news, but Bemis's case is evidence of the sort of network to which a church gave access and how members of a congregation could always be sure of a helping hand when necessary. While individualism reigned in the secular world, community spirit and consideration for others thrived within the closeted circles of the religious communities. All the more important, then, to belong to a church, to which you could turn in time of need.

But, man of faith that he was, Peder Sather's benevolence also extended beyond his own religious circle. In March 1861, for instance, he and Edward Church were both on the board of the San Francisco Port Society. This society had been instituted to help indigent and often alcoholic sailors by providing them with food, clothing, and shelter, not only by promoting their social welfare, but also by ministering to their spiritual needs and bringing them to salvation through preaching the gospel. It would be wrong, though, to see this venture as being solely a demonstration of missionary zeal and morality, San Francisco at this time was so notorious for gambling and crime, drunkenness and prostitution that the area around the docks was dubbed "the Barbary coast." Nevertheless, his seat on the board of the Port Society puts Peder Sather in the company of men who reacted against what they regarded as a general moral decline in society and whose faith had taught them that there were other values than the purely monetary. Because the problem, as those with plenty of money often found, was that happiness did not always increase with the thickness of one's wallet.

This does not, however, alter the fact that the spirit of the times was considered by many to be both vulgar and materialistic, and not only on the West Coast. Two of Peder Sather's friends in New York, Peter Naylor and

Benjamin Haxtun, wrote in the *New York Times* of the need for "a more refined taste and cultivated social bearing in the community." They had attended a lecture at the Mercantile Library which had been so interesting that they wanted to thank the man who had given it and they urged him to give it again so that he could share his thoughts with still more people. But the man whom they had heard speaking was not just anyone; his name was Francis Vitton, a famous lawyer and professor of theology. Naylor and Haxtun were convinced that with his lecture he could help to foster "a nobler public sentiment."

In 1861, when the Civil War broke out, Peder Sather and his friends appear to have been pillars of the community and guardians of public morals. Sather had his hands full, what with his work for charitable and religious societies, the board of the university, the Grand Jury, and the chamber of commerce. And on top of all of this, something happened which was to have major consequences for the bank. In April 1861 Edward Church contracted typhus and died shortly afterward. He was forty-seven years old. As a result, James Hutchinson was promoted from cashier to manager, and the bank changed its name to Sather & Co. And Sather & Co. it would remain as long as Peder Sather lived.

Edward Church's death coincided with the start of the Civil War, but, since the state was so far away from the battlefront, the lives of ordinary Californians were not greatly affected by the conflict. Nonetheless, a fierce debate did flare up between supporters and opponents of the northern states and Abraham Lincoln, when the southern states seceded from the Union and formed their own Confederate States of America, in protest against Lincoln's stance on slavery. In California only 28 percent of the population had voted for him—a minority which, in all probability, also included Peder Sather. Ever since his time in New York he had been a fierce opponent of slavery and a staunch supporter of equal rights for black people. Sather was a great admirer of Abraham Lincoln and hoped for victory for the Union army, now under the command of his good friend General William T. Sherman. Despite strong pro-Confederate feeling among its inhabitants, California placed two volunteer brigades at the disposal of the Union, and an announcement in the press in 1863 names Peder Sather as one of those businessmen who gave his employees permission to enlist.

During the first years of the Civil War, Peder Sather lost two of his closest friends and colleagues: first Edward Church, in 1861, and then, in 1863, Francis Drexel, who died of injuries sustained when he fell onto a train track and was run over by a train in Philadelphia. On the sudden death of his father Anthony Drexel took over the running of Drexel & Co. He retained the company's head office in its hometown, but also maintained his association with Robert Winthrop, the man who had been running the company's branch in New York since 1859. Winthrop was a personal friend of Peder Sather—and of Theodore Roosevelt Sr., father of the future president.

In San Francisco Peder Sather continued to expand his activities in the insurance business, an extremely lucrative one in a city so subject to earthquakes and fires. He was now a shareholder in the Firemen's Fund, one of the largest fire insurance companies on the West Coast, popular with customers because it donated a certain percentage of its profits to a relief fund for firemen and their families.

In a history of the Firemen's Fund published in 1929 Peder Sather was praised for all that he had done for the company. In this book, occasionally marred by purple prose, he is described as a "tower of strength" in the organization, an accolade conferred on him mainly for his actions in the aftermath of the Great Fire of Chicago in 1871. The Firemen's Fund had had to pay out huge amounts in claims, its coffers were almost empty and the company was in danger of closure when Peder Sather granted the company a fifty-thousand-dollar overdraft to keep it afloat.

The sinking of the *SS Central America* in 1857 and the subsequent enormous losses incurred by businesses not covered by insurance led to a great demand for shipping and cargo insurance, and the Civil War did nothing to lessen this demand. In 1864 Peder Sather was a shareholder in both the Home Mutual Insurance Company and the California Insurance Company, along with men such as bookkeeper Henry Lee, Senator Charles F. Lott, and Samuel Merritt. An insurance company which, over and above its normal services, offered insurance against directly war-related risks—particularly those facing seamen and ship's passengers—could be said to have been capitalizing on the Civil War, and those associated with such a company could be accused of being profiteers. I am not certain whether this label could also be attached to Peder Sather, but a financier he was and would always be.

Around this time, however, Sather also become involved in another, quite different venture. Only a couple of months after the outbreak of the Civil War a new national relief agency was set up in New York to provide medical aid for wounded soldiers, care for the dying, and help for their families. With hundreds of thousands wounded and dying on the battlefields this organization, the United States Sanitary Commission, was faced, right from the start, with an insurmountable task. A year later, however, steps were taken to set up a parallel agency, known as the Christian Commission, whose remit was the same as that of the Sanitary Commission, although it also aimed to bring the gospel to the soldiers. A great many of these young men were, it was said, "sons of pious parents. They go away from the blessings and from the restraints of home and from the influence of the sanctuary." Abraham Lincoln was patron of the Christian Commission, and during its first year this organization distributed countless Bibles and New Testaments to the hospitals and sent more than three hundred Christian ministers out to the battlefields. The ministers were to act as "a medium of communication between the Christian parents and their wounded, sick and dying sons, and from the latter to their home circles; in a word to do for our brave men on the battle-field what their father and mother would do for them if they might."

In December 1864 the Christian Commission opened an office in San Francisco, with Peder Sather as its treasurer and James A. Roberts as manager. Roberts was one of the three men who had helped to save Drexel, Sather & Church in 1857 and he was also on the board of the Baptist Church.

The San Francisco branch's work consisted of making door-to-door collections and organizing bazaars and fairs. Its inaugural meeting was held at Platt's Music Hall in the presence of the Reverend C. P. Lyford, a representative from the head office in Philadelphia. Lyford gave a two-hour-long talk which was continually interrupted by applause from the packed hall. He described in detail how the organization's valiant agents went out into the trenches, risking life and limb to take food, clothes, and medicine to the soldiers while also "introducing the subject of religion to them whenever the opportunity presented itself." And now, when it was opening an office in San Francisco, the Christian Commission simply could not be seen to have fewer resources than the Sanitary Commission. Reverend Lyford concluded by informing the audience that all donations could be delivered to Mr. Sather, the banker, on Montgomery Street.

When he finally stepped down from the lectern the pastor was asked by members of the audience if he would sing a song for them—"The Battle Hymn of the Republic." The lyrics to this hymn had been written in 1861 by Julia Ward Howe, a well-known writer, pacifist, and abolitionist, and it had become one of the most popular songs of the Civil War because of its anti-slavery sentiments. After asking the audience to join him in the chorus, Pastor Lyford blithely broke into song. And sitting there listening to him was

Peder Sather, graying now, but straight-backed, with accounts ledgers and collecting boxes at the ready.

From the report of this meeting in the *San Francisco Bulletin* it is clear that the members of the Christian Commission were considered an odd bunch. A journalist from the *New York Times* was also in San Francisco at this time to cover the situation there, and what he wrote only reinforced this impression. While out walking in Montgomery Street one day he had been virtually attacked by a lady from the commission. She was selling tickets for a bazaar and would not let the poor newspaperman go until she had shoved a ticket into his pocket and extorted five dollars from him. The last he saw of her, she was on the other side of the street, pouncing on another victim while crying out warnings against giving money to the Sanitary Commission—according to her, a thoroughly un-Christian organization.

The Christian Commission might have been regarded as a bit of a joke, but it carried on with its work undaunted. In January 1865, after a tour of the West Coast, Pastor Lyford returned to San Francisco, where a farewell meeting was held for him prior to his departure for Philadelphia. The commission's treasurer, Mr. Sather, also attended this meeting, I presume, and would once more have had the pleasure of hearing the pastor speak. The Reverend Lyford was able to report that he had been very well received wherever he went, on account of the gospel he was sure, but, he added, his own unassuming manner might also have had something to do with it. He was dreading leaving California, he said, because he would soon be going back to the battlefields and was afraid of being killed. He did not exactly look kindly on the fact that the troops were now being fed soup and chicken, custard and jelly, and that these meals were washed down by beer and wine. Pastor Lyford sighed. Pastor Lyford shuddered to think what he was liable to see down there. Why, when he was in the army he had marched for miles and fought the hardest of battles on nothing but dry biscuits and bad coffee.

As treasurer of the Christian Commission Peder Sather also came in for his fair share of ridicule in the press. Not that he was ever mentioned by name, but everyone knew the identity of "the well-known banker" who week in, week out was the butt of so many jokes. In the spring of 1865 the papers were full of anonymous items, particularly from contributors writing under the pseudonyms Verbum Sat and Verbum Sap—from the saying *verbum sat sapient est:* "a word to the wise is sufficient," or "enough said." It looks, though, as if the author of these satirical pieces may have been Mark Twain, who was working as a journalist in San Francisco at that time and lived on Rincon Hill.

The controversy over the Christian Commission sprang from the organization's appeals for donations from both individuals and groups. In the spring of 1865 an amateur dramatics society had staged some performances in a private home in South Park, a new middle-class residential area not far from Rincon Hill. Such entertainments, or "parlor theatricals" as they were called, were very popular throughout the country. This particular dramatics society had decided to donate the takings from one of its shows, ninety dollars in all, to the Christian Commission. According to the newspapers, the organizer of the entertainment—referred to only as "No. 20 Hawthorne Street"—had duly called on "the well-known banker" the following day to make the donation to him, but when Peder Sather heard where the money came from he refused to accept it. In the treasurer's opinion, the amateur dramatics society's activities were of such an immoral nature that its money was not acceptable.

This was what had outraged people and sparked off the feud. Some people sided with Sather and wrote letters saying that in a city as sinful as San Francisco, swarming as it was with gamblers, thieves, liquor salesmen, cheats, and counterfeiters, shouldn't all such disreputable characters be forbidden from supporting worthwhile causes? And, it was asked: "Does not the amateur actor, like the professional one, assume the appearance of passions and emotions he does not actually feel? Does he not put on the dress and manner and use the language of some fictitious character? What is this but counterfeiting? And is not counterfeiting falsehood, and is not falsehood sin?"

Others criticized the treasurer in the most scathing terms: "is the 'Christian Commission' a body organized for charitable ends, or for the purpose of obtruding on the community the pharisaical doctrines which its officers may happen to entertain on questions of religion or morality?" Was the money from the theatricals so dirty that the soldiers would be infected by it. Were theatrical entertainments one of the seven deadly sins? Was it true that the banker had likened the donation to "the receipts of a dram shop or drinking-saloon"? Did he consider it no better than a false check?

Criticism of Peder Sather reached even greater heights when "No. 20 Hawthorne Street" disclosed details of what had happened on the morning when he had gone to present the donation to Sather. On the way there he had met Pastor Lyford, who had been furious when he learned where the money came from. The two men parted and the organizer of the theatricals had carried on down to Montgomery Street where Peder Sather had gladly accepted the ninety dollars. He and the gentleman from Hawthorne Street had then had a pleasant chat. But when, in the course of this conversation, the latter happened to mention Lyford and how angry he had been, Sather suddenly announced that he could not accept the money after all.

When this story was printed Peder Sather was accused of being not only a Pharisee, but a coward as well. Surely he was capable of using his own judgment? Or was he nothing but a yes-man. What if Pastor Lyford had instructed him to accept donations presented in silk purses, but not cash that came in burlap sacks?

As yet, no one from the Christian Commission had spoken up in Sather's defense and the banker's own lips were firmly sealed. But after the feud had been raging for some weeks an extraordinary meeting of the board was held at the bank and a statement then issued to the press. The excuse given in this for the rejection of the donation was so unlikely that no one believed it. In any case Peder Sather could not win: if he had been swayed by Pastor Lyford's opinion then he was seen as being spineless; if the decision had been based on his convictions then he was branded a hard-line puritan.

I suspect that Mark Twain may well have been the man behind Verbum Sat and Verbum Sap, for one thing because the tone of these pieces is not unlike that of Twain's newspaper columns—caustic and witty. But there is something else which tends to support this theory. Three years later, Mark Twain fell in love with a girl by the name of Olivia Langdon. To begin with her father, a San Francisco banker, was unsure about the match, so he asked an old friend to make some discreet inquiries as to Twain's character. This old friend happened to be James Hutchinson, Peder Sather's manager.

One of the people whom James Hutchinson contacted was James Roberts, a long-standing ally of Sather's and president of the Christian Commission. Mark Twain was also an acquaintance of Roberts and must have felt quite sure that the latter would give a good report of him and thus clear the way for him to ask for Olivia's hand. He could not have been more wrong. James B. Roberts's verdict on Mark Twain read as follows: "I would rather bury a daughter of mine than have her marry such a fellow." Such a damning reference may have been by way of a payback from a friend of Sather's to one of his enemies. But what is worse: Roberts's vicious attack on Mark Twain highlights his own appalling view of women and the morals held by a guardian of public morality. This, together with the fact that Peder Sather also forbade

Mary Emma from seeing *her* sweetheart, throws a shocking light on the lot of middle-class daughters back then.

Sather was pilloried over the "parlor theatricals" controversy, accused of being cowardly, straitlaced, and hypocritical; it almost looks as though someone had it in for him. The whole affair was really far too trivial to merit so much press coverage at a time when the Union army was winning on all fronts and the Civil War was almost over. Peder Sather never defended himself: he met all accusations with silence. He was at the peak of his banking career, he was a well-known figure in the city, and evidently had as many foes as friends. At the heart of the matter lay a rigid form of religion adhered to not only by Sather, "the well-known banker," but by the entire Christian Commission. Peder Sather, the jovial wine drinker of the 1850s, seems intent on denying to others the pleasures that he himself had indulged in ten years earlier, but from which he now abstained. However, he did not allow his own local conflict to overshadow what was happening on the battlefront. On March 15 the *New Orleans Times* printed an item which suggests that the Christian Commission in San Francisco had already gone down on its knees to send up prayers of thanks for the Union army's victory. The newspaper reported that the commission wished to honor President Lincoln with a gift. Its choice had fallen on a gold pen in the shape of a quill set with diamonds. Peder Sather contributed to this fine gift, but Lincoln was never to have the pleasure of using it, because on April 11, 1865, he was assassinated at Ford's Theater in Washington.

Four days later, when the news reached San Francisco, the leaders of the National Union Party announced that they would be arranging a grand mourning procession through the city. Fifteen thousand men—soldiers, civilians, firemen, representatives of the trades, the arts, and commerce—marched down Montgomery Street in total silence. The street was draped from end to end in flags and banners. The women were all dressed in red, white, and blue. The hush was broken only by the dull thud of cannon fire. People crowded together on rooftops and in windows to watch the procession. The bands played "The Battle Cry of Freedom." People joined in the chorus, wiped away tears, and sobbed into handkerchiefs. In the center of the city and up on the hills the church bells began to chime. As they did so the flags were lowered to half-mast and the whole city came to a standstill. Somewhere in the throng was Peder Sather, no longer just a face in the crowd, but the well-known banker on the corner, where the doors were closed and the offices empty for the day. Peder Sather with a black silk hat on his head and sorrow in his heart.

SIXTEEN

The Haunted House

When Peder Sather resigned from the university's Board of Trustees, one of the reasons he gave for doing so was that "various circumstances" had arisen to which he could see no end. He did not say what these circumstances were; he only apologized for having to resign and said that his decision was final. There was none of the hesitancy here that he had shown when accepting his seat on the board.

Events had occurred that were to have long-lasting consequences; circumstances of a very different nature from the deaths of Edward Church and Francis Drexel and in no way connected to the standing of the bank, to duties, responsibilities, or overwork. All the indications are that these had more to do with a problem within the family, more specifically with the youngest daughter, Mary Emma.

During the 1860s the Sathers stayed for long periods of time at the old schoolhouse in Alameda; this we know from tax records and articles and notices in the press. This idyllic, sheltered peninsula close to Oakland was becoming an increasingly popular place to live, and with ferries shuttling back and forth every half-hour Peder had no problem getting to and from the city and the bank. Indeed, with the family in the country suburb, the ferry trips across the bay, and his work in the financial district, this was not unlike his life in the 1840s when he was working in Manhattan and living in Brooklyn.

There were close on fifteen hundred people living in Alameda in 1860: Germans, Irish, British, and a scattering of Chinese and black people. Most were manual laborers or farmers, but among them too were quite a few merchants and businessmen, lawyers and doctors: people who had moved out here either because of the climate, which was milder than in San Francisco, or the growing belief that it was a good idea to keep work and home life separate. After a hard day at the office there was nothing quite like coming home to the cozy family nest, to hear the birds singing in the trees and enjoy the dinner that was all ready and waiting for you, while the sun set over the Pacific, the shadows lengthened, and the woods grew still.

Alameda was separated from the mainland by marshes and wetlands, a paradise for geese and quail, pelicans and herons. Oak trees grew in pleasant groves, their low, dense crowns forming leafy evergreen canopies. In the spring the meadows were a mass of yellow and orange poppies whose petals, blown off by the breeze, fluttered down to land on the bright-green grass and lie there, shriveling up like dying embers. At midsummer the peninsula was baked by the sun, brown and tinder-dry. It was bounded on three sides by the Bay and to landward by the marshes, but plans were now afoot to fill in the wetlands with earth and build a bridge across the marshes to the mainland.

Deer, powerful and alert, grazed in the backwoods, nibbling and chewing leaves. In ponds and lakes ancient turtles paddled lazily about, their gray, watchful heads just above the surface. Snakes dozed on sunny slopes, hummingbirds whirred through the air, raccoons padded through the undergrowth, hidden by the night, hidden by the thick morning fog, hidden by the dense thickets, overgrown and impenetrable. What business did human beings have here?

As yet the houses were well spread out, one here, another in the woods, secluded, perfect for anyone looking for peace and quiet. The old schoolhouse had no near neighbors, nor was it likely to have, lying as it did on a large property that Sather had bought in 1854. Ten years later, when he purchased another tract of land further north on the peninsula, he would become the biggest landowner in Alameda.

When darkness fell, little lamps were lit in the schoolhouse, none of them capable of lighting up the huge rooms, but bright enough for night prowlers to see that it was inhabited. During the day, children strolling down the paths through the woods would stop and stare at the house, point at the funny-looking tower, and make up stories about what it might be, giggling, sniggering, wondering. On Sundays the occasional walker, having lost his way in the backwoods, would come out here only to discover that he had strayed onto private land.

There was an Indian burial ground on the property, a steep mound clearly visible in the landscape, as big as a soccer pitch. The local people were well aware of what lay inside it and they were shocked when word got around that

Peder Sather wanted to build a mansion up there for his son. He had apparently claimed that the burial mound was actually a natural formation, but never had it opened in order to find out for sure one way or the other and no house was ever built there. The mound was not opened until 1892, in connection with the building of a new road. And the locals were shown to have been right all along. Found inside were complete skeletons, pieces of cups and bowls, jewelry, and masses of seashells.

For Sarah and her daughters, used to living in New York, which in 1860 had a population of close on a million, the animal life, the flocks of birds, the flower-strewn meadows, the shrubs, and the brushwood cannot entirely have made up for what they had left behind, even though they could always pop across to San Francisco, a city smaller than Brooklyn and a veritable village compared to Manhattan. Young Peder went to the bank with his father and the girls went to the Young Ladies' Seminary in Benicia, but how did Sarah spend her days? Did she stay at home with the three servants and take tea with Mrs. Myers?

The school in Alameda had been built in 1855 and was originally called the Oak Grove Institute, but later changed its name to the Alameda Collegiate Institute for Young Ladies and Gentlemen. It being the first school on the peninsula quite a lot was written about it in later years. The general opinion was that it ought to be preserved and turned into a museum, nonetheless in 1913 the old schoolhouse was demolished to make way for a road.

In May 1893 a long article about the school and its history appeared in the *San Francisco Chronicle* under the sinister headline "The Haunted House." This was also the caption underneath the drawing of the school that accompanied the article, and the whole piece was subtitled "The Sather Mansion in Alameda."

The *San Francisco Chronicle* was one of the city's biggest newspapers and was read throughout California. In 1893 Peder Sather had been dead for seven years, but the schoolhouse—now dilapidated and moss-grown—was still owned by his estate. The article had been inspired by a wish to restore and preserve the school. According to the *Chronicle* Peder Sather had never made any attempt to maintain the building and never set foot in it after 1865, when the family stopped using it.

An initial description of the isolated location and of a schoolhouse that was anything but cozy and homelike inside was followed by various details which more than suggest that the Sather family had not been happy in that house. The gist of the article, which concerned Mary Emma, tallies with the biographical notes given to me by Kathleen Bruguiere Anderson and with other sources. This article in the *San Francisco Chronicle* may therefore help to explain what Peder Sather meant when he wrote that various circumstances made it impossible for him to carry on as a trustee of the university. The following account is based on the details given in the *Chronicle* on May 21, 1893.

The schoolhouse had lain empty for some years before the Sathers moved into it. Bushes and shrubs, left to grow unchecked, had closed in around it, their branches scraping against its walls. It contained eighteen rooms, some of which had been used as dormitories, others as offices, classrooms, and kitchens. Swing-doors, like the ones in western saloons, led onto wide corridors. The doors could neither be closed nor locked, so the slightest sound from the tiniest nook or cranny could be heard all over the house. Not only that, but the rooms were so big and the ceilings so high that even someone as tall as Peder Sather looked small in them.

It would have taken a lot more than the six family members and the three servants to fill those eighteen rooms with life. Sarah Sather, sensitive and highly-strung by nature, had never liked the place, and objected to moving there. She was too timorous to want to explore the house and find out what might be tucked away in its many dark corners and cubbyholes. She hated the huge shadows that danced around the circles of light thrown by the meager lamps. She wanted Peder to try to rent the place out and build a new house for them on another plot of land, along with a house for Peder Jr., to be completed by the time he was ready to take over the bank. But the family went on living in the old schoolhouse, despite the fact that Sarah was unhappy there.

Senator Leland Stanford, the future founder of Stanford University, had also been considering making his home in Alameda. He knew Peder Sather and asked him if he could buy from him the patch of land on which the Indian burial ground lay. Sather would have sold it to him on the spot, but Sarah felt that the price the senator was offering was far too low and prevented the sale from going ahead. Leland Stanford can hardly have been short of cash, however; he was in the process of making a fortune from the building of the transcontinental railroad, linking the East Coast and the West Coast, which was completed in the spring of 1869. Instead of moving to Alameda, Stanford bought a large stretch of land in Palo Alto, where he made his permanent home and later founded the famous university.

The *San Francisco Chronicle* gives the impression that Sarah was not without influence where her husband was concerned, and not mean with money either. This supports my theory that she came from a well-to-do family and that despite her nervous disposition she did have some sort of hold over Peder. Why he should have insisted that she put up with living out in the Alameda scrub, is another matter. Was it simply in order to save the building from going to rack and ruin?

To a lady of quality the schoolhouse might otherwise have seemed a fine enough residence. Built in the southern style, it had broad front steps leading up to a portico that ran the full length of the building. At the back of the house were the old boarding school kitchens, the larder, and storerooms, large enough to cope with the biggest social gatherings.

More than anything, though, what caught the eyes of passers-by was the square tower room on the roof. What might that be used for? they wondered. The *San Francisco Chronicle* wrote that the young people of Alameda still told stories of having seen a mysterious figure at the window up there, and the grown-ups would never forget the tragic events that had taken place in the old schoolhouse: Mary Emma, the family's youngest daughter, had gone mad after her father forbade her to marry the man of her choice, of whom he did not approve. She eventually became so deranged and violent that she had to be confined to the house, and people strolling past would sometimes catch a glimpse of her through the tower windows.

Mary Emma went on living at home for many years, but her condition did not improve. Instead it gradually deteriorated, making life difficult for everyone. It was only a matter of time before her parents would have to find a place for her in an asylum. Her illness had been triggered by her father's refusal to let her have anything to do with the man she loved, but it seems unlikely that the ructions this caused were to blame for the fact that she did not get better. Nonetheless, the article in the *San Francisco Chronicle* calls to mind James Roberts's words concerning any possible alliance between his own daughter and a man like Mark Twain. The daughters of wealthy families were not free to wed whomever they chose. Marriages were arranged more in order to safeguard fortunes and property, and to avoid any drop in social status or other scandalous loss of prestige. It is a well-known fact, of course, that bachelors would court the daughters of rich men in order to get their hands on the family fortunes, and that a young girl could end up in the clutches of a Lothario who did not necessarily love her. And if there was one thing that parents—and, more especially, the family breadwinners—feared it was this. Another case in point is that of Senator Charles F. Lott, an associate of Peder Sather's in the insurance business and a man said to be so well loved by the

FIGURE 15. Mary Emma Sather, 1865. Photographer: William Shew, 421 Montgomery Street, San Francisco. Courtesy of Eva Helle.

people of California that they grieved every time he went to Washington, but of whom other, somewhat less flattering, stories were later told. Lott too had a daughter whose marriage he prevented, and when he died she was left in her brother's charge. Only when the latter too was dead was the girl free to marry the man she loved, who had stayed true to her all those years.

The national census of 1870 shows that at that point Mary Emma was still living at home, as were her sisters, including Caroline who was by then thirty-four years old. I have found no evidence of Mary Emma being committed to an asylum before this time. The first psychiatric hospital in California had opened in 1853, and since it was in Stockton, not far from San Francisco, Sarah and Peder could have visited Mary Emma as often as they wished had they sent her there. But they didn't, and knowing what conditions could be like in such asylums one can well understand why not.

In 2003 the astute and incisive writer Joan Didion published a book entitled *Where I Was From,* a memoir of her childhood and youth in

Sacramento and of six generations of her family's history, starting with her great-great-grandparents, who came to California during the Gold Rush. In this Didion described the unspeakable treatment of psychiatric patients on the West Coast during the latter half of the nineteenth century. Asylums were hidden well out of the way, the main point of them being to isolate the patients from society in order to protect it from them. None of them received any treatment to speak of; asylums were little more than prisons in which the mentally ill were left to rot.

The number of psychiatric patients here was much higher than in any other state, and Joan Didion believed that asylums in California were used as a means of exercising widespread and heavy-handed social control. Anyone who showed any signs of abnormal or eccentric behavior, of being any kind of social misfit, risked being declared insane. The same applied to old people, drunks, the mentally backward or those commonly regarded as "simple." The most human of conditions could be cited as causes of mental illness, from homesickness to fear of fires or earthquakes. In the 1870 census one Californian out of every 489 was registered as being mentally ill; ten years later this figure had risen to one in 345. According to Joan Didion these statistics contrast sharply with the way in which Californians have always liked to present themselves as open-minded and more tolerant than the people of other states.

As a source, the article in the *San Francisco Chronicle* should not be taken entirely at face value, even though the information given in it has been corroborated by others. Considering what Didion says about psychiatric institutions at that time, Peder and Sarah might not have had any choice but to keep Mary Emma at home. The tower may have been a last resort when her ravings were at their worst. The only way up to it, the *Chronicle* says, was by a ladder. The question is: was it better for Mary Emma to be shut up in a tower room at home than in an asylum in some out-of-the-way spot? My job is not to judge, but to tell a story, and in any story of mental illness shame also has a part to play. From that point of view the house in Alameda could have been useful when it came to concealing how seriously unhinged Mary Emma could sometimes be. Likewise, a man such as Peder Sather might have felt that the rural surroundings would have a soothing effect on the girl. It was widely believed that fresh air and country living could cure all manner of ills. Thus, the whole family found itself, for the moment, with its hands tied.

And yet: other sources say that during the 1860s "all sorts of hospitality" was extended to guests at the house on Rincon Hill. So the Sather family must have spent a fair bit of time there. As indeed they did—confirmation of this can be found in the tax records for 1863, the year in which Sather gave up his seat on the university Board of Trustees. In that year he was registered as resident in Second Street, truly a man of rank and standing with, according to tax records, "four horses in the stable, five carriages in the outhouse, a piano and a silver plate, 210 ounces."

This address does not fit, though, with what we know of Mary Emma and the situation in the house in Alameda. Not that the one necessarily excludes the other, since the sources I have consulted are somewhat imprecise as to dates, referring only to "the 1860s." Mary Emma may have had her good spells; at other times—when the Sathers had guests, for example—it might have been impossible to have her in the house on Rincon Hill. On such occasions Sarah and Peder always had the house in Alameda and Mary Ann Fowler, one of the servants who had been with the family for years, to take care of Mary Emma.

Mental illness was such a taboo subject back then that it is not so surprising if those sources who remember the family's life on Rincon Hill make no mention of Mary Emma. Although, it is true, they may simply have been exercising an understandable discretion. Nostalgic memoirs written by individuals who themselves belong to the upper levels of society tend not to dwell on the sadder recollections, which is fair enough. Or it could be that Mary Emma's parents did all they could to keep her hidden and prevent word of her condition from getting out.

Just as Timothy Ball was saddened by the fate that befell Peder Dysterud in Indiana, I find it hard to remain unaffected when writing about the trials and tribulations of the Sather family in the 1860s. The very best of intentions can have the most dreadful consequences, and everyone can be hurt by them. Life is not a sum that can be solved simply by adding up the numbers. Not everything in life can be worked out by means of logic and reasoning. A conclusion, however neat, may still not tell the whole truth.

There is no byline attached to the article in the *San Francisco Chronicle,* so for all we know it was nothing but gossip. But the writer, whoever he or she was, clearly had something against Peder Sather and his choice of address, and more than hints that he was unreasonably hard on Mary Emma. Put this together with the feud surrounding his involvement with the Christian Commission and a picture begins to emerge of an individual who, at the height of his career, had serious problems at home and was regarded by the outside world as a moralistic sort of man.

In 1865 the family was once again registered as living in Alameda, where Sather was listed as the resident with the most capital and highest earnings; any man looking to marry one of his daughters would definitely have been making a good match. In that same year the San Francisco newspapers rated Sather as one of the wealthiest men in the city, along with the blue jean manufacturer Levi Strauss; Benjamin Davidson, agent for the Rothschild banking concern; Mayor Thomas Selby; Senator Charles F. Lott; and George Johnson from Bergen, the Norwegian-Swedish Consul General.

When writing about a Norwegian immigrant born two hundred years ago who has left only sparse and very faint traces of himself it would be unwise to be too definite in one's assertions; far better to be aware of one's own limitations. As the narrator here, I am on the outside and on foreign ground, to a much greater extent than passers-by in the scrubland of Alameda. But like them I cannot help but wonder about what an unhappy family must have lived in that house and what an unhappy father Peder Sather must have been, no matter how successful he was as a banker.

During those years there seems, though, to have been one matter to which he remained committed and that was the fight against slavery and the living conditions of black people. In January 1865, when the Civil War was drawing to a close, Peder Sather became one of the founding members of the Californian branch of the American Freedmen's Aid and Union Commission, an organization set up to help freed slaves by providing them with food, clothing, jobs, accommodation, and schooling. The governor of California was elected as president of the commission, and Senator Leland Stanford and Peder Sather as vice-presidents.

The following August, Peder Sather's name appeared in an "independent call" signed by several thousand citizens of San Francisco. In this they begged a number of Republican and Democrat politicians "of the highest capacity, the purest integrity and the most devoted loyalty to the country and the Union to join forces to ensure that the Union's principles also on slavery would be adhered to." The president of the commission invited all citizens to attend a mass meeting in Platt's Hall on Montgomery Street. Women, in particular, were urged to come along—space had been reserved for them in a special gallery, the announcement said.

Undertakings like this and others I have mentioned could perhaps be dismissed as charity, alms dispensed by the rich to the poor or even a form of penance for one's own wealth. I would rather see it as a mark of a social conscience; it reminds me of a note in an old census record about a poor boy living at Nordstun Nedre Sæter: "on the Farm from Compassion."

Peder Sather still kept in touch with his brother Christoffer in Odalen, but there is little to suggest that he took the opportunity in his letters to tell him about the situation in the family. Peder does, though, show his concern for the people back home. In December 1867, when his brother Lars died, leaving a wife and children on Spigset Farm, Peder wrote to Christoffer to tell him that he had transferred, through Shipley & Co. in London, eighty-five pounds sterling, which was equal to around 380 *speciedaler*, and that this could be collected from the Christiania Kreditbank: "It will, I suppose, be necessary for you to go into Town when you receive this," he writes. The money was for the widow and her children, to pay off the debt on the farm, and here Sather adds something which shows that he was not a member of the old school where the equality of the sexes was concerned. Of the rights to Spigset Farm he says: "It is my wish that they should all have an equal share in it, Girls as well as Boys."

This letter is written on the notepaper of the banking house of Sather & Church, with the name of the firm's former partner in brackets in the letterhead. In 1867 Edward Church had been dead for six years, but Peder Sather was obviously not the sort to waste paper just because the bank had changed its name to Sather & Co. This letter might, therefore, be proof that those who described Sather as frugal were right, and this may also have been one of the main reasons for his success. In which case it's no wonder that he was so upset by Peder Jr.'s extravagance and self-indulgence.

The letter of December 7 is concerned only with Odalen and how things are with everyone there: confirmation, again, that he had not blanked out the past or forgotten anyone at home. His questions and comments are so detailed that he seems almost to be picturing every one of them: Lars's widow in the winter cold, the fatherless children whom he hopes will be able to have a "decent Upbringing." He pictures them, he thinks, he writes, sitting there in his office on Montgomery Street while the December rain pours down and a miserable, wet Christmas approaches. "Greetings to Friends and Family from your devoted Brother."

Peder Sather could probably have bought the whole of Odalen, half of Hedmark County, and a bit more besides had he so wished, but in this case it was merely a matter of dollars to the tune of around 380 *speciedaler* to a widow and her children. He cares about them, of course, but he appears to have kept careful account of all financial transactions, whatever their nature—a habit that had taken him from strength to strength in the banking world. At the end of August 1866 he had, for example, purchased the lot on which the bank sat for fifty-five thousand dollars. Since 1863 it had occupied premises on the northeast corner of Montgomery and Commercial Streets, with a frontage of thirty feet on Montgomery Street and sixty feet on Commercial. In pictures the building does not look particularly imposing, and although it had three floors to it the upper floors were rented out. According to the employment records Sather & Co. had a staff of no more than ten or thereabouts. On the other hand, no bank on Montgomery Street could be described as small or insignificant. On the contrary, one of the richest men in the San Francisco area was to be found behind that modest thirty-foot frontage on one of the best streets in town.

In the fall of 1866 Peder Sather was in New York together with—according to the ship's passenger list presented on their return to San Francisco on November 24—"a daughter." Such lists never gave the names of wives or children; in this respect they were considered no better than third-class passengers. We have no way of knowing, therefore, which daughter this was. It may have been Caroline, if she had to go to New York for treatment, or possibly Mary Emma. Sather had been advised to have her admitted to Burn Brae, a private mental hospital just outside of Philadelphia, where Anthony Drexel lived. Burn Brae had opened in 1858 under the direction of Dr. Robert Given. This hospital was the first in the country to offer conversational therapy, and in 1867 it was considered to be the best of its kind in America. It was situated in an idyllic spot on Drexel Hill and looked like a grand Victorian manor house with its white-painted window frames and ivy-covered walls.

Inside, Burn Brae had been designed to be as much like home as possible, with elegant drawing rooms, paintings on the walls, a library, and a piano. The hospital had all the facilities necessary to promote the well-being of its patients, including its own farm, which supplied fresh eggs, fruit, and vegetable, and kept horses on which they could go for long rides. It also had cricket pitches, tennis courts, and a swimming pool. There were concerts in the evenings, readings and lectures with discussions afterward, and dinners worthy of the finest restaurants. This was a clinic for the country's upper classes, rather different from sending your daughter to an asylum in Stockton, but it was a long way from home. So when Mary Emma was eventually admitted to Burn Brae it was good to know that Anthony Drexel was nearby and could check that all was well with her.

When Peder Sather and "daughter" left New York on November 1, 1866, they must have done so in some haste: back in San Francisco there had been an outbreak of typhus and Peder Jr. had caught the disease. First he was racked by fever and chills and suffered from incessant diarrhea; then his whole body became covered in a painful, suppurating rash. His face, the soles of his feet, and palms of his hands were the only areas not affected. After this the boy grew more and more delirious until he had lost his wits entirely.

Peder Dysterud Sather died on December 13. He was just twenty-one years old, only a couple of years older than the cousin after whom he was named, who had passed away at Red Cedar Lake at Christmastime 1838. The funeral service was held at home on Rincon Hill, in the presence of family and friends, the papers said. Afterward the coffin was taken to Lone Mountain Cemetery. Peder Sather had picked out a burial plot on a hill with a view of the city. He had a spiraling white marble column made and set over the grave. There it could stand pointing toward the heavens while Peder Sather sank into the depths of despair. It was said that he took the loss of his son very hard, and that he never got over it. Of his surviving children, Josephine was now the only one who was fit and well.

SEVENTEEN

Never Sather & Son

A year after Peder Jr. died James Hutchinson and his wife Coralie had a son. Birth records show that they named the boy James Sather Hutchinson, and it seems reasonable to assume that there was a direct connection between Peder Jr.'s death and the choice of name.

As manager of the bank James Hutchinson was Peder Sather's right-hand man and Coralie was Edward Church's sister-in-law. It may be that the couple wished to comfort the grieving father by giving their son his name. If so, then this only goes to show how close-knit the circle around Sather was. Hutchinson also cherished hopes that the bank might one day be known as Sather & Hutchinson, but instead, as he remarked somewhat ruefully in an interview given when he was an old man of ninety-three, he had had to be content with being one of the reasons why the bank was called Sather & Co., and not Sather Bank. This suggests that Sather wanted to maintain full control of the bank, even though his manager may have aspired to change that state of affairs. And if *that* is so then it speaks of an inner circle that was not just a nest of warmth and friendship but also a hotbed of fawning and flattery.

James and Coralie Hutchinson's marriage in the early 1850s had been preceded by a lengthy courtship, or so Anthony Tasheira noted in one of his letters. Tasheira did not like Coralie; he felt that she put on airs and said that he had never seen a woman who looked so insincere, not even her sister Letitia Church.

James Hutchinson was a pale, thin man of average height, he had a long face and a pursy little mouth—Coralie did not find him particularly attractive, but he was so exceedingly unctuous and obliging that she knew he would be an easy catch. Anthony did not believe for one minute that James really loved Coralie either; he suspected that it was not for love, but for other reasons entirely that he fluttered and flitted around her whenever she came swanning past with her nose in the air.

Coralie lived with her sister and Edward Church in the house next door to Sather's on Rincon Hill. James Hutchinson lodged nearby with the Turnbulls and never missed an opportunity to pop round to the Churches on some pretext or other, or to the Sathers' if he knew that Coralie would be there. Anthony had a strong suspicion that Hutchinson had a secret plan to marry his way to a directorship, but Coralie played it very cool. Whenever he so much as tried to have a word with her she would don her coat and bonnet and announce that she needed some fresh air.

At some point, though, according to Anthony, she must have had a change of heart, because late one evening he and Speer Riddell received word that she and James Hutchinson were to be married—at eight o'clock the next morning no less. The wedding was to take place at the home of Peder Sather. Neither Anthony nor Speer Riddell slept well that night, and were so tired in the morning that they barely managed to shave and grab a bite to eat before stumbling out of the bank, dressed in their best and making their way up to Second Street. Their stomachs were rumbling by the time they knocked on Sather's door. Inside, however, they were astonished to find no sign whatsoever that a wedding was to be held there. No table had been set and there were only three or four other guests present apart from Peder Sather, among them the minister, who demanded to be paid twice the normal fee, arguing that it was highly unusual for people to ask to be wed so early in the morning and in a private home at that.

Edward Church was there, as distant as always and all ready to go to the bank, and Letitia was so carelessly attired that, in Anthony's opinion, she might as well have been in her dressing gown. The bridal couple had not gone to any trouble over their appearance either; the wedding ceremony was held in the drawing room, it was over in a matter of minutes, and the newlyweds then drove off in a carriage—off on their honeymoon it was said, but when they came back two or three days later Coralie was in a foul mood. She said they had had such a terrible row that as far as she was concerned the marriage was over. This was not, however, the case. In due course James became manager of the bank and in 1867 Coralie gave birth to a boy who would carry on the name of Sather.

Giving one's children the surnames of other people is, it has to be said, a very symbolic act, but Peder Sather had given his son Peder Dysterud's name, Anthony Drexel had called one of his sons after George Childs, and now the

Hutchinsons had seen fit to follow suit. It's touching, it's puzzling—an act which speaks volumes, but which cannot fully be explained, unless as a token of a culture which considers family names so sacred that they simply cannot be allowed to die out.

If this was their real reason, then the Hutchinsons succeeded beyond all imagining. James Sather Hutchinson would become one of California's leading mountaineers, a monument raised to his honor in Yosemite National Park. There on a little plaque his middle name can still be seen, but no one today realizes that this was the name of a banker from Montgomery Street in San Francisco, who hailed from a farm in Odalen, Norway. But perhaps more than anything what this story of Hutchinson the suitor and Hutchinson the bank manager and name chooser tells us is that the clique surrounding the bank was an incestuous one. This impression is only reinforced by the knowledge that at least two of the bank's employees were Freemasons—namely, those hungry young men who raced up the hill, dressed in their best shirts, to attend a hastily organized wedding at the home of master of ceremonies Peder Sather.

But in 1867 all of this was far in the past, Anthony was dead, Edward Church was dead, and the year before Peder Jr. too had died, all three of typhus. In San Francisco the risk of infection appeared to be as great as it had been when Anthony was prospecting for gold in Tuolumne. Back then Peder Sather had advised him to spend a dollar a week on vegetables to stave off sickness, but here were three men who had succumbed even though they all had good homes, good incomes, good hygiene, and access to all the fruit and vegetables they could want. But in a city like San Francisco, bounded on three sides by salt water, with very few freshwater springs, a hopeless sewage system, and an extremely dense population the danger of contagion was ever present and epidemics spread like wildfire. Sanitary conditions were appalling and the city stank.

The Sathers might have been less at risk of infection had they been living in Alameda, but a newspaper item from the fall of 1867 states that Peder Sather had rented the schoolhouse in the woods to the newly established Alameda Seminary. So the family were now back on Rincon Hill for good, at a time when the population of San Francisco was nudging a hundred thousand and the city was undergoing major changes. After the Civil War there had been a sharp increase in productivity; columns of smoke rose from the chimneys of iron foundries, sawmills and shipyards, shoe and clothing factories.

This led to the emergence in the city of a new and clearly defined working class, and of a moneyed elite far wealthier than that produced by the Gold Rush. This new wealth stemmed from the silver deposits recently discovered at Comstock, about one hundred miles from Grass Valley. The amount of silver found here put the gold discovered during the Gold Rush totally in the shade. It gave rise to an upper class that built virtual palaces containing ballrooms big enough to accommodate three to four hundred guests—residences that made the Sather family home look like a cottage in comparison, and in some books that was in fact what it was called: "a cottage."

Apart from the information that Peder Jr. died of typhus in 1866, I have not been able to find out much about the years following the family's move back to Rincon Hill after the Civil War. From occasional items in the newspaper it appears that Sarah may have been involved in charity work, especially in aid of unwed mothers, although her generosity seems to have had its limits: fifteen dollars here, twenty dollars there. Nonetheless, membership of one or two charitable foundations did at least help to get her and her as-yet-unmarried and in some cases troubled and ailing daughters—none of whom was getting any younger—out of the house. While their parents might have considered it a disgrace to have their daughters marry beneath them, it did them no credit either to have a house full of potential spinsters. Not only that, but a single girl who was no longer in the first flush of youth was regarded as a poorer and poorer match with each year that passed. Sarah herself had been almost thirty before she married, so how happy was she with this situation? Well, at least she was the wife of one of the city's most prominent men and could sweep along Montgomery Street in a gleaming carriage drawn by four gray thoroughbreds.

Peder Sather was pushing sixty, his hair and beard were almost white. He was always to be found in his office behind one of those tall windows, hunched over piles of correspondence from Luther Lawrence and Anthony Drexel. But did the ships ever bring anything from Norway? Yes, they did. Most of the banks that had sprung up during the Gold Rush had gone under, but Sather & Co. had survived all the crises. So was Peder Sather content? Yes, he was. James S. Hutchinson, the bank manager, took care of all the day-to-day work and Mr. Sather could spend as much time as he liked strolling through the streets whenever he needed a bit of exercise and some fresh air. The papers called him a notable, an eminent citizen, a dignitary. As a banker he was reputed to be so trustworthy that his word was as binding as a signature on a contract. He rose from his desk, told Hutchinson he would be out for half an hour, took his silk hat from its hook, and left the bank. Heads turned as soon as he started to walk down the sidewalk: there goes the well-known banker! That tall man? Yes, that tall man. The one walking so slowly? Why is he walking so slowly? Is he unwell?

One of the first things that Europeans newly arrived in San Francisco remarked on in letters home was the way people there charged along the sidewalks as if on their way to some very important meeting, when in fact they were only out to buy a tin of pipe tobacco or do some window shopping. Why all the hurry? Had these Californians never heard of walking simply to let one's thoughts run and ideas surface?

Another thing was that, when asked, the local people would tell visitors of all the wonderful sights to be seen in San Francisco, but when asked what these wonderful sights were the only thing they could think of was a bunch of sea lions down by the baths! Or so one Parisian commented wryly in a letter home, although this same person did also add that the San Franciscans' love of their city was in itself such an interesting phenomenon that it made up for almost everything else.

In his letters to relatives and friends in Norway, did Peder Sather mention how he felt about the city or was he only interested in hearing how things were in Odalen? There is no way of knowing, because the letters are gone. Did he know that he was a grandfather, that Petrine had three children? Did he say anything of how wealthy he was or how difficult things could be with Mary Emma in the house? It's highly unlikely. The first would sound too much like boasting, the second would sound too awful. His letters were those of a country boy from Odalen, his life that of a San Francisco banker, and there was no reason to mix these two.

When in San Francisco I always take a walk down Montgomery Street, still a key financial center, full of skyscrapers and deep shadows, banks and constant breezes. Beneath the asphalt is a sailing ship from the 1850s; it has lain there since the harbor was filled in all those years ago. But the same sun still shines down on it, the rain falls as it did back then, raindrops the size of small eggs pelting down onto faces and hands.

To stand on the spot where the bank lay is like standing outside a rehinged door that now swings inward instead of out. On the corner of Commercial Street, where Sather & Co had its offices, there was a gaslight, the one under which the peculiar news vendor had his pitch, and directly opposite was Sorbier's, a French restaurant, and the shoemaker's from which Nelson Cook collected Speer Riddell's boots. Same spot, different time. In 1867, as today,

Montgomery Street was a central thoroughfare. It no longer runs along the waterfront, though, as it did when Peder Sather arrived here in 1851 and could see it from the deck of the ship far out in the roads. Just up the road is the Wells Fargo Museum, whose archives I thought might contain a letter or two from Peder Sather. But no, they are all gone.

Picture Peder on a summer's day in San Francisco, where it is always a little chilly. He shivers. It is even colder up on Rincon Hill where the breeze is always stronger. The clatter of horses hooves over the cobbles, the clang of heel-glazing irons, and rumble of carriage wheels— Montgomery Street is a canyon full of sounds that echo all over the town. Silk hats and bowlers, and wasn't that Sheve the photographer who just walked past? Bonnet ribbons fluttering in the breeze; full-length black capes like mourning sails on a schooner. Should he take a walk over to Lone Mountain? No, he can't go to Lone Mountain because if he does he won't be able to pull himself away. He passes beneath green awnings, has to duck his head and put a hand to his top hat, bow to fate, bow his head and say nothing, it's a fine day after all, and there are, after all, always the days between the nights, and isn't that Samuel Merritt coming down the street in that green carriage?

I can almost feel the straining of the lathered horses, some pulling street-cars, others pulling loads of sugar, iron, flour, or timber. I can almost hear the flapping of the sails in the harbor and the water gushing from the ferry wheels; almost feel the acrid reek of the coal furnaces stinging my nostrils, catch the whiff of horse dung and of beef served at a linen tablecloth in the establishment belonging to two puritanical gentlemen from Boston. The gardens on Rincon Hill cast a veil of scents over the city—from acacias, roses, freesia—there to mingle with the aroma of malt from a brewery and the sharp tang of salt water. Same place, different time: and in this time shift a car horn sounds like the ringing of the bell on a gleaming green Wells Fargo stagecoach drawn by six whinnying horses.

By 1867 Nelson Cook had been in Peder Sather's employ for almost twenty years. Nelson it was who headed down to the post office as soon as the stage-coach had passed the bank door—it rattled so loudly over the cobbles that you never had to wonder what it was that had just sped past, horses frothing at the bit, their flanks running with sweat, nearing journey's end after the last stage across desert plains and over mountain ridges.

Nelson's wife Anna's skills as a seamstress were in great demand. She must have earned much more than her husband; there seemed to be no end to the influx of people to the city and customers were queuing up to have pretty summer dresses or lightweight suits made. Unemployment on the East Coast had risen again, compelling people to go west on overcrowded ships: in just nine months in 1868 sixty thousand new immigrants arrived in California.

But this was a very different world from the one to which the prospectors had come a couple of decades earlier: back then you could never tell whether the man crouched in the river, sifting water from sand, searching for a glint of gold, was a lawyer or an iron founder. The nouveaux riches silver barons had introduced new class divides to the city along with a decadence and style of life hitherto unseen in San Francisco. This new upper class liked nothing better than to get all dressed up, go to parties, and lounge around the hotels of Monterey, where the gentlemen played cricket and the ladies twirled their parasols and protected their complexions from the sun. These parvenus would rather have died than be seen wearing the same outfit for more than a few hours at a time, so the queues at the tailors' and dressmakers' were long and the materials being handled were more costly than ever before: the finest wrinkle-free Chinese silk and the lightest wools from Kashmir. The nights of cutting and sewing were also long when the year was one constant round of suppers and soirées, masked balls and charity dances, finishing off in the wee small hours with a charming cotillion.

These society gatherings were always reported in the newspapers, which could fill page after page with the names of those present: guest lists that the reporters had wangled out of waiters or servants. But I have still to see Peder Sather's name or that of anyone in his family in those countless, long, and closely written columns. Which may mean that he moved in other, less peacock-like circles, in more exalted, dignified company, where the extravagant lifestyle of these new millionaires was eyed with dismay. A glance at the house on Rincon Hill is enough to dispel any notion of Sather as a man who paraded his wealth, even if his son had been more interested in spending money than in earning it, and had thus incurred his father's wrath.

Sather himself did have a reputation for being thrifty. This was, after all, a man who still used company notepaper that ought to have been destroyed years ago, a man who had grown wealthy by scrimping and saving and who ventured nothing without considering the consequences. Letters from Odalen regularly landed on his desk at the bank, notes regarding widows and fatherless children, interest and debts. Such letters represented unintentional measures of how far he had come, reminders that must have caused him to feel a pang whenever Nelson walked in carrying more bags of gold pieces from the Mint, whenever he struck a good property deal, whenever he stroked the flanks of his four gray carriage horses, whenever he bought a mahogany dressing table for Sarah or hung a gold necklace around her throat—if, that is, she was in the mood to receive such a gift. Sarah was, after all, an unpredictable lady, sweet-tempered or sour as the mood took her.

The position of women in nineteenth-century society was such that they have for the most part been forgotten by posterity, as if they had lived only to bear children and die. Consequently not that much is known about Sarah either, despite the fact that she was married to Peder Sather for forty-six years. Even her descendants can provide no information about her—to Kathleen Bruguiere Anderson her great-great-grandmother was just an unknown face in a cracked frame. Only in fragments of sentences does one catch an inkling of her; in the article on the house in Alameda, for instance, in which she is described as being highly-strung and delicate, but which also gives the clear impression that she was much preoccupied with money and would therefore sometimes force Peder into making decisions he was not necessarily happy with.

Attempting to build up a portrait of an individual who lived and died in anonymity may not be the wisest of undertakings, but if you mean to dig her up again you have to start somewhere. One person who took the liberty of breaking this law of wisdom, however, is Sterling Dow. Dow was a professor at Berkeley in the 1960s and a holder of the Sather Chair in Classical Literature. In this capacity he wrote a book about the Sather professorships, in which he asks the same questions that I have asked, as to how Peder Sather can have been so completely forgotten when he had, in fact, not only been a cofounder of the university, but also one of its most important patrons. Dow knows nothing of Sarah's life, because no one does, but in front of him as he writes he has the pictures of Sarah and of Jane Krom, and much more is known about the latter. Having studied the images of these two women, set there side by side, Dow asserts that Peder's wives must both have been powerful, demanding women. This might sound like pure male chauvinism, but only if it is a bad thing for a rich man's wife to have power and make demands. Of Sarah he says that she looks forbidding and old-fashioned, seeming to belong to an earlier century. Dow draws no other conclusions, except to hint that Peder Sather's private life may have been problematic.

The picture Dow studied, probably taken in the late 1860s, was of Sarah in late middle age. To me, as to Dow, Sarah seems a somewhat unforthcoming character: it's very hard to imagine her with a glass of wine in her hand on a jolly evening at the Turnbulls', or even, for that matter, enjoying a cup of coffee in the sunshine on the veranda. She seems out of place, doubtful, tight-lipped, and unbending. Who knows why? In the letter to his brother Christoffer from December 1867, Peder does not say a word about Sarah, he writes as if he were quite alone, reveals nothing personal, about himself or the family. He speaks only of Odalen, of greetings he wishes his brother to pass on to kith and kin and those he has received or hopes to receive.

That December letter, written in his office on Montgomery Street—with no willful Mary Emma to disturb him, no ailing Caroline (now over thirty) around, no strong, healthy, much admired Josephine—says nothing of any of them. There Peder Sather sits in the bank, it is December, it rains all day long, Montgomery Street is dark and wet and the gas lamp outside sheds a greenish-yellow light on the driving rain. There is no one on the street, but behind the rehinged door lies, not an office, but a den, a refuge, a treasure. Here Peder is alone, as he used to be on Rincon Hill.

In the winter of 1867–68 Sather is at the height of his career, his name constantly being mentioned in the press, rendering even the most trivial of news stories more appealing to the ordinary people who would never pass through the turreted front gate on Rincon Hill. In May 1868 the *Alta California* printed a story, one which was also picked up by the *Salt Lake Daily Telegraph*, of an interesting—to its readers—incident involving the banker's garden. It had occurred around nine o'clock one morning. Mr. Sather was nowhere to be seen, he had risen and gone out early and was now at the office. The morning fog was lifting and Sarah and the girls—were they in the house? Did they hear a rumpus and run to the windows? What did they do when they saw what was happening out there?

A Mexican vaquero had been driving a herd of cattle down Harrison Street toward the harbor where they were to be loaded onto a cargo boat. Outside the Sather house the drover sprang down from his horse to tighten his saddle girth. The lead steer saw its chance to escape and went thundering through the Sathers' front gate, which happened to be open. It then proceeded to flatten everything in its path: flowers and bushes, cypress trees, birdbath, and sculptures. The drover raced after the steer, but just when he thought he had the desperate creature under control it charged at a tree protected by wire netting—and got its horns entangled in the wire. With a mighty heave the steer tore itself free and bounded off to the opposite end of the garden with the drover in hot pursuit. He almost caught it with a neat throw of his lasso, but the animal ripped the rope apart as if it were a piece of string. According to the papers, a gentleman who had sought refuge under a pine tree along with a little boy was almost impaled like a worm on a fishing hook. Could that have been James Hutchinson with his two-year-old? Then the steer caught sight of a marble statue of the Greek goddess Psyche, made a run at it, rammed it with its horns, and the goddess toppled to the ground, her neck broken, her head rolling in the grass. Eventually the bull wandered into a corner, its horns were lassoed and it was led out of the ruined garden.

An insignificant little incident, but one that offers some small insight into the banker's life in 1868. It tells past and present that he had a marble statue of Psyche in his garden, this man who had grown up among redcurrant and blackcurrant bushes at Nordstun Nedre Sæter.

It was not long, though, before the Sather family found itself faced with devastation of a much worse order. Rumor had it that a main highway was to be built across Rincon Hill. Second Street was to be widened considerably; it would cut through the foot of the hill and end in a 130-foot gully which came to be known as the Second Street Cut. The Sather's garden would be demolished in the process and the house left teetering on the edge of a steep drop. The street's residents would only be able to gain access to their homes by way of ladders, something which would, in effect, make it impossible to live there. The purpose of the new road was supposedly to save the horses from having to haul heavy loads up the slopes from the city center, but this was just a smokescreen. The man behind these plans was, in fact, a property speculator by the name of John Middleton. Middleton had bought a large number of building lots to the south of Rincon Hill, and if he could force a road through to them he would be able to sell them at a vast profit.

The whole of San Francisco was up in arms when word of this got out— the residential area of Rincon Hill was the pride of the city. The newspapers were bombarded with letters of protest, neighbors on Second Street met to discuss what could be done, but soon realized that it was useless. John Middleton had hired lawyers, he had gone behind the backs of the city councilors and acquired allies among the state politicians in Sacramento. By the late fall of 1868 it was only a question of time before the first charges of dynamite would be detonated, and before then the houses would have to be vacated. Most of them were poorly insulated and poorly soundproofed; they were also standing on sandy, unstable ground. The building work would take about a year. Where were the Sathers supposed to live in the meantime, and what were they to do when it was finished?

In 1868 Peder Sather had been away from Norway for thirty-six years and had never been back to visit his homeland. Neither Sarah nor his daughters had seen the place where he had been born and grown up. Hans Rees was the only person to have gone there, and probably Lucinda, Jane Krom's sister, too, since Hans, Lucinda, and all their children are registered as having been in Norway in 1860. They had visited Odalen, had seen the house of his forefathers, had met Christoffer and brought back the greetings that had prompted Peder to reestablish contact with his brother, to sit in his office in the evenings writing letters home. They could not live on Rincon Hill for the next year anyway, so perhaps the time was right for a longed-for reunion.

———

EIGHTEEN

Among Friends on Wall Street

Peder Sather came to a decision: he had been in America for half a lifetime and his letters from Christoffer were his guarantee that there was a way home to Odalen. They had brought it all back to him: the sound of the River Sæter on a spring evening, the taste of freshly strained milk, the smell of birch burning in the stove, the warmth of the room in the early morning when the floor was still cold! No, it was all too much! Plant potatoes, see the first curled-up leaves climb quietly toward the light, grow into full, leafy, flowering heads above the ground and ten times as many tubers below! See his forefathers' farm, visit his parents' graves, the graves of Anne and Lars. No, no, they live on in your heart, they are gone only for those at home. And winter—it can quite unsettle you, the thought of winter, the one season you really miss: pitch-seam boots stiff with the cold; snow squeaking on leather. Oh, snow; snow falling soft and hushed, piling up in drifts, and you have to clear it, thrusting a shovel into the fresh, white powder. And if anyone spoke did you have to say anything? No, when you came home after thirty-six years everything went without saying.

Peder Sather told his friends in San Francisco that he was going home to Norway and would be away for at least six months, possibly longer. The whole family was going, Sarah and the girls; it was time to show them where he had spent his boyhood, as it says in the biographical notes filed at the California Historical Society in San Francisco.

In books on Norwegian emigration Peder Sather is described as being a central figure in the small Norwegian colony in San Francisco, but other sources say nothing of this, so it is hard to tell what it actually meant and I can well understand why historians have been unable to elaborate on this point. I have exactly the same problem with my knowledge that Peder Sather,

George Childs, and Anthony Drexel were close friends: I cannot tell what they talked about or what they did when they met on an evening in Philadelphia. I have to confine myself to establishing that they did have such an evening together.

There were really too few Norwegians in San Francisco to sustain any sort of independent association; instead a common Scandinavian Society was formed, but anyone wishing to check its records and find out who belonged to it and what they did is out of luck. The society's files were lost in the huge earthquake that struck the city in 1906. But the very fact that Sather mixed with other Norwegians and Scandinavians is significant, reinforcing as it does my impression that Norway never completely lost its hold on him, that he dreamed of going back sometime, and that it was a long time since finding money for the fare had been a problem.

The only other Norwegian whom I have come across in the course of my research is the Mr. Johnson whom Anthony Tasheira said that Peder Sather had met and who was in all probability Bergen-born George Johnson, the Norwegian-Swedish consul general. I am basing this assumption on the fact that a lot of the Norwegians in San Francisco were seamen or craftsmen, who worked on the coastal steamers, on the ferries in the bay, or were carpenters employed in the shipyards. A note in one newspaper tells of a drunk man found lying perishing in the gutter without a penny in his pocket. This man, who later died, was a Norwegian, but it's unlikely that he was ever a member of the little Norwegian Society founded in the 1850s or of the Scandinavian Society formed when the Norwegian organization was dissolved some years later.

Peder as a central figure among local Norwegians? Not among poor, drunken Norwegians. As we know, Peder Sather was actively involved in projects dedicated to dispensing clean shirts and the gospel to the down-and-outs in the harbor area, and he seems more likely to have frequented the homes of those of his compatriots who had, as they say, made their mark: merchants and businessmen, like Knut Henry Lund from Moss, just south of Christiania, who also served for some years as consul general. Lund had a large import-export business dealing mainly in steel, and was often away on long journeys to Europe and the Orient, while Sather still had not managed to make the trip back across the Atlantic. What did he answer when asked if he wasn't soon going to pay a visit to Norway? That he did not actually have an answer?

It could also be, of course, that he had simply been getting on with his life without Norway being a big issue to him or important enough for him to take the boat back there. But the fact was that Norway did matter to him; even in his early days in New York he mixed with other Norwegians, played host to men such as Søren Bache and was so well-known in the Norwegian community that new immigrants arrived from Norway already armed with his name and address. And then there was Bernt Dysterud, who came to visit his Uncle Peder in 1855 and stayed with him for almost a year. So—Peder Sather did not care about Norway?

That Peder and his brother Christoffer went twenty-four years without getting in touch indicates that for both men their pride outweighed their need for each other and this was possibly another reason why Peder did not go back, but the two devoted brothers were now reconciled and what better time for a visit to Norway than in 1868, with Rincon Hill facing long-term devastation and the Sather home uninhabitable.

But if there really was something holding him back and leaving him lost for an answer whenever he was asked why he didn't go back to visit Norway, it might have been the one thing that he had never been able to put behind him, something that still haunted him: Ingeborg Knudsdatter, from Lakkergaden in Christiania, and Petrine, his daughter. Petrine was four years older than Caroline, so in 1868 she would have been in her mid-thirties. She had been married for years to Johan Christian Andreas Encke, a master builder from Kiel. The couple lived in Christiania, at number 4 Nytorvet, now Youngstorget. By the winter of 1868–69 Petrine had had three children by Johan: Christian, who was a mechanic, and two daughters, Ragna and Aagot. In 1869 Petrine would have a fourth child whom they named Peter David. So the Peder Sather who was at that point considering taking his family to Norway already had three grandchildren there, his girls were their aunts, and the children's mother was his daughters' half-sister.

From that sequence of names—Peder, Petrine, Peter—it seems clear that Ingeborg had not kept her father's identity secret from Petrine and that she had told her daughter of the circumstances surrounding Peder Sather's departure from Norway. A letter that I came across later in my research shows that she knew he was in America, knew where he was living, what business he was in and how well he was doing. But was that a good enough reason not to go home? A child born out of wedlock? Well, for a man who waited twenty-four years before getting in touch with his own brother, a man with such a reputation for trustworthiness; a pillar of the community, guardian of public morals, and God-fearing man who had chosen to be baptized and saved through total immersion in order to start a new life; a man who was governed by contemporary ideas of honor, pride, and shame—for such a man it would not have been easy to go to Sarah and say: I have a daughter in Norway, she is only three or four years older than our own dear Caroline.

I have no idea how Peder can have received letters from Petrine, whether he replied to her or helped her financially. All of this has gone to the grave with them, and there it will lie for all eternity.

In September 1868 the university at Berkeley was officially opened, and on October 6 Peder Sather was ready to set out for Norway. He had said it and he meant it. The Sathers left San Francisco around noon on the steamship *Oregonian*. Their faithful servant Mary Ann Fowler accompanied them on the voyage, while James Hutchinson was charged with running the bank and finding a new house for the family to move into on their return.

They must have been in a hurry to leave, because if they had waited a few months the transcontinental railroad would have been completed and the family could have traveled to New York by train in about a week. Instead they had to go by the usual route, by steamer down to Panama; but the newer ships were faster and the whole journey could be done in less than ten days. Nor did they lack for any comforts on board—Peder Sather had bought first-class tickets. Every member of the party had their own cabin and at dinner a string quartet helped to lighten the mood and aid the digestion. As usual the ship called in at Acapulco to take on coal and more passengers, and when they reached Panama the weather there was like high summer.

From Panama they took the train to Aspinwall: a journey of only a few hours now. The locomotive and its string of yellow wooden carriages wound their way along the narrow track over forest-clad mountain ridges and through dense, damp jungle. Branches swished against the windows, parrots fled shrieking from the din of the engine and the black smoke pouring out of the smokestack. Passengers who, thirty years earlier, had crossed the Isthmus of Panama on donkeys or on foot, in canoes or on small paddle steamers, really had to pinch themselves. Prior to 1855, even the strongest and healthiest young people could fall prey to such deadly diseases as typhus and malaria. Now travelers could sit and drowse in comfortable bamboo seats and be served lemonade and tropical fruit. In Aspinwall another ship would be waiting to carry them north to New York—as long as the tide was in, allowing it to anchor off the gently sloping shore.

Aspinwall was the sort of place that people were happy to get away from as quickly as possible: a few clusters of houses bounded to the front by swampland and to the back by a dense wall of jungle. Only ship's officers and a few foreign dignitaries had houses of any decent standard, the rest were tumble-down shacks. But the Sathers were lucky; their ship was there waiting for them, in deep water offshore, and after passengers had been checked for weapons they were rowed out to it, with barely a backward glance at the weather-beaten wooden shacks on the shore, the flocks of turkeys flapping around the buildings, or the mules asleep on their feet under sloping palm trees.

The Sather family could sit up on deck in the fine weather as the paddle steamer churned its way between the islands of the Caribbean, past the blue mountains of Jamaica and the green hills of Cuba. But as the ship neared New York and the temperature dropped day by day, all of its passengers gradually retreated indoors, the gentlemen to the smoking room and the ladies to their own lounge. There sat the three sisters, all of them unmarried and two of them very fragile. Caroline, the eldest, was thirty-two, tall, dark and blue-eyed. Then came Josephine, twenty-seven and as tall as her sister, but with gray eyes like her father's, dark and pretty with her smooth hair parted in the center and drawn back into a bun at the nape of her neck. And Mary Emma, her hair done in exactly the same way, the youngest at twenty-five, was seated there too, dreamy-eyed and trying to put on a brave face. And with them, their mother, of whom so little is now known and who must have been at least sixty-two years old.

Now Sarah and the girls were going to be accompanying Peder to ice-cold Norway, to Christiania, to Lillestrøm from where they would take the new Kongsvinger railway line to Disenå station. There they would alight to be met by banks and mounds of snow, frozen rivers and drooping, white-cloaked pine branches; by steaming horsebacks and jingling sleigh bells. Then they would be wrapped in sheepskin rugs and whisked off through the gloom to the farm where Peder Sather had been born. The reek from roaring fires would sting at their nostrils long before they reached the house and the frost flowers on the windows would make it impossible for them to see who was waiting inside. Weatherwise they could not have picked a worse time, but they would have had to spend some time in New York first, to see family and friends there and organize their passports before setting out across the dark and stormy Atlantic.

New York City now boasted a million inhabitants, which made it the largest city in the country. In twenty years the population had doubled. In Brooklyn it had tripled; with its four hundred thousand inhabitants the once peaceful suburb had been completely transformed. This was a very different place from the one that Sarah and her daughters had left in 1858. They had lived here for over twenty years, while on Rincon Hill they were still regarded as newcomers, mainly because they had moved back and forth so much between Alameda and San Francisco.

When mother, father, and daughters stepped ashore in New York the streets were covered in slush and ice, giving them a foretaste of winter in Norway. I can just picture the tall, lovely Sather sisters caught in the yellow-green light of the gas lamps, clad in thick, full-length fur coats, their faces shaded by broad-brimmed hats. After weeks of traveling by train and ship they cannot get to the hotel quick enough. Peder Sather is shivering inside his coat and the sort of beaver-skin cap rich men wore in the winter. The sleet slants down through the beams of the streetlamps as the trunks are lifted into one coach while the Sathers climb into another.

Then, no doubt, they drove off to the elegant Fifth Avenue Hotel in Madison Square, since this was where Peder and Sarah Sather usually stayed when they were in New York. The Fifth Avenue Hotel was still a favorite rendezvous for the top people in financial, political, social, and artistic circles, just as it had been when Abraham Lincoln wrote his famous speech in one of its rooms. Old pen and ink drawings of the interior show suites complete with elaborate fireplaces and fabulous bathrooms, a lofty dining room with rows of long tables ranged under crystal chandeliers, and a menu featuring the choicest seafood dishes prepared by the best chefs in town. The library offered a wide selection of newspapers, magazines, and books and was always full of men reading and chatting while puffing on bent pipes and sipping their drinks. The women, meanwhile, would retire to the comforts of the ladies' drawing room where they could sit back and relax on rosewood chaise longues next to windows draped in dark-green brocade, their aching feet resting on rugs of the finest Oriental silk.

As the hotel became more and more popular, so one splendid mansion after another began to spring up along Fifth Avenue. In 1869 the Astor family had its home there, and right across the street from them one of Peder Sather's friends was in the midst of finishing what was to be the street's grandest residence. This friend was Alexander Turney Stewart, an Irishman who had come to America in the 1820s. With him from Ireland he had brought a batch of lace and linen purchased with money he had inherited. By 1850 Stewart was the biggest retailer in America, thanks to his idea that it might be worthwhile gathering all sorts of shops together under one roof. Thus Stewart founded the world's first department store, known as the Marble Palace. He was the first retailer in the country to offer a mail-order service, and was soon raking in a million dollars a year. Stewart went on to open similar stores in major cities in America and Europe, and in 1869 he was one of the wealthiest men in the country, close on the heels of the Astors, owners of such establishments as the exclusive Waldorf-Astoria Hotel.

In January 1869, two months after Peder Sather arrived in New York, President Ulysses S. Grant offered Alexander T. Stewart the post of secretary of the Treasury, but his appointment was rejected by the Senate because the law prohibited merchants or importers from holding such office. Later, Anthony Drexel was also offered this post, but turned it down. Drexel and President Grant were personal friends, and if Drexel was shy, Grant was not much better; it was said that the slightest compliment could cause him to blush from top to toe.

Grant was a regular visitor to Philadelphia, where he was always made welcome by George Childs at his place in the country, which lay right next door to Anthony Drexel's summer house. Childs also invited Mark Twain to stay while Grant was there, the two met in 1866 and immediately became friends. Twain persuaded Grant to write his memoirs by promising to help him to get them published. The end product proved to be a rare work of military history.

Peder Sather had a network of contacts that included members of the country's absolute elite; this is, in part, what makes him one of the most unique—not to say enigmatic—Norwegian immigrants of the nineteenth century. To my constant despair, the sources I have consulted confine themselves to determining which circles he belonged to and say nothing of how he came into contact with these different people in the first place. It looks, though, as if it was the Drexel family, and Anthony in particular, that introduced Peder Sather to a world which might otherwise never have been open to him.

A family that had never been outside the country needed to organize passports, so one day in the middle of January 1869 Peder Sather took a cab from his hotel to the office of his friend William Farnham, who was a notary public on Wall Street. Unfortunately Farnham began by asking him for something that Sather had not even thought about before leaving San Francisco. Because he was foreign-born, in order to obtain an American passport he had to provide proof of his American citizenship. It was thirty-seven years since Peder had left Norway and now, when he had at long last made up his mind to go home, it seemed that he was to be prevented from doing so by his own short-sightedness. His certificate of citizenship was filed away among his private papers in a locked cabinet, so no one could get at it and forward it to him.

Sather explained the situation to William Farnham, who, to his delight, thought he knew of a way round the problem. Farnham was pretty certain that a copy of the necessary document had to be filed at the issuing office, and if Peder could remember where he had been presented with his certificate of citizenship Farnham would go there and collect it. Sather was certain it had been at the Marine Court in 1839, so that should have been that problem solved. He was told to come back to the notary public's office on January 18, by which time Farnham would have got hold of the document. His passport would be ready for him to sign the next day, in the presence of two witnesses as prescribed by law. Sather had already arranged for two friends to act as witnesses. One was Anthony Drexel, who happened to be in town at that time, the other was Robert Winthrop, managing director of Drexel & Co. on Wall Street, the bank which had taken over from Peter Naylor as Sather & Co.'s agents in New York. Anthony Drexel had gone into partnership with Robert Winthrop six years earlier, but was not sure whether to continue this association. The bank's branch in New York made an annual net profit of three hundred thousand dollars, an excellent result, but one which might be even better under a different director.

Peter Naylor was the father-in-law of both the late Edward Church and businessman Benjamin Haxtun, a close friend of Peder Sather's from his time in New York. Sather had used Naylor as his financial agent since the 1850s and it was Naylor and Haxtun who, some years earlier, had written an article in the *New York Times* regarding the need for "a more refined taste and cultivated social bearing in the community." Peter Naylor and Robert Winthrop were also closely related, both being sons-in-law of Moses Taylor, for almost thirty years the influential director of the National City Bank of New York, a forerunner to today's Citibank. I take the liberty of naming all of these men because they were, each and every one, leading figures on Wall Street—which makes the call for a more refined taste and cultivated social bearing all the more interesting.

According to what Peder Sather told the notary public, he had become an American citizen in 1839, but when William Farnham called at the Marine Court to pick up the certificate which would testify to this it could not be found. Farnham then went to every court he could think of in the city in search of the vital piece of paper, but drew a blank at every one.

As a friend of Peder Sather, and therefore biased, Farnham had asked another notary to deal with the matter for him and eventually had to inform his colleague that his search had been fruitless. Farnham thought the certificate must have been destroyed in a fire, although there had been no fires at any

FIGURE 16. Part of Peder Sather's passport application, New York, January 13, 1869. Shows the signature of Anthony J. Drexel, Peder Sather's close friend. Courtesy of Fold3.com.

of the places he had checked. His fellow notary informed him most humbly that he was prepared to waive the formalities, seeing that his honor Mr. Farnham knew the esteemed Peder Sather personally. Peder Sather's difficulties in obtaining a passport are described in a seven-page document stored in the U.S. National Archives. What this does not give, however, is the reason why Farnham never found the certificate: Peder Sather did not in fact become an American citizen until July 17, 1847, fifteen years after coming to New York. And his certificate of citizenship was not issued by the Marine Court but by the Common Pleas Court. How could Sather have forgotten that?

By 1847 he was also the father of a son, Peder Jr., the last of his children, born in 1845. So there may have been legal and hereditary reasons for his decision to take American citizenship at that particular time. Or it could be that he had waited as long as he could before giving up his rights as a Norwegian citizen.

Peder Sather's application for a passport contains a word-for-word repetition of what Anthony Drexel and Robert Winthrop said of Peder Sather when they presented themselves at the office of the notary public on January 19, 1869: "We are well acquainted with said Peder Sather and know him to be a gentleman of high personal and social standing and of unimpeachable truth and veracity." All three had then signed the application and lastly the notary had stamped it with the American seal. Two days later Sather went back to collect the passport, this time accompanied by Anthony Drexel; he and no one else was to testify that Sather was who he said he was.

When Sather's daughters called at the notary public's office to collect their passports they brought Mary Ann Fowler, their faithful governess, nurse, maidservant, with them as witness. As for Sarah, as a married women she could travel on Peder's passport. In it her name appeared in a note in the margin advising that she was traveling abroad with him.

Now, with all their papers in order, the Sathers were free to set sail for Norway, for the land of snow and ice, the Norwegian language, the girls' father's odd vowel sounds, for Nordstun Nedre Sæter, to get to know the person he had once been. But they never made it to Norway or to Nordstun. Either Sather changed his mind or he had never really meant to visit his homeland at all. Maybe it was just something he told his friends. In which case it seems likely that something was preventing him from going back— something or someone. For a long time I thought I knew where the Sather family actually went, because in the margin of Sather's passport application there is a note in William Farnham's jagged handwriting: "Morocco bound," it says. I took it, therefore, that the family was *bound for* Morocco, a popular destination with wealthy Americans in those days. But I had of course completely misunderstood. I realized my mistake when I eventually managed to make out the last word in the note: "requested." So in fact this was an instruction to the bookbinder. Peder Sather had requested that his passport be *bound* in fine Moroccan leather.

I have, however, found a few clues to where the Sather's may have spent their time abroad. In August 1869 the *New York Times* reported that Peder Sather, his wife, and daughters were in Paris, and that on the twentieth of that month they had attended a reception, or dinner, or something of the sort at 3 rue Scribe. This happens to have been the address of Anthony Drexel's branch in the French capital, and George Childs had also gone to Europe just after Christmas in 1869. Anthony Drexel is known to have visited Europe every year, staying among other places at Karlsbad, famous for its spa and a favorite haunt of wealthy Europeans and Americans. It seems very likely, therefore, that the tubercular Peder Sather, the neurasthenic Mary Emma, and the physically frail Caroline would visit this resort.

Sather & Co. collaborated with several banks in Europe. In 1870 it had partners in London, Paris, Dublin, Hamburg, Bremen, Berlin, Leipzig, Kassel, Cologne, and Frankfurt—quite an itinerary, you might say. Men like Hans Rees and Knut Henry Lund, George Childs, and Anthony Drexel did not go to Europe for a vacation, but to do business, and more often than not they traveled alone. The list of banks was also a list of their contacts, a well-organized man's world. They met at the spas, too, setting up office there for weeks or even months, as Anthony Drexel did at Karlsbad. But this was not the world the Sathers moved in; they were traveling as a family, new to foreign parts. The English newspaper the *Anglo-American Times* regularly published lists of Americans traveling to Europe via London. And the lists that I have found show that, although Peder did take the opportunity while in Europe to meet up with his best friends and associates, and to strengthen his international banking connections, he was not there solely on business. In 1869 the Sather family spent time in Rome, Naples, Dresden, and Hamburg, and made several visits to Paris, where George Childs and Anthony Drexel also happened to be staying. In other words, the Sathers were, at least to some extent, doing the classic Grand Tour.

When the captain of the Atlantic steamship *Cimbria* presented his passenger list to the port authorities on arrival in New York on April 27, 1870, on it were the names of Peder Sather, Caroline Sather, Josephine Sather, and Mary Emma Sather, but not of Sarah Sather. Did she sail home earlier? With friends perhaps?

The steamship's manifest also states that the *Cimbria* had sailed from Hamburg. So Peder Sather came that close to Norway, to Christiania, the Kongsvinger line, and Disenå station before leaving Europe and setting out once again for the other side of the world.

NINETEEN

Under the Fever Trees

While the Sathers were in Europe five hundred men and tons of dynamite had blasted a cleft almost 130 feet deep through Rincon Hill. New times were coming: up ahead the factories awaited, behind lay a world in ruins. To reach their homes residents first had to clamber some way up the side of the gully and then climb up long ladders. When they reached the topmost rung and peered over the lip of the cleft, it was to find that the gardens were gone and the houses were teetering on the edge of the slope. The residents of Second Street were afraid that sooner or later the winter rains would wash away so much earth and sand that the houses would be dragged with it into the abyss.

James Hutchinson had managed to find a house for the Sathers in Oakland, a large and very grand mansion which they took over from bookkeeper Henry Lee, Harriet's husband and Eliza Tasheira's son-in-law. Many people wondered what had possessed a bookkeeper to buy a house like that. What had in fact happened was that he had been rash enough to try going into business for himself, with disastrous results. According to *The Morning Call:* "Lee was in the stream of the first great Oakland real estate boom. But he overreached himself and he is thought to have lost in stocks, so that when Mr. Sather returned home from Europe, Mr. Lee transferred all his property to him. In the booming times Mr. Lee started out to build a fine residence and as the boom increased his ideas became more extravagant until his plans of a $15,000 house grew to the outlay, it is said, of $104,000. This house became costly because of the great expense in finishing it with fine woods and decorations. At one time no less than six Italian decorators were engaged in beautifying the interior."

Henry Lee was now flat broke and out of work. He and his family had moved into a small apartment in San Francisco, and Henry stayed home with

FIGURE 17. Sather house in downtown Oakland. Original address: Twelfth Street, between Grove and Castro; from 1879: 664 Central Avenue. This is where Preservation Park Museum is located today. Courtesy of the Oakland Public Library.

their four children while Harriet, his wife, supported the family by teaching school. The 1870 census reveals that Eliza was living with the Lees, keeping house for them.

There is much to suggest that Peder Sather was one of those from whom Henry Lee had borrowed money; a note in the *Oakland Tribune* reveals at any rate that he bought the property for next to nothing, although it was one of the biggest in town, with stables, a coach house and gardens that covered a whole block.

From now on the Sathers were going to be living very graciously indeed, in a mansion with two stories plus attics. It towered majestically over the street with its oriel windows, covered veranda, and circular, domed conservatory. The windows were tall and narrow with white frames, and behind the massive oak-paneled door lay a reception room in which to welcome business associates, while the rooms beyond this were reserved for close family and friends. Peder Sather had a low, finely wrought stone wall built around the property, then set about laying a wooden sidewalk. He also had two eucalyptus trees planted down by the front gate; before too long they would sprout long, drooping branches that would give off the most refreshing scent.

Eucalyptus trees were often called "fever trees" because it was believed that they could cure disease, and the Sather household needed all the remedies it could get.

The new house lay on Twelfth Street, on the site of what is now the Preservation Park museum. As elsewhere in Oakland, Twelfth Street was lined with oak trees. In old photographs these trees show up as dark, gloomy blotches, but in fact it was the oaks which, with their dense green foliage, lent character to Oakland, during the long, dusty summers.

In 1870 the streets of Oakland were home to almost ten thousand people. Samuel Merritt had been mayor of the town until 1869. He had become a wealthy man and was a generous benefactor. Medical man that he was, he bequeathed a hospital to the town, and there was just as much celebration when he paid out of his own pocket for the damming of a tidal lagoon, causing the waters to rise and spread further inland to form the saltwater lake now known as Lake Merritt. No one had ever imagined such a thing was possible, but in 1870 little sailboats were skimming the waves off its beaches; children were swimming in it and the people of the town promenading up and down the shorefront.

Long before this Peder Sather had purchased three hundred acres of land on the hills around the lake—the Sather Tract as it was called. When the family moved to Oakland he arranged for the planting of hundreds of trees on its slopes and laid out a system of paths fanning out from the lake. Together with Samuel Merritt he had bought another, similar piece of land alongside the lake, a joint purchase which was to lead to a lot of trouble when it came to settling the estates of the two men.

Samuel Merritt was still single, living on the outskirts of the town with a staff of Chinese servants. When one of his brothers died he invited his sister-in-law and her children to come and live there—he was not happy living alone. Samuel Merritt measured six-foot-two in his stocking feet and was plumper than ever, as broad as he was tall. He was a somewhat eccentric and much-loved character, and a good mayor. And his popularity was in no way lessened when he won the battle between towns in the district to become the western terminus of the transcontinental railroad. This created jobs and made Oakland the first town so far to have a direct link to New York and the rest of the continent. Now people from the San Francisco area could travel to the East Coast swiftly and in comfort, and people from the east could easily come and visit them. It was with the coming of the railroad that California truly became a part of the United States.

One of Peder Sather's best Norwegian friends, Hans Rees, was still living in New York. He had come there as a shoemaker from Norway and he had done no worse for himself in the leather goods business than Sather had in banking. Since the mid-1840s, when the two had worked together for a few years, Rees & Hoyt, the company that Hans owned along with his sons and his partner William Hoyt, had become one of the biggest in its field. In 1870 Hans and his wife, Lucinda, were back in New York after living for some years in Milwaukee, Wisconsin. Thanks to the new railroad Hans and Lucinda Rees and Jane Krom, who was still friendly with Sarah and Peder, could see the Sathers as often as they liked and the journey from New York only took a week.

The new residence, with its stables, coach house and enormous garden was no small responsibility. The garden didn't tend itself for one thing; a gardener laid out paths that wound around neatly clipped shrubs, exotic trees, stunning floral displays, sparkling fountains and classical statues with dreamy faces. The garden was said to be a real showplace in Oakland, a spot that drew many admiring eyes. These were great days for landscape architects, they designed the loveliest public parks and private gardens. Urbanization and industrialization had created the need for green open spaces in towns and cities, places in which to relax, stroll, and enjoy picturesque, man-made scenery. The most famous landscape gardener was Frederick Olmsted, the designer of New York's Central Park, who would shortly be commissioned to develop a plan for the campus of the new university at Berkeley.

Peder Sather was no longer just a well-to-do middle-class gentleman, he was now a member of the upper class. He was registered as being a "capitalist" by profession in tax records and censuses, and the house in Oakland certainly fitted well with that epithet. Peder and Sarah Sather would never leave this house, the question was whether their daughters ever would. Mary Emma was still living at home and had been well enough to go with them to Europe—proof perhaps that she did have her good spells—but her mental problems were by no means over.

A man like Peder Sather did not sell real estate unless it was necessary, so, like the other leaseholders on Second Street, he rented his house out to someone prepared to take the risk of living there, and he very quickly found a tenant, a young writer by the name of Charles Warren Stoddard, who had published his first volume of poetry, entitled simply *Poems,* in 1867 and was now making a living by writing for the local newspapers. Stoddard made notes about the house and the property as a whole, so once again I am able to cite a writer as one of my sources. The first was Walt Whitman with his poem "Crossing Brooklyn Ferry" and a third is to come.

Stoddard noted that part of the front garden had been blown up, and this meant that he had to use a door at the back of the house, but this was so narrow that he had to edge his way into the house—a rambling pile that was in a terrible state. One day he noticed a man climbing up the ladder to it with a sketchpad under his arm. The stranger sat down with his back to the house, looked at the view, and began to sketch it. Stoddard did not want to disturb him, and the man out there did not seem to realize that someone was actually living in the house. Stoddard noticed him sitting there several days in a row and was extremely embarrassed to find, when he finally spoke to him, that the stranger was none other than the famous writer Robert Louis Stevenson.

Stevenson had recently arrived from Paris, where he had met and fallen head over heels in love with a married lady from San Francisco; now he had come to the city hoping, as he told Stoddard, to meet her and ask for her hand.

In the meantime Stevenson had met Samuel Merritt, who knew a lot of artists. Merritt often took Stevenson out sailing on the bay in his yacht; there is an old photograph of them posing on the deck together with a number of ladies in summer frocks and big hats. When one considers that Peder Sather and Samuel Merritt had been friends for over twenty years one can't help wondering whether behind the facade which, according to my sources, he appears to have presented, he may still have yearned for a more free-and-easy life than that of the respectable family man. Was that it? Did they all dream of having greater freedom than family life would allow?

Charles Warren Stoddard and Robert Louis Stevenson soon became firm friends and spent their evenings together drinking wine and talking and talking in Peder Sather's ramshackle house. Stoddard said Stevenson seemed to him to be something of a romantic and a dreamer, and he could not understand it when his famous colleague said that he found the house charming and inspiring. The property must have made a strong impression on Stevenson, though, because he used it as the model for a house in his novel *The Wrecker*, published in 1892 and made into a film in 1927. The house appears in chapter 8 of the book, along with a detailed description of the precarious sandy cliff on which it sat, of toppled cypress trees, their roots pointing skyward, of the rickety ladder leading up to the property from the bottom of the gully, of the greenhouse full of geraniums and walls covered in ivy, of the wind that shook the old pile to its foundations in the summer and the torrential rain that battered against the walls in the winter, boring into the sand until the building swayed in the mire and looked set to slide into the abyss at any minute.

Did Peder Sather ever climb up the ladder himself to look at his property? Did he sit down with Stevenson to talk about Paris, which they had both recently visited? Did he have anything to tell regarding the effects of the Franco-Prussian War, which had been raging while he was in Europe, or had he been oblivious to that—simply going from bank to bank while Sarah and the girls gazed dumbstruck at Michelangelo's works. And what would he have said of Stevenson's reason for being in San Francisco? Or did he stay well away from the ravaged house and garden where, back in the 1850s, life had been full of the joys of bachelordom? That was a closed chapter now. And for me all of this is a closed book. I teeter on the slopes of imagination at the thought that my own tale is encompassed by a still greater, but forgotten story.

While Sather was abroad his manager, James Hutchinson, had done a bit of dealing in the real estate market and had bought a considerable number of lots in Oakland, which was gradually developing into something more than a township outside of San Francisco. In the 1870s Peder Sather was not only a successful banker, he was also a major landowner. Twenty years earlier he had purchased key tracts of land in Alameda, and he also owned a farm in nearby San Pablo Creek. The Sather Ranch covered an area of 1,150 acres, some of this arable land, the rest good pasture for beef or dairy cattle. According to the newspapers it lay close to the railroad line and was well supplied with fresh water. He held onto all of these properties, as well as several others in San Francisco, until his death. According to William Sturm, librarian at the Oakland Library History Room, for decades there was also a railroad station named after him—Sather Station in Oakland, a Southern Pacific station located at the corner of High and San Leandro Streets.

Peder Sather seemed by now to have consolidated his position as a banker and become an older and well-established personage; the somewhat younger Anthony Drexel found himself in a rather different situation. He had long felt that Robert Winthrop was not pulling his weight and did not make enough effort to stay up to date on international affairs. Drexel had secretly decided to end this association and look around for another partner.

While he was considering this move, Anthony Drexel received a letter from an American financier in London, Junius Spencer Morgan. He wrote that he had a bright, but rather disheartened son whom he was hoping Drexel might have a word with, and possibly find an opening for at the bank. So Anthony Drexel invited the young man to his home in Philadelphia and very quickly realized that he was faced here with a rare financial genius. The young man's name was John Pierpoint Morgan, and in 1871 he and Drexel became partners.

That same year saw the completion of the Drexel Building, so big that Anthony Drexel was now the owner of the most expensive building on Wall Street. He made Morgan president of the bank in New York while he remained in Philadelphia. Thus began the career of the later so famous and notorious J. P. Morgan, a financier unlike any America had ever seen before and one of the most significant names in the history of American and international finance.

Peder Sather retained Anthony Drexel as his main collaborative partner, an association that involved regular trips to the East Coast, but in 1870 they were living in two different worlds: Sather the local capitalist in the small town of Oakland, Drexel at the top of the American financial pyramid. Peder Sather had so many friends on the East Coast, though, that one cannot help wondering whether he ever considered moving back there. Or did he refrain from doing so in order to save running into Jane Krom too often? The climate in California was good for his health and that was the main thing, after all; and as a banker maybe it was better to be a big fish in a little pond than a little fish in a big one.

In the early 1870s Peder Sather was usually to be found among the guests at official dinners and receptions in San Francisco. In January 1872 the newspapers noted that he had attended a magnificent banquet given at the Grand Hotel in honor of a delegation of Japanese diplomats who were visiting the country to open up new trade channels. One minute the reporters were comparing the banquet to the feasts of King Ahasuerus described in the Book of Esther, the next with the bacchanalian revelries of ancient Athens—while emphasizing, for the sake of propriety, that the alcohol consumption at the Grand Hotel had been far more moderate than that in the Greek capital.

Present at the banquet were the governor of California and various ambassadors and consuls, including the Danish consul. Also among the guests were several of Peder Sather's friends: Thomas Selby, now the ex-mayor of San Francisco, Bancroft the bookseller, Shreve the goldsmith, and James Roberts, former president of the Christian Commission. The rector of Grace Church had been invited to bless the dinner, which he did, the papers said, to everyone's satisfaction. He then said a short prayer that "was listened to with marked interest, indicating that the occasion and the sentiments it called forth were appreciated by those present." The somewhat awestruck journalists concluded their reports with detailed descriptions of the eight-course dinner, a menu consisting of an impressive selection of meat, fish, and fowl, superb sauces, every conceivable variety of vegetable and potato, pies and petit fours, cakes and desserts, wines and champagne, not to mention sherry or cognac with the coffee—and all of the finest quality.

Peder Sather, Esquire, is unlikely to have drunk anything but water, for when, around this time, a group of gentlemen who were horrified by the drinking habits in Oakland proposed that the town council should ban the sale of alcohol, Sather added his name to the petition. He was still a man of faith, and a member of the board of the Oakland Baptist Church, which he supported generously. The church itself was extremely grand and imposing and its bells could be heard all over town when they called people to services. Sather also carried on indefatigably with his humanitarian work; one minute providing aid for earthquake victims in remote Lone Pine, an old prospecting town where fifty-two out of fifty-nine houses were flattened, the next helping the people of Portland, Oregon, where several thousand were left homeless by a big fire in 1873.

Peder Sather, a capitalist who did not need to work, or to give away so much as a dollar if he didn't feel like it, was working hard and giving away more money than ever. Still, though, he was now living in the sort of mansion in which he had been in service as a young man, and if this had been his goal when he emigrated from Norway then he had certainly achieved it. But the family had not long been settled in Oakland before it was overtaken by old troubles and new sorrows.

Neither Caroline nor Mary Emma was getting any better, and now it was Josephine's turn to incur her father's wrath. Sometime between 1870 and 1873 Josephine fell madly in love with a young man of French origin, Emile Bruguiere. He was by all accounts the handsomest, most well-dressed and most charming young gentleman in San Francisco—a proper dandy. But he had no money. Josephine's feelings for him were not just a passing fancy and it was not long before her father was forbidding her to have anything to do with her sweetheart. When they went on meeting anyway he refused to see either of them—which seems to suggest that Josephine had eloped with Emile. It must have been very hard on the young couple, to have her father wash his hands of them like this, but Josephine was made of stronger stuff than Mary Emma. For a long time it looked as if Peder would never change his mind, and while this war of attrition was being waged Christoffer died in Odalen. So Peder never did get to see him again, the brother with whom he

FIGURE 18. Josephine Frances Sather, 1865. Photographer: William Shew, 421 Montgomery Street, San Francisco. Courtesy of Eva Helle.

had become reconciled, but with whom he had had no contact for twenty-four years. Something had seized up inside him, in order to preserve what had to be saved at all costs. His honor perhaps?

Eventually Peder Sather did relent and take pity on the young couple. Josephine and Emile Bruguiere were married in the drawing room at home in Oakland on October 23, 1873, by William Kip, the bishop of California. Whose part Sarah had taken in all this we do not know. But if she supported Peder it must have been hard to be a daughter in the Sather family, and if she sided with her daughters this must have led to serious clashes between husband and wife and turned this mansion, too, into a haunted house.

Once Josephine and Emile were married, however, Peder could not do enough for them. He gave Emile a job at the bank and bought the newlyweds a big apartment on Sutter Street in San Francisco. Six years later Josephine and Emile had four sons: Peder—named after his grandfather—Emile, Francis, and Louis. For Josephine, unfortunately, things turned out much as her father had feared: Emile the dandy had a roving eye, but she forgave him everything.

The Sathers' troubles were not yet over though. Only a few months after Josephine's and Emile's wedding, Caroline contracted typhus. She died on March 31, 1874, at the age of thirty-eight. The local women's temperance society had been planning to hold a mass rally in Oakland on the day on which Caroline was to be buried, but this event was postponed due to the funeral, the *Oakland Tribune* announced. The funeral service was to be held at home, it said, and carriages would be waiting at the landing stage to pick up any of Caroline's friends coming across on the ferry from San Francisco. Caroline was buried next to her brother Peder in the cemetery in San Francisco, and to her too Peder Sather raised a spiraling white marble column.

In the same year that Caroline died, Mary Emma was admitted to Burn Brae, diagnosed as suffering from "dementia"—a blanket term which at that time covered just about every form of mental illness, but which doctors today say may only have meant that the patient was not capable of looking after herself.

On January 23, 1875, the *Oakland Tribune* published a list of residents with mail lying uncollected at the post office. One of these was "Miss Mary Emma Sather," but there was no longer any Mary Emma in Oakland; she had crossed the continent, had spent a week on a train, accompanied by nurses, accompanied by misfortune, accompanied by her parents to Philadelphia and Burn Brae, the elegant manor house on Drexel Hill and the most modern psychiatric clinic in America. There she would remain for the rest of her days, as a patient of Dr. Robert Given, the hospital's founder.

So. the 1870s had got off to a sad start for the Sathers. And while Peder's friend William Turnbull was socializing with Cornelius Vanderbilt in New York, enjoying fun-filled days at the races and lively evenings in Newport or at the most expensive hotels in Saratoga where, according to the *Hartford Daily,* "they play euchre and whist for little or nothing, being too rich to bet," the Farrar family had been struck by disaster after disaster. Charles Farrar had been running the bank in Nassau Street with his nephew Luther Lawrence ever since Sather left. Luther, who was still single, suffered however from rheumatism and in June 1870 he set out for the hot springs in Arizona, which were supposed to have a therapeutic effect. He died on the way there, all alone in a hotel room, and his coffin was taken home to his mother in Pepperell. That same year, in Brooklyn, Charles Farrar's only son died of typhus and in 1874 Charles himself died. The bank carried on, run now by Luther's brother, but it was the end of an era, also for Peder Sather. Anthony Tasheira, Edward Church, Francis Drexel, Luther Lawrence, and Charles Farrar—all gone. Meanwhile, Peder Sather had lost three children and seen his favorite daughter sink into madness.

And now new crises were brewing for the bank, for industry and for the financial sector. An unnamed employee of Sather & Co. disappeared from work and was found dead some days later on a beach not far from Oakland. This happened at a time when the authorities in San Francisco were issuing annual reports on the rise in suicides. The 1870s was a time of economic depression and in San Francisco low wages and high unemployment drove workers to organize themselves for the first time. The new unions attracted thousands of members, but the front they formed also represented a racist attack against the Chinese, who had been regarded as pariahs ever since the Gold Rush. But when the transcontinental railroad was built they were the ones who did the heavy work, along with the Irish. The railroad was finished now, though, and the "Chinamen" were pouring into the city looking for other employment. The white workers regarded this as a huge threat to their jobs, the unions only served to fuel their contempt for the already stigmatized Chinese, and no one made any protest.

At national level President Ulysses S. Grant was about to trigger another financial crisis. The release of large quantities of silver into circulation had led to rampant inflation and on the advice of Anthony Drexel, Grant pushed a bill through Congress which stated that in the future the national bank would only hold gold reserves and not silver. This prompted a drastic drop in the value of the silver being mined and the silver coinage in circulation. A number of banks were forced to close, and in 1875 the crisis spread to the West Coast, where the Bank of California, the biggest commercial bank in the state, was particularly hard hit. Under William Ralston's leadership the bank had issued countless loans to the large silver-mining companies in Comstock, Nevada. These loans were granted with the assets of the mining companies as surety, and during the boom years of the 1860s the bank raked in massive profits.

Assuming that the income from the silver mines would go on flowing into the bank's vaults, Ralston took out huge loans which he then spent on projects such as the Palace Hotel in San Francisco, one of the most modern, most enormous, and most luxurious hotels in the world, boasting a thousand rooms, seven thousand windows, and hydraulic elevators.

The hotel was to be opened with much pomp and circumstance in the late summer of 1875, but just before this grand opening Ralston had to close the bank. The flow of income from the mining companies had dried up, the vaults were empty, and he was personally unable to honor the bank's own loans, which had financed the building of the hotel among other things. Neither the board nor the shareholders had been informed of this situation and the time was coming when Ralston would have to lay his cards on the table.

Although Peder Sather had refrained from speculating in the silver market, even Sather & Co. did not remain unscathed by inflation and the losses it brought in its wake. Sather may not have been a gambler, but in 1875 everyone was affected, even solid banks founded on the traditional principles of safe investment and risk spreading.

It was in the hysterical atmosphere of the silver market that the term *bonanza* was coined, cropping up first in Comstock where the biggest lodes had been found. The word bonanza is Spanish for calm seas, fair weather, or smooth sailing and was what sailors would wish each other when setting out to sail seas that might engulf them. Peder Sather was not the type to let a chance go by, but this time there was a risk of losing money. For the sake of his own interests he kept a cool head, and when one remembers that he always had Anthony Drexel to advise him, it seems that Sather & Co. was in no immediate danger.

Sather did not remain untouched, however, by the eventual fate of William Ralston. Because the self-styled "cashier" of the Bank of California was the brother of Andrew Ralston, Sather & Co.'s attorney. Andrew had offices on the floor above the bank and one day he came down to see Peder and told him that William was on the verge of a breakdown and that he feared the worst.

Peder Sather got in touch with Anthony Drexel, and within just two days obtained assurances that both Sather & Co. and the Bank of California could count on receiving financial guarantees. Thus Sather had come up with a solution to the problem, for his own bank and for William Ralston, who had now barricaded himself inside the Bank of California where he was informing the board of the situation and being asked to tender his resignation. Things were very chaotic and outside the bank furious customers and shareholders large and small were gathering to demand their money.

That same morning Peder Sather called a meeting at which he would make a statement regarding the news of the guarantees from Anthony Drexel. As always in such times of crisis, a bank would invite customers and the general public to gather outside the bank. According to the *San Francisco Bulletin,* when Peder Sather stepped out onto the sidewalk to announce the good news he was "the very picture of confident tranquility."

The first thing Sather did was to reassure investors in the Bank of California. He had been in touch personally with colleagues in the east who had promised to help William Ralston out of this tight spot. Peder Sather could, therefore, assure them that the bank would be back in business again very soon. Sather & Co. would not be hit by the silver crisis, he said, because Anthony Drexel and John Pierpoint Morgan had given him clear indications that the market would soon recover. They would also issue him with all the necessary credits should these, for some reason, become necessary.

In the meantime William Ralston had left the Bank of California by a back door and gone straight from there to North Beach, where he was in the habit of taking his morning swim. And on this August day, too, the bank director went swimming; not parallel with the shore, though, but out to sea. When he did not return a search was instituted, but William Ralston was later found drowned. With Peder Sather's help Ralston's brother Andrew had tried to prevent just such an accident. As for the Bank of California, Sather's predictions were proved right; the necessary capital was forthcoming and a month later the bank was open for business again.

TWENTY

Peder and Jane

In October 1881 Sarah and Peder paid one of their many visits to Burn Brae to see Mary Emma, who had now been there for six years. Afterward they went to New York and checked in at the Fifth Avenue Hotel. While there Sarah developed a fever and had difficulty breathing. A doctor had to be called and she was diagnosed as having pneumonia. For two weeks she lay in bed at the hotel, while her condition steadily worsened. And on October 31, she passed away. She was seventy-four years old. A mother with three children in the grave was now following them there.

Peder Sather was faced with a long, sad journey back to Oakland. Sarah was to be buried in San Francisco and her coffin would be traveling with him on the train. But he had not been totally alone during the days he had spent by his wife's deathbed. Dr. James Watson, the Sathers' family doctor in Brooklyn, had been there by her side with him. Jane Krom had sat with him too. And, since Jane was Lucinda's sister and Hans Rees's sister-in-law, it seems likely that they were also there to give Peder their help and support.

Jane was born in 1824 and met Sarah and Peder Sather for the first time at Lucinda's wedding to Hans Rees in 1844, so by 1881 he had known her for thirty-seven years. She was a sturdy, buxom woman of fifty-seven, fourteen years younger than he. Sources say that she became a widow the year before Sarah's death and that her husband's name was John Read or Reade, although no one, myself included, has been able to discover who exactly he was. What is certain, however, is that Jane had remained unmarried for many years and in the census records from 1880 she is once again registered as "single" and living with her sister. Jane had had no children, either, and when asked about this later she became very angry and refused to answer. If Peder was a proud person then Jane was no less so.

FIGURE 19. Jane Krom Sather, 1824–1911. Married to Peder Sather, 1882–86. Painted in 1892 by her friend William Keith, Scottish-American painter, 1838–1911. Courtesy of the Bancroft Library, University of California, Berkeley.

Of all the people who could have accompanied Peder back to Oakland, besides Dr. Watson, it was Jane he chose, and he informed his friends in the Fifth Avenue Hotel clique of this. The train pulled out of Grand Central Station, setting out on the long journey to the West Coast, through cities, through townships, through forests, across deserts and mountains. It was November, it was snowing, then raining, the pallid November light fell through the window of the reserved compartment in which Peder sat with Jane by his side, while Sarah was now traversing a much greater continent.

Sarah had never made it to Odalen, but the woman sitting next to him on the train had always had an intimate, personal acquaintanceship with Peder's native land through her sister. Lucinda had been there, according to the Norwegian census she had been married there, and she and Hans had taken their children, Jane's nieces and nephews, there. So Jane had always been kept up to date with what was going on in Norway and, unlike, Sarah, was not dependent on what Peder did, or did not, tell her.

American sources contain quite a bit of information on Jane, so much that one would think that Peder had never been married to anyone but her. But till now no one has been able to say how she first got to know the Sathers, only that she "had known him since Mr. Sather's partnership with Francis Drexel was established." I have, however, unearthed evidence that puts the relationship between Jane and Peder in a quite different light. It was of a much more personal nature than the official version given in other sources would lead one to believe.

And when one also knows that Jane, this woman fourteen years Peder's junior who sat next to him on that train as it chugged on toward Oakland, was his bride-to-be, one's thoughts start to run along another track. This knowledge sets a parallel story rolling, a tale of feelings, of secret feelings, denied to a man of pride and honor. Such a story rushes across the century with a couple in love on board, while "John Read or Reade" is lost among all the thousands of Americans of similar name.

Jane and Peder on their way to the empty mansion in Oakland, with Sarah in her coffin in another car. Here is a chapter that is far more like something out of a romantic novel than any tale I could weave from dusty papers from some archive. Two trains were in fact steaming through the morning mist and the evening gloom, beneath setting suns and rising moons, while sleep evaded Jane and Peder and Sarah would never wake: a train of sorrow, carrying old hurts with it and a train of longing, bound for its first moments of joy. Hans Rees and Peder Sather had more in common than the fact that they were friends, Norwegians and immigrants who had done well for themselves; they had also fallen for girls from the same family.

Which is not to say that Peder Sather ever broke his marriage vows. On the contrary, he seems to have been willing to sacrifice just about anything for the sake of his pride and his honor. So Peder and Jane must have been made of the same stuff, since they appear to have had the strength to wait for each other, even if it took a lifetime.

In 1881 Peder Sather was seventy-one years old, his hair and his beard were white and thinner now than they had once been. In a picture taken only a couple of years later he is crinkling his eyes cheerily, as if William Turnbull had just spun him some yarn and was waiting to see his response. Fifty-seven-year-old Jane, who had grown up in a stone cottage on a small farm, has the look of a queen about her, a queen born on the wrong side of the blanket who claims the throne with a witty remark and regally ascends it.

Before leaving for Oakland with Peder, Jane had lived for a while in Landis, Vineland, a "model" community in New Jersey based on the principles of equal rights for women, temperance and a love of nature. This last reflected a trend at that time and was a reaction against urbanization and industrialization; it was a movement which was given a voice early on by the philosopher Henry David Thoreau in his classic work from 1854, *Walden; or, Life in the Woods*.

Landis was in the countryside, but Jane was a city person and had lived for many years in New York. Of her early life only bits and pieces are known— that she grew up, for example, as one of fifteen children in Marbletown in Ulster County, north of New York. The way she is presented in the sources I've consulted you would think she had only been born on the day that she became Peder's wife, appearing out of nowhere in the shape of the widow of an unidentified husband.

But Jane had known Sarah and Peder Sather for almost forty years, had known the children since they were babies. Josephine, waiting on the platform to meet her mother's coffin, was well aware of who would be with her father when he got off the train now approaching: this eccentric spinster who lived with her sisters, loved company, and had always come out to Brooklyn with Hans Rees and Lucinda. Jane was like a funny aunt, plain-spoken, self-assured, and always ready with the sort of biting remark that caused some to gloat and others to giggle.

When Peder Sather arrived back in Oakland with a much younger woman by his side, people there must have considered it quite fitting and by no means improper for a widow with no family, a woman with all the vigor of youth and the authority that comes with age to be there to help and comfort an elderly, grieving widower.

A brief death notice in the San Francisco papers said that "Mrs Sather ... was a very estimable lady, much beloved among a wide circle of acquaintances and friends in Oakland, where the family resides, and in this city, to whom the news of her death is a great shock." It's hard to know whether there was any truth in these statements; the tone is hackneyed and more reminiscent of the stuff printed in the society columns. There is no mention in the obituary of Sarah's maiden name, and no real personal details. She goes to her grave as a relatively anonymous figure, nothing more than the wife of Peder Sather.

It is much more interesting to imagine this traveling companion from New York, this solid, commanding figure, among all those grieving friends and acquaintances. When the funeral service was over, the coffin was carried out of the parlor and everyone filed quietly after it. Only a few sniffles were heard, the swish of skirts, the creak of the parquet flooring and the ticking of Peder's innumerable clocks. The black-clad funeral party, ladies with mourning veils covering the faces and gentlemen with bowed shoulders, stepped through the front door and the rain battered against their faces—November was a wet month. Peder walked at the head of the procession, right behind the coffin, together with Josephine, Emile—and Jane? Or did he leave her to bring up the rear. Out by the front gate, where the fever trees shivered and rustled, their scent faint in the chill air, the carriages were waiting to take the mourners down to the ferry, with Sarah's horse-drawn hearse leading the cortege. Then they crossed the bay, sailing over its leaden, ponderous waters. More carriages were waiting in San Francisco, where Sarah was laid to rest alongside her son Peder and her daughter Caroline, far from the first of her children to die, little Mary Augusta, who lay in a cemetery in Manhattan.

Jane is reported to have stayed with Peder for several months. She then returned to New York; but while together the couple must have been making plans because it was not long before Jane was back at Grand Central Station to take the train to Oakland once again—this time on her way to marry Peder. She arrived in Oakland in the early hours of October 28, 1882, and they were wed that very evening, surrounded by friends. The wedding ceremony took place in the same room as the funeral service for Sarah, almost a year to the day since the latter had died in the hotel in New York.

Right from the start Jane seems to have been welcomed with open arms. She and Peder were married by the Reverend Granville Abbott of the Baptist church, a man who had known Sather and his family for years. The marriage would hardly have met with approval had there been the slightest suspicion that Jane had been Peder's mistress. And the haste with which the wedding was arranged says something about the rules that applied when it came to a man and a woman living under the same roof. This puts one in mind of an early morning on Rincon Hill when Peder Sather arranged the marriage of James Hutchinson and Coralie, with two tired and hungry young bank clerks as witnesses and Letitia Church looking as if she had barely managed to pull a comb through her hair and wipe the sleep out of her eyes. Why the hurry? Because propriety dictated it. The act of love was to be conducted within wedlock and nowhere else.

Jane was an ardent supporter of women's suffrage, and it was not long before she had become a leading member of the local branch of Sorosis, the first professional women's club in America, founded in New York in 1868. Its aim was to bring together women who were interested in literature, the arts, journalism, and current affairs and to promote their right to be accepted by professional organizations within these fields on an equal footing with men. As a girl Jane had attended a small country school with just one classroom, and whether she had had any education other than that is not known. But in 1882 there were academics within her close family, an indication of the sort of environment she came from. Jane's nephew, Lucinda's and Hans Rees's son, was John Krom Rees. John had followed in his father's footsteps, starting out as a tanner, but ending up as a professor of astronomy and mathematics at Columbia University in New York.

Jane was happy in Oakland, living in a neighborhood where a lot of staff from the university also had their homes, and sources say that she and Peder were exceptionally hospitable. Among the other people living in that part of the city was a little boy called Jack London. He had been born on Third Street in San Francisco in 1876 and the family moved to Oakland in 1879. Jack would later take private French lessons with Lilian Remillard, daughter of the multimillionaire Peter Remillard who lived right next door to Peder and Jane. Literary historians are sure that the Remillard family home was used by London as the model for the Morses' house in *Martin Eden,* which was published in 1909. Remillard had worked his way up from nothing by manufacturing bricks and when Lilian, later the Countess Dandini, took over the company she became even richer than her father. She lived to a great age and gave an interview to the *Oakland Tribune* as recently as the 1960s. In this she mentions that she knew Peder and Jane very well. They were a popular couple in the neighborhood, she says, but unfortunately she does not elaborate on this statement.

I have found no evidence of the young Jack London ever having met Peder Sather, but I like to think that they might often have seen one another when Jack was out walking his dog Rollo, passing Peder's front gate, plucking at the drooping eucalyptus branches that sprang back, leaves rustling, when he let go of them.

But even if Peder never did speak to Jack London, an article in the *San Francisco Chronicle* is proof that Jane and the writer did cross paths at one point. They met when the world-famous soprano Emma Nevada gave a concert in San Francisco while touring the United States with a young Pablo Casals, one of the greatest cellists in the history of music. After the concert the two musicians were invited to a party arranged by the wife of William Sharon, the owner of a large silver-mining company, who more or less had a monopoly on silver mining in Comstock. This had made Sharon one of California's wealthiest men, and the couple lived in lavish style in their mansion, the Casa Monata, in Piedmont, Oakland.

The party for Emma Nevada and Pablo Casals was held on a mild spring evening. Scores of the Sharons' friends and acquaintances were assembled at their home to meet the two musicians. As usual with such events the complete guest list was published in the newspapers; on it were the names of Jane Krom Sather and Jack London. Reports said that the tables were sumptuously decorated with floral arrangements of lilies and acacia, cherry blossom and masses of orange and yellow California poppies. Guest flocked around the two artists and helped themselves to canapés, fruit, and drinks. Picture Jane that evening: she is wearing a dark-green gown adorned with a profusion of lace and a ruffled collar. Next to her stands Lilian Remillard and beside her a dark, young man who had already started writing. At the library in Oakland Jack London had got to know Ina Coolbrith, a famous poetess who was the librarian there. She read what he wrote and came to mean so much to him that London later called her his "literary mother."

Jack London also studied for a while at the university at Berkeley; horse-drawn omnibuses went all the way out to it and the terminus lay where Sather Gate stands today. But in between his writing and his studies he could be found among the guests at cultural events hosted by the local beau monde. In my mind I see him and Jane beneath the crystal chandeliers, Jack with a glass of champagne in his hand and Jane firing off witty retorts. She is in her element, both impressive and bizarre in her evening finery. Oh yes, in my mind's eye I see them both listening, transported, to the soprano and the cello while the singing and the music pour out of the open windows and the fresh spring air flows in.

Jane was a well-read individual and regarded as something of an intellectual; she held literary salons at her home and attended everything in the way of cultural events in Oakland and San Francisco. In the university archives at Berkeley I found a letter from the artist William Keith, addressed to his friend John Muir, one of America's first conservationists and to this day a well-known scientist. Keith wrote: "Dear Muir, can't you come down next Saturday. I told Mrs. Sather that you might be here—she is coming in just to meet you. She is the widow of the Banker. She has given a great deal of money to the University and is a very interesting personality."

Peder and Jane were both very sociable, extrovert characters, and they had a good life. Their coachman, who had been with Peder for over twenty years, would drive them out to the ranch at San Pablo Creek. Two Scandinavian ladies looked after the house for them, one Danish, one Swedish. And although the newlyweds often sat in the library at home in the evenings they did not spend all their time reading. Peder Sather had found himself a wife who loved to play cards and who ran a whist club which met regularly. So now he could get out his own packs of cards again. The house also had a billiard room and sometimes he would invite old friends over for a game.

It seems by all accounts that a new and better life had begun for Peder Sather. He was to be seen working in the garden, an elderly man at peace with himself, with a cheerful, sprightly lady by his side. The one person for whom things did not get any better was Mary Emma, almost forty now and an inmate of Burn Brae since 1874. In the Philadelphia census of 1880 her entry reads like a biography reduced to ashes, where the only words still legible are: spinster, madwoman, Norwegian father, American mother.

Peder Sather had for many years been on the board of the Society for the Prevention of Cruelty to Children, and he retained his seat on it until his death. In 1885 the society presented a report which stated that in one year two hundred children had been placed with families or in children's homes, and they were all doing well.

But Peder's health was failing and according to a couple of sources there were times when Jane was more like his nurse than his wife. James Hutchinson saw to the day-to-day running of the bank and the results gave no cause for complaint. In the summer of 1883 the *New York Times* published a list of California's wealthiest men, and yet again Peder Sather's name appeared on it, together with that of the governor and people like blue jeans manufacturer Levi Strauss and railroad magnate Leland Stanford.

Peder Sather was still on the board of the California Insurance Company and the Baptist Church. He is also still listed as a member of the California Academy of Natural Sciences. And along with Samuel Merritt he is named as a supporter of the Berkeley School for the Deaf. When President Ulysses S. Grant, the great hero of the Civil War, died in July 1885, Oakland city council formed a committee to organize an outdoor memorial service. Peder Sather, Samuel Merritt, and Peter Remillard were asked to arrange this event, for which they put together a program of songs, poetry readings, and music. Ulysses Grant was a Republican and Peder Sather's presence on the committee tends to suggest that he was of the same political persuasion, an assumption that is borne out by his great admiration for Abraham Lincoln.

By the fall of 1886 Peder's health had deteriorated considerably. In the September he attended a wedding at the Baptist church with Jane, but was confined to his bed for months afterward. What was wrong with him, if it was not complications arising from his tuberculosis, we do not know. In December the newspapers published several bulletins stating that he was much worse and that the end was not far off. Clearly, Peder himself had feared that this was the case, because in April of that year he had written a long and very detailed last will and testament in which he appointed Anthony Drexel to be Mary Emma's guardian after his death. The wording of this particular clause is strong and moving: everything humanly possible had to be done to ensure that his daughter had as good a life as she could have. He urges Drexel to: "give such attention and exercise such care over my . . . daughter as shall secure her as much comfort and happiness as possible." On December 21, Peder Sather made substantial alterations to his instructions regarding the administration of his assets, and shortly afterward he had a stroke. On December 28, 1886, after four years of marriage to Jane, he died at home in Oakland, aged seventy-six.

The funeral ceremony was held in the same place as Sarah's, the same room in which he and Jane had been married. It was a strictly private affair attended only by those closest to him. This time too the Reverend Granville Abbott conducted the service and led the congregation in prayer. A trio consisting of a husband and wife and a young girl sang two hymns—"Beyond the Smiling and the Weeping" and "Along the River of Time." In a simple metal coffin Peder Sather was carried to the family burial plot in San Francisco, to lie there forever next to Sarah and two of his children.

Word must have reached Petrine in Christiania, now Oslo, that her father had died and had left a fortune to his heirs. Who brought the news to her? Petrine had been widowed some years earlier, she had five children and was not exactly rolling in money. And yet in 1879 she could afford to send one of her two sons, Christian, to America; more specifically to Philadelphia. Here Christian, a mechanic by trade, stayed with the famous Norwegian-American engineer and inventor Tinius Olsen, who, among other things, later supplied machinery for the Drexel Institute. So from 1879 Peder Sather had a grand-child living in Anthony Drexel's hometown. Coincidence? Surely not. Sather had arranged on the quiet for Christian to come to Philadelphia and paid for his upkeep there for years. If I am right, it was Christian who wrote to Petrine to tell her that Peder was dead.

On May 17, 1888, the *San Francisco Bulletin* reported that a Norwegian lady by the name of Petrine Encke had "assigned all her interest in the Peder Sather estate for a presumed consideration of $50,000 paid by Mrs. Josephine Bruguiere of San Francisco." "Mrs. Encke's name," the paper added, "has never appeared in the will or elsewhere, so far as is known, and who she is and what this means is a moot question."

Petrine would not have received so much as a cent had she not been able to document that she was, in fact, Peder Sather's eldest daughter. I found a picture of her in the archives of the Norwegian newspaper *Aftenposten,* and the resemblance to her father is striking.

Christian, still a bachelor and described in a Norwegian census as "sickly and unemployed," returned home to his mother. Not long afterward, his brother Peter David emigrated to America. He became a doctor in St. Paul, Minnesota, and later in Brooklyn, and married the Swedish born opera singer Inez Odquist. There are a good many descendants of the couple living in America today, all of them direct successors of Peder Sather.

Christian stayed with his mother, Petrine, and in the 1890s he was the owner of an elegant tenement building on Christiania's exclusive west side. With her legacy from her father Petrine had purchased several fine properties and generously bestowed apartments on her grown-up children. The illegiti-mate girl child born in the slums of Lakkergaden on the east side of Christiania, as the daughter of Ingeborg Knudsdatter and Peder Sather, had become one of the wealthiest women in the city.

TWENTY-ONE

In Memoriam

I, Peder Sather, residing in the City of Oakland, County of Alameda, State of California, and now engaged in the business of banking in the City and County of San Francisco, said State, being of sound mind and memory, do hereby make, publish and declare this to be my last will and testament in manner following, that is to say: First. I give, devise, and bequeath, unto my friends Anthony J. Drexel, and Benjamin Haxtun, of the City of New York . . .

So read the first lines of Peder's Sather's will. The language is measured and precise, the details arranged systematically. The rise and fall of the words lends them both lightness and weight and keeps them flowing on, from one point to the next.

Now obviously these lines can simply be read as legal formalese, but I would also venture to describe that "I, Peder Sather" as a statement of identity, containing as it does a Norwegian first name and an Anglicized surname. In 1832, when he left Norway and came to New York, he called himself Peter; when he left this life and set out for life everlasting he did so as Peder. "I, Peder Sather" speaks of a Norwegian in American guise.

In my search for information on Peder Sather his name has often given me problems. Three variations on his first name exist—Peter, Pedro, and Pedar—and in different contexts his surname has been misquoted as Sotter, Saether, Sathier, Dather, Prather, Souther, Father, and Lather. The older the papers, the more misinterpretations there are, especially in newspapers. This reminded me that emigration is like a double vanishing trick—you are neither in one place nor the other.

The typewritten copy of Sather's will amounts to fifteen pages. It is the longest of all the documents he left behind him and is arranged in chapters, like a short novel. These chapters dealt more with the principles relating to the dividing up of his estate than with figures, so they actually concealed more than they revealed. In addition to the bank in Montgomery Street, his liquid assets, and the stocks and shares he owned at the time of his death, Peder Sather also owned various pieces of real estate in San Francisco, including whole blocks and countless lots in Oakland, Brooklyn Township, San Pablo Creek, and the Alameda peninsula. How great a fortune he left probably even he did not know, but some sources have put it at six million dollars, others at eight or even ten million. His life's work, summed up in dollars. But a life's work that takes the form of money has a way of disappearing. When the money is gone it's all gone. So what the will says about how the money was to be administered is vital. And on this point Peder Sather was clearly in some doubt, because over the years he altered his will several times, the last time just before he died. A capitalist's thoughts on the administration of his own money are in themselves worth knowing, not least when we are talking about a fortune amassed by an immigrant who started with nothing.

Peder and Jane had been married for just four years and Josephine Bruguiere and her sons were shocked to hear that Peder had left Jane in charge of managing a large proportion of his fortune. They were equally shocked when they learned where this money was to end up, namely at the university. This had not been specified in the will, but it became evident from the decisions Jane made.

Read as a biographical document, the will provides confirmation of how close the friendship between Peder Sather and Anthony Drexel remained throughout their lives. The fact that Peder appointed Anthony as Mary Emma's guardian is in itself proof of that. And that he asked his friend not only to take care of her after he was gone, but "to secure to her as much comfort and happiness as possible," shows just how fond of and worried about Mary Emma her father was. He had known the Drexel family for almost forty years—hidden somewhere here is a great and unwritten story about the friendship between these two men. The will does, however, testify to Anthony's unique position among Sather's many friends.

While passersby could view the house and the garden from the outside, and I have studied all their splendors in pictures, Peder Sather posthumously ushers later generations over the threshold. This he does by listing in his will a whole lot of items which he wants Jane to keep. This list speaks for itself, detailing exactly what he wished to leave to whom, what some people might like to have and what Jane might be interested in holding onto. Here is just a brief extract from this list; an inventory that takes the reader on a tour of the Sather mansion, room by room:

> One large crayon picture of myself. A square-backed easy-chair, in the library. One medium-sized Japanese vase, in dining-room. One gold and blue Damascus vase. One round enameled box. One decanter-shaped vase. One sewing-machine. One walnut work-table. One enameled work-box. One mahogany arm-chair. Two chairs with upholstered seats. Two cane-seat chairs. One rocking-chair, red seat. One bedstead, with bedding, which she occupies. One down silk quilt. One walnut bureau, in dressing-room. One rosewood commode. One small iron safe. One walnut night-commode. Six Chinese plates. Three small French plates, red borders. One large Chinese bowl. One pink vase, with stand. One Roman striped-Afghan. One picture of Miss Julia Grey, in frame. One large chest. One large trunk. One Limoges vase. One small, dark vase. The plants in the conservatory.

From this list there emerges a picture of what Peder from Nordstun Nedre Sæter believed an upper-class home ought to contain: a reception room, for example, and not a plain porch; a dressing room, not merely a hook on the wall for shirt and pants; and a library was essential, lined from floor to ceiling with books. A house such as this also had to be graced with antiques and fine Persian rugs, hand-painted china, furniture in choice woods, and original paintings. None of which could be said to have been a standard part of the décor back in Odalen, not even on a decent-sized farm. This list is proof, rather, that the move from Norway to America had also been a social and cultural emigration, and as such it can tell us not only what Peder Sather learned along the way, but also something of his hopes and dreams.

Peder had made this list of all the things Jane was to have in case anyone tried to claim them for their own, and the only person likely to do so was Josephine. Was it really necessary, though, to state the obvious—such as that Jane be allowed to keep her bed and her sewing machine? Surely he wouldn't have left his wife to sleep on the floor after he was gone, or to make do with needle and thread when one of her garments needed mending? Of course not. In the end Peder realized that it was pointless to itemize every single thing and simply wrote that she should of course keep anything she wanted.

Josephine received an inheritance so great that it enabled her to face the future without having to worry about money, and this she used to lead an exceedingly extravagant high-society life on the West Coast, in France, and in Newport, Rhode Island, not far from New York, a favorite high-society stomping ground. In Newport she built "Castlewood," a palatial summer residence which, without a word of exaggeration, made the house in Oakland look like a log cabin. And in 1890, when Mary Emma died at Burn Brae at the age of forty-seven, under the terms of the will her share of the inheritance passed to Josephine. When Mary Emma died, I say, but Peder's and Sarah's youngest daughter's life was not a parenthesis, nor is she merely an incidental character in this story. She passed away on December 17 and was laid to rest in Woodlands Cemetery in Philadelphia, far from family, far from friends but, one hopes, with Anthony Drexel there to see her laid to rest.

In the press, speculation was rife as to how the banker from Montgomery Street would have apportioned his assets and what would happen now to the bank and its customers. This interest derived from the fact that Sather & Co. was a private concern, inasmuch as the bank's assets were its owner's assets. According to the *Daily Alta California* the bank was valued at $1,255,366. Would all of that now go to his heirs? His will reveals Peder Sather's thoughts on this: Sather & Co. was to carry on as before, without any interruption. And that was what happened. Sather & Co. changed its name to the Sather Banking Company, with James Hutchinson continuing as manager. In 1897 the bank changed its name again, this time to the San Francisco National Bank, which was incorporated into the Bank of California in 1910.

Shortly after Peder Sather's death, Jane set off with some women friends to spend some months in Europe. After that, she continued to travel, leaving a lawyer and real estate agent by the name of Dingee to manage her money in her absence. She became embroiled in a dreadful dispute with this man when she discovered that he had embezzled around a hundred thousand dollars from her. It was at this point that Jane Krom Sather wrote to Lyman Gage, secretary of the Treasury during Theodore Roosevelt's presidency, asking him to intervene. And to make quite sure that Gage knew exactly who Peder Sather was, Jane emphasized the fact that her husband had been an intimate friend of both Anthony Drexel and George Childs.

A lot of people were out to get their hands on Jane's money and this angered and upset her. In July 1888 she set out on a months-long trip to Alaska, going on from there to New York to visit Lucinda Rees, who had been a widow since Hans's death in 1885. In 1889 one of the Rees's sons committed suicide, and soon after this Lucinda moved to San Francisco to stay with one of her daughters. Relations between Jane and Peder's two surviving daughters were decidedly frigid, and when Mary Emma died, Jane was in Europe. In Oakland she lived alone with her two female servants and must at times have felt very lonely. According to neighbors, the garden was left to go to rack and ruin, and it can't have been pleasant, living in that big house all on her own. Jane was a bit of a character and journalists never missed an opportunity to make fun of her. They kept watch on her day and night and reported on every single, little occurrence.

Around midnight on one particular November night she happened to look out of a window and spot a couple of men lurking around the front gate. A moment later they rang the doorbell. She did not dare to go downstairs, so instead she opened the window and asked what they wanted. The men said she had to come down and open the door; they wanted to show her two sidewalk planks that had come loose. Jane was not that easily fooled, though. She told them to clear off, but afterward she felt so nervous about being in that enormous house all by herself that she could not sleep. "MRS SATHER SUSPICIOUS" the headline in bold capitals trumpeted above a report of the incident in the paper the next day, following this up with a wry comment about her now having her own emergency line to the police station. Another night, around one o'clock, she was woken by shuffling sounds outside the parlor window. Thinking it must be burglars, and since she was alone in the house, she immediately called the police. But she had no cause to get into such a panic, the newspapers said, it was only a couple of reporters looking for a comment from her on some rumors about a remark she had made at the whist club.

Reporters noted when Jane Krom Sather was at home, when she was out traveling, where she had gone, whom she was traveling with, and when she was expected to return. Her every movement was recorded, even if she was only going shopping. On one occasion her carriage horses bolted, the coachman was thrown from his seat and Jane herself was slung out of the carriage and badly hurt. She could have been killed, and the headline next day read: "MRS SATHER'S NARROW ESCAPE."

Jane felt so vulnerable and anxious that she eventually asked an unmarried nephew from New York, Reuben Krom Hawk, to come and stay with her. In return she would pay for all his needs. After a couple of years, however, he started trying to extort money from his elderly aunt, while Jane, for her part, took a dim view of the fact that he had found himself a lady friend. They fell out and she eventually kicked him out of the house. Her nephew responded by taking her to court. In the court report Jane comes across as a sharp-tongued old dame. "Why did Mr. Hawk leave your home?" the judge asked her. "Because he wanted to, I presume." Jane replied. "Was that the only reason?" the judge inquired. "I do not keep people very long at my home," came the tart retort, "they become tiresome, and when they do I want them to leave."

Society ladies were beginning to find Mrs. Peder Sather a little too eccentric, and she had very little in common with most of them anyway. Like Peder she was an active supporter of the temperance movement and hosted meetings of the local branch of the society at her home. When the poet, pacifist, and feminist Julia Ward Howe was in the San Francisco area she stayed for several weeks with Jane, who was well known for seizing every opportunity to improve her mind. According to professor of history Leon Richardson, speaking in an interview, she was always to be found in the auditorium when some gifted lecturer was visiting the university at Berkeley. "Jane K. Sather was a woman who was interested in her own educational development and did everything possible for it." She was, he said, "well-read . . . thoughtful, and she went to important lectures. When big men came along or big women she went to hear them, took pains to keep up to date, to keep up to the minute, so that her judgment was never a snap judgment, it was a judgment based on her investigation of things."

Jane Krom appears to have been Sarah's direct opposite: modern, childless, independent, and highly unconventional. And it says something about Peder Sather that he should have chosen to marry her of all people. She shared his own thoughts on education and enlightenment. The objects in the house in Oakland can just as easily be regarded as symbols of a country boy's longing for culture and personal growth as of a banker's snobbish pretensions. Peder Sather was not born into the upper classes, but that is where he ended up, and viewed in that light the piano in the drawing room, the books in the library, and the paintings on the walls can be taken to represent something more than superficial décor.

Jane became friends with the president of the university, Benjamin Ide Wheeler, a man who lived and breathed for that seat of learning. His opinion of the moneyed classes shines through in one of his lectures, which was printed in the *New York Times*. In it, Wheeler says that one of the most regrettable consequences of wealth is that it isolates the rich from the rest of the world. People who do nothing but move between their country homes in Newport and Palm Beach, enjoy dining late on French cuisine, and only marry and divorce within their own ranks are living in a bubble. In Wheeler's view, individuals of judgment and foresight were rarely to be found among those for whom luxury was the be-all and end-all.

The share of his fortune which Peder Sather had left in Jane's hands went to the university that he had helped to found. She presented the first endowment in 1900, and this was used to fund the Sather Chair of Classical Literature and to build up a general library as well as a library devoted to legal books and publications, the Sather Law Library. She also donated to the university a piece of real estate in Oakland worth $150,000, which the university would later be able to sell for many times that sum.

In May 1903 President Theodore Roosevelt paid a visit to the university and Benjamin Wheeler invited Jane to the reception for him. Roosevelt crossed the bay to Berkeley on a tugboat, escorted by a virtual armada of small boats. The wharf and the streets up to the campus were thronged with children and adults waving flags and clutching flowers. Theodore Roosevelt, the youngest president in the history of the country, was in sparkling form, waving and shaking the hands of people lining the route. His carriage rolled slowly along the road, escorted—at the president's own request—by a troop of black cavalrymen: a personal protest against racial segregation in the army. The cortege arrived at the campus to find thousands gathered to hear him speak, and what Theodore Roosevelt had to say made everyone sit up and take notice: society, he declared, not only needs practical men and women, it also needs thinkers and dreamers.

Among those who heard Roosevelt speak and were in the president's party, when it went on afterward to dinner at the university president's home, was Jane. There is a picture of her standing next to Benjamin Ide Wheeler, wearing a dress that led spiteful journalists to remark that she looked like a lady from the time of Louis XIV. But Jane liked to dress up and for this occasion she had donned her very best bib and tucker: rustling skirts of the heaviest brocade; a bodice of snowy lace bedecked with quivering chiffon bows and jingling chains. Beneath a hat adorned with feathers and tempting-looking silk fruit, the ghost of a smile is visible, a smile from Shokan, from the stone cottage and the thirty-eight books, from women who span and wove.

In those days the campus was a secluded parklike spot that almost blended with the surrounding countryside. The university buildings were dotted here and there across the grounds with picturesque lanes and paths winding between them. Right from the start the university had been a public institution, and it now offered courses in a wide range of subjects, from the humanities, mathematics, and the natural sciences to agriculture and engineering.

The town of Berkeley was starting to spring up around the campus, but as yet there was nothing to mark the main entrance to the university. This gave Jane the idea for what was to become Sather Gate, the monument she would raise to Peder's memory. But why a gateway? Possibly she knew that part of the land on which the campus stood had originally been donated by Peder. According to Lawrence Emerson Nelson's *Redlands: Biography of a College*, in 1866 Sather made provision for the university in a codicil to his will, "granting the college much of the present city of Alameda." For some reason, and much to Peder Sather's surprise and dismay, there was a disagreement regarding this proposal, one which is commented on in a letter cited in Nelson's book which says: "Please advise the board as a fiscal measure to treat him in the matter of his offer of the Alameda property with the respect which such kindness demands. He has as yet received no intimation that his kindness has ever been appreciated and naturally feels grieved." "Later," Nelson continues, "his widow ignored the college, erected Sather Gate and Sather Campanile at the University of California." So with Sather Gate Jane may have been covertly alluding to this earlier episode.

The main entrance to the campus was completed in 1910; it had cost forty thousand dollars to build. On this occasion too Jane was ridiculed in the press. Sather Gate had been decorated with eight panels showing eight nude figures—four male and four female. Many people were shocked by the nudity and demanded that they be removed. Word had it that the demand had actually come from Jane herself, that she was the prudish one. But this was not the case, as a letter from Jane to the secretary of the regents proves. In this she says that if people were not enlightened enough to be able to differentiate between nude and naked then it was all the same to her. A few years ago, in connection with its centenary the gate underwent restoration work to the tune of one and a half million dollars. This brought it back to the condition it was in when Jane saw her monument to Peder completed.

Jane later donated two hundred thousand dollars to the university for the building of Sather Tower, the 307-foot campanile. And again spiteful tongues wagged when it was reported that Jane had vetoed plans for the building of a pond next to the campanile because she was afraid that its smooth reflective surface would tempt male students to look up the skirts of the female students on the sly. Other people felt that the campanile was nothing but a megalomaniac woman's monument to herself, and that the money could have been more usefully spent. Snide comments of this sort were silenced, however, when Jane presented the money for the two professorships, one in history and one in classical literature. By dint of sound management of the Sather funds, the university was able, in 1991, to establish a third Sather professorship, the Peder Sather Chair in History. As the donor of something in the region of a million dollars she was now one of the university's great benefactors. Some historians believe that Jane donated her own money, from before her marriage to Peder Sather, and that she was married for a while to one of Anthony Drexel's business partners. But this is not true, since Jane's possible first husband's name was John Read (or Reade), while Drexel's associate was William Read. It should also be said that the campanile was financed by the sale of Sather's shares in the Firemen's Fund Insurance Company.

With her donations, the childless Jane was acting quite in Peder Sather's spirit and it is thanks to her that his name has not been utterly lost to oblivion. In the fall of 2012 the Peder Sather Center for Advanced Study was opened on the campus—yet another memorial to the Norwegian who cofounded the university. And so a historic circle was closed.

Jane spent her last years quietly in Oakland, surrounded by Peder's clocks and cared for by her Danish housekeeper and Swedish nurse. On a December day in 1911, as the wind swept down Twelfth Street and the rain shook the fever trees, Jane Krom Sather passed away peacefully in her own bed—a woman unlike any other. Her one last wish had been that she should be laid to rest for eternity next to Peder. And if there was no room for her there, she wished to be cremated, she said, and her urn buried in the grave. But she did not get her wish; Josephine would not allow it. When she heard that Jane had donated a substantial proportion of her father's fortune to the university, she went to court to try to get the money back, but her suit was unsuccessful. She did, however, manage to prevent Jane from being buried in the family grave in San Francisco. Instead her body was taken to Mountain View Cemetery in Oakland and interred in a plot belonging to a friend, Francis Smith of Oakland. There she rests today, together with a dozen members of and friends of the Smith family, while her beloved Peder is interred at Colma, just outside of San Francisco.

Josephine climbed further and further up the social ladder, but this cost money and her inheritance from her father was steadily dwindling. After several years of lavish socializing she was forced to leave her summer residence in Newport, where she had been living far beyond her means. Not that this left her without a roof over her head, though—she simply moved to one of her other homes.

History speaks well of Josephine; she was a languorous beauty, generous and loved by all, sources say. Her son Peder became a cancer specialist; Francis was a groundbreaking art photographer, Emile a musician and opera librettist, while Louis found it enough just to live from day to day and never left Josephine's side.

After Castlewood finally went under the hammer, Louis and Josephine—who had been widowed in 1900—lived for long spells in Paris, but often went back to New York to see friends. This was also what they were planning to do in August 1915, although the First World War had broken out by then and the Atlantic was swarming with German U-boats. Josephine, in Paris, was worried and not sure what to do. She had first canceled the tickets, but then, because Germany had promised that no civilian ships would be touched, she changed her mind, rebooked, and boarded the liner *SS Arabic* along with Louis, her French chambermaid Margaret, her chauffeur, and her two bulldogs.

The ship had not long left Liverpool and was sailing just off the Irish coast when the thing that Josephine had been dreading actually happened. The *Arabic* was torpedoed by a German U-boat and went down. Only two American citizens were lost and one of them was Josephine. Louis had managed to hold on to his mother for a while, but then he was hit on the head by a spar from the wreck, was knocked out, and lost his grip on her. When he regained consciousness his mother was gone. The bulldogs, meanwhile, had been picked up by one of the lifeboats. One month later the drowned heiress's body was washed ashore not far from the small Irish town of Queenstown. And so the voice of the only daughter of Peder and Sarah who could have passed on her father's story was tragically stilled, and all that is left today are a few memorabilia.

BIBLIOGRAPHY

This bibliography has several sections, in the following order: Books and Journal Articles Cited by Page Number; Other Books and Journal Articles; Newspaper Articles; Archives; Sources in Archives; City Directories; U.S. Census Reports Listing Peder Sather; Oral Sources.

BOOKS AND JOURNAL ARTICLES CITED BY PAGE NUMBER

American Baptist Home Mission Society. *Annual Report, 1853*, p. 279. New York: American Baptist Home Mission Society, 1853.

———. *Annual Report, 1884*, p. 8. New York: American Baptist Home Mission Society, 1884.

———. *The Home Mission Monthly*, p. 195. New York: American Baptist Home Mission Society, 1882.

———. *Proceedings of the American Baptist Home Mission Society at Its Fiftieth Anniversary Meeting, San Francisco, May 24th–26th*, p. 53. San Francisco: American Baptist Home Mission Society, 1882.

Anthony, Charles Volney. *Fifty Years of Methodism: A History of the Methodist Episcopal Church*, p. 86. Charleston, SC: Jarreth Printing, 1952.

Armstrong, Leroy, and J. O. Denny. *Financial California: An Historical Review of the Beginning and Progress of Banking in the State*, p. 137. San Francisco: Coast Banker Publishers, 1916.

Asher, John R., and George H. Adams. *Pictoral Album of American Industry*, p. 40. New York: Asher & Adams, 1876. Repr., New York: Rutledge Books, 1976.

Bancroft, Hubert Howe. *Chronicles of the Builders of the Commonwealth*, vol. 6, p. 566. San Francisco: Historical Company Publishers, 1892.

Barker, Malcolm E. *More San Francisco Memoirs, 1852–1899*, pp. 39, 126, and 131. San Francisco: Londonborn Publications, 1996.

Bemis, Stephen Allen. "Recollections of a Long and Somewhat Uneventful Life," p. 62. Unpublished MS, St. Louis, 1932. Washington, DC: Library of Congress. American Memory Historical Collections.

Bjork, Kenneth O. *West of the Great Divide: Norwegian Migration to the Pacific Coast,* p. 138. Northfield, MN: Norwegian-American Historical Association, 1958.

Brown, Ira Cross. *Financing an Empire: History of Banking in California,* p. 228. Chicago: S. J. Clarke Publishing, 1927.

Childs, George. *Recollections,* p. 33. Philadelphia: J. B. Lippincott, 1890.

Clarke, Dwight L. *William Tecumseh Sherman: Gold Rush Banker,* p. 376. San Francisco: California Historical Society, 1969.

Clausen, Clarence, and Andreas Elviken, eds. *A Chronicle of Old Muskego: The Diary of Søren Bache, 1839–1847,* pp. 50–51. Northfield, MN: Norwegian-American Historical Association, 1951.

Cook, James M. *Annual Report of the Superintendent of the Bank Department of the State of New York,* p. 81. Albany: State of New York, Bank Department, December 31, 1858.

Comstock, David Allan. *Brides of the Gold Rush,* pp. 312, 313, 320, 321. Grass Valley, CA: Comstock Bonanza Press, 1987.

Deutsch, Monroe E., ed. *The Abundant Life: Benjamin Ide Wheeler,* pp. 338–40. Berkeley: University of California Press, 1926.

Dow, Sterling. *Fifty Years of Sathers: The Sather Professorship of Classical Literature,* pp. 23–36. Berkeley: University of California Press, 1965.

Ellsworth, Lucius F. *Craft to National Industry: A Case Study of the Transformation of the New York State Tanning Industry,* p. 194. North Stratford, NH: Ayer Company Publishers, 1975.

Ferrier, William Warren. *Origin and Development of the University of California,* p. 503. Berkeley: Sather Gate Book Shop, 1930.

Foote, Horace S. *Pen Pictures of the World,* p. 394. Chicago: Lewis Publishing, 1888.

Fisher, Victor, Michael B. Frank, and Dahlia Armon, eds. *The Mark Twain Papers,* vol. 3, *1869,* p. 53. Berkeley: University of California Press, 1992.

Gerber, John C., Paul Baender, Walter Blair, and William Gibson, eds. *The Works of Mark Twain,* pp. 138, 533. Berkeley: University of California Press, 1981.

Harris, Susan K. *The Courtship of Olivia Langdon and Mark Twain,* p. 75. Cambridge: Cambridge University Press, 1996.

Helfand, Harvey. *University of California: An Architectural Tour and Photographs,* pp. 40, 45. New York: Princeton Architectural Press, 2002.

Hinkel, Edgar, and William McCann. *Oakland, 1852–1938,* pp. 386, 499–50. Oakland: Oakland Public Library, 1939.

Homans, J. Smith, ed. *The Bankers' Magazine,* p. 457. New York: J. Smith Homans, 1888.

Hoover, Mildred Brooke. *Historic Spots in California,* p. 23. Stanford, CA: Stanford University Press, 1932.

Kirkeby, Birger. *Sør-Odal bygdebok,* vol. 6, pp. 382–87. Skarnes, Norway: Skarnes Kommune, 1990.

Langford, Laura Carter Holloway. *Famous American Fortunes and the Men Who Made Them,* pp. 187–90. New York: J. A. Hill, 1889.

Lapp, Rudolph M. *Blacks in Gold Rush California,* p. 107. New Haven, CT: Yale University Press, 1977.

Lockwood, Charles. *Suddenly San Francisco: The Early Years of an Instant City,* p. 90. San Francisco: Examiner Division of the Hearst Corporation, 1978.

Loomis, Noel M. *Wells Fargo,* pp. 42, 82, 124. New York: Clarkson N. Potter, 1968.

Lovoll, Odd Sverre. *The Promise of America: A History of the Norwegian-American People,* p. 233. Minneapolis: University of Minnesota Press, 1999.

McDonald, Edward D., and Edward M. Hinton. *Drexel Institute of Technology, 1891–1941: A Memorial History,* p. 5. Philadelphia: Haddon Craftsmen, 1942.

Merritt, Frank Clinton. *History of Alameda County, California,* vol. 1, p. 577. Chicago: S. J. Clarke Publishing, 1928.

Miller, Paul. *Lost Newport,* p. 17. Carlisle, MA: Applewood Books, 2010.

Morehouse, Henry Lyman, and Thomas Jefferson Morgan. *Baptist Home Mission Monthly,* nos. 3–4, p. 195. New York: Baptist Home Mission Society, 1881.

Nelson, Lawrence Emerson. *Biography of a College,* pp. 27–28. Redlands, CA: University of Redlands, 1958.

Norkross, Frank. *A History of the New York Swamps,* p. 107. New York: Chiswick Press, 1901.

Northern California Writers' Projects. *San Francisco, the Bay, and Its Cities,* pp. 208, 218, 402. San Francisco: Hastings House Publishers, 1940.

Parker, Cornelia Stratton. *Wanderer's Circle,* p. 2. Cambridge, MA: Riverside Press, 1934.

Preservation Park Museum. *Through These Doors: Discovering Oakland at Preservation Park,* pp. 15–16, 42–43. Oakland: Preservation Park, 1996.

Reid, Robert W. *Washington Lodge No. 21. F. & A.M. and Some of Its Members,* p. 200. New York: Washington Lodge, 1911.

Roinestad, Søren. *A Hundred Years with Norwegians in the East Bay,* p. 94. San Francisco: R & E Research Associates, 1963.

Rottenberg, Dan. *The Man Who Made Wall Street: Anthony J. Drexel and the Rise of Modern Finance,* pp. 46–48, 202–3. Philadelphia: University of Pennsylvania Press, 2001.

Sherman, William Tecumseh. *Memoir,* p. 376. New York: Penguin Classics, 2000.

Shumate, Albert. *A Visit to Rincon Hill and South Park,* p. 70. San Francisco: Tamalpais Press, 1963.

Stadtman, Verne A. *The University of California, 1868–1968,* p. 191. New York: McGraw-Hill, 1970.

Stein, Barbara R. *On Her Own Terms: Annie Montague Alexander and the Rise of Science in the American West,* p. 115. Berkeley: University of California Press, 2001.

Stevenson, Robert Louis, and Lloyd Osborne. *The Wrecker,* p. 14. London: Cassells, 1892.

Todd, Frank Morton. *A Romance of Insurance,* pp. 48, 83, 87. San Francisco: H. S. Crocker, 1929.

Twain, Mark. *Early Tales and Sketches,* p. 533. Berkeley: University of California Press, 1979.

Tønsager, Hans. *Barndoms- og ungdomsminder om Henrik Wergeland,* p. 46. Kristiania: Cammermeyer, 1897.

University of California. *Endowed Chairs of Learning,* pp. 20–22. Berkeley: University of California Press, 1947.

Verbarg, Leonard H. *Celebrities at Your Doorstep: A Selection of Knave Personalities from the Sunday Tribune,* pp. 39–40. Berkeley: Alameda Historical Society, 1972.

Whittelsey, Charles Barney. *The Roosevelt Genealogy, 1649–1902,* p. 76. Hartford, CT: Whittelsey, 1902.

Whittemore, Henry. *History of Masonry in North America from 1730–1800: Together with a History of Several Lodges of Houston County, New Jersey,* p. 117. Whitefish, MT: Kessinger Publishing, 2003.

Willey, Samuel H. *A History of the College of California,* p. 243. San Francisco: San Francisco Historical Society, 1887.

Wilson, Neill Compton. *400 California Street: The Story of the Bank of California,* p. 68. San Francisco: Bank of California, 1964.

Woodbridge, Sally Byrne. *John Galen Howard and the University of California: The Design of a Great Public University Campus,* p. 122. Berkeley: University of California Press, 2002.

Woods, Samuel D. *Lights and Shadows on Life on the Pacific Coast,* p. 228. New York: Funk & Wagnalls, 1910.

Wright, Benjamin Cooper. *The West, the Best, and California, the Best of the West: A Story Of Some of the Principal Features in the Business Life of the Golden State,* pp. 157, 203. San Francisco: A. Carlisle, 1913.

OTHER BOOKS AND JOURNAL ARTICLES

Alexander, James B., and James Lee Heig. *Building the Dream City.* San Francisco: Scottwall Associates, 2002.

Andersen, Arlow William. *The Norwegian-Americans.* New York: Twayne Publishers, 1975.

Bagwell, Beth: *Oakland, The Story of a City.* Oakland: Oakland Heritage Alliance, 1982

Baker, Joseph Eugene. *Past and Present of Alameda County, California.* Chicago: S. J. Clarke Publishing, 1914.

Ball, Timothy H. *Encyclopedia of Genealogy and Biography of Lake County, Indiana: With a Compendium of History, 1834–1904.* Chicago: Lewis Publishing, 1904.

———. *Lake County, Indiana, 1834–1872.* Chicago: J. W. Goodspeed Printer and Publisher, 1873.

Barry, Theodore. A., and Benjamin. A. Patten. *Men and Memories of San Francisco in the Spring of 50.* San Francisco: Bancroft, 1873.

Barth, Gunther. *California's Practical Period: A Cultural Context of the Emerging University, 1850s–1870s.* Berkeley: Center for Studies in Higher Education and Institute for Governmental Studies, University of California, 1994.

Biddle, Cordelia Frances. *The Conjurer.* New York: Thomas Dunne Books, 2007.

———. *Deception's Daughter.* New York: Thomas Dunne Books, 2008.

Bostwick, Henry Anthon. *Genealogy of the Bostwick Family in America.* Columbia, SC: Bryan Printing Company, 1901.

Boucher, Francois. *American Footprints in Paris.* New York: Boucher Print, 2007.

Bowen, Robert, and Brenda Bowen. *San Francisco's China Town.* San Francisco: Arcadia Publishing, 2008.

Brands, Henry Williams. *The Age of Gold: The California Gold Rush and the New American Dream.* New York: Anchor Books, 2002.

Brentano, Carroll, and Sheldon Rotblatt. *The University in the 1870s.* Berkeley: Institute of Governmental Studies, 1996.

Bruce, John. *Gaudy Century, 1848–1948: San Francisco's One Hundred Years of Robust Journalism.* New York: Random House, 1948.

Bruguiere, Francis. *26 photographs.* San Francisco: H. S. Crocker, 1918.

California Academy of Sciences. *Proceedings of the California Academy of Sciences.* San Francisco: California Academy of Sciences, 1873.

Colby, Robert. *Cornelia and Jess, A Love Story.* Available at Friends of the High Lakes website, www.friendsofthehighlakes.com/Cornelia_and_Jess_A_Love_Story.pdf (accessed June 25, 2013).

Didion, Joan. *Where I Was From.* New York: Vintage International, 2003.

Enyeart, James. *Francis J. Bruguiere: His Photographs and His Life.* New York: Alfred A. Knopf, 1977.

Ernst, Robert. *Immigrant Life in New York City, 1825–1863.* Syracuse, NY: Syracuse University Press, 1994.

Ferber, Linda S., and Asher Brown Durand. *Kindred Spirits: Asher B. Durand and the American Landscape.* Brooklyn: Brooklyn Museum, 2007.

Ferrier, William Warren. *Ninety Years of Education in California, 1846–1936.* Berkeley: Sather Gate Bookshop, 1937.

Finley, John. "Banks and Banking in California." *Overland Monthly,* no. 1 (1896): 81–103.

Finley, Moses. *The Ancient Economy.* Berkeley: University of California Press, 1973.

Gilman, Daniel Coit: "How Pioneers Begun a College." *Overland Monthly* (March 1875): 287–90.

Gjerde, Jon, ed. *Major Problems in American Immigration and Ethnic History.* Berkeley: University of California Press, 1998.

Hansen, Gladys, ed. *San Francisco: The Bay and Its Cities.* New York: Hastings House, 1973.

Hinkel, Edgar, and William McCann, eds. *Oakland, 1852–1938: Some Phases of the Social, Political and Economic History of Oakland, California,* vol 1. Oakland: Oakland Public Library and the Works Progress Administration, 1939.

Hittell, Theodore. *History of California,* vol. 3. San Francisco: N.J. Stone, 1897.

Holloway, Laura Carter. *Famous American Fortunes and the Men Who Made Them.* New York: J. A. Hill, 1885.

Hughes, Edan Milton. *Artists in California, 1786–1940.* Sacramento, CA: Crocker Art Museum, 2002.

Hyneman, Leon. *World's Masonic Register.* Lawrence, Luther S. Banker, 164 Nassau Street, New York City, Metropolitan Lodge, chapter 21. Philadelphia: J. B. Lippincott, 1860.

Jones, William Carey. *Illustrated History of the University of California, 1868–1901.* San Francisco: Frank H. Dukesmith, 1895.

Kerr, Clark. *The Gold and the Blue: A Personal Memoir of the University of California.* Berkeley: University of California Press, 2003.

Koford, Henning. *Samuel Merritt: His Life and Achievements.* Oakland: Kennedy, 1938.

Lotchin, Roger W. *San Francisco, 1846–1856: From Hamlet to City.* Lincoln: University of Nebraska Press, 1979.

Millard, Bailey. *History of the San Francisco Bay Region.* Chicago: American Historical Society, 1924.

Miller, James. *New York As It Is; or, A Stranger's Guidebook to the Cities of New York.* New York: J. Miller, 1866.

Mørkhagen, Sverre. *Farvel Norge.* Oslo: Gyldendal, 2008.

Norris, Kathleen. *The Venables.* New York: Warner, 1972.

Orcutt, Samuel: *A History of the Old Town of Stratford and the City Bridgeport, Connecticut,* vol. 2. New Haven, CT: Press of Tuttle, Morehouse & Taylor, 1886.

Pelfrey, Patricia. *A Brief History of the University of California.* 2nd ed. Berkeley: Center for Studies in Higher Education, University of California, 2004.

Perry, Mark. *Grant and Twain: The Story of a Friendship That Changed America.* New York: Random House, 2004.

Ræder, Ole Munch. *America in the Forties.* Minneapolis: University of Minnesota Press, 1929.

Rasmussen, Louis J. *San Francisco Ship Passenger Lists,* vol. 2. Colma, CA: n.p., 1966.

Reed, Ishmael. *Blues City: A Walk in Oakland.* New York: Crown Publishers., 2003.

Richards, Rand. *Historic San Francisco: A Concise History and Guide.* San Francisco: Heritage House Publishers, 2007.

Schall, Rebecca. *Historic Photos of San Francisco.* Nashville, TN: Turner Publishing, 2006.

Semmingsen, Ingrid. *Drøm og dåd: Utvandringen til Amerika.* Oslo: Aschehoug, 1975.

Soulé, Frank, John Gihon, and James Nisbet. *Annals of San Francisco.* New York: Appleton, 1855.

Stadtman, Verne, et al. *Berkeley at Mid-Century: Elements of a Golden Age.* Berkeley: Berkeley Public Policy Press, 2002.

Starr, Kevin. *California: A History.* New York: Modern Library, 2007.

Staub, Geraldine P., Carolyn T. Cotton, and Ann Preston. *Francis Martin Drexel, 1792–1863: An Artist Turned Banker.* Philadelphia: Drexel University, 1976.

Sterling, George. *The Evanescent City: George Sterling and Francis Bruguiere.* San Francisco: A. M. Robertson, 1916.

Taper, Bernard, ed. *Mark Twain's San Francisco.* Berkeley: Heydey Books and Santa Clara University, 2003.

Tocqueville, Alexis de. *Democracy in America.* London: Penguin Classics, 2003.

Trollope, Frances. *Domestic Manners of the Americans.* London: Penguin Classics, 1997.

Tucker, Elizabeth. *Campus Legends: A Handbook.* Greenwood Folklore Handbook Series. Westport, CT: Greenwood Press, 2005.

Twain, Mark, and Charles Dudley Warner. *The Gilded Age: A Tale of Today.* London: Penguin Classics, 2001.

Watson, Kent, and Peter van Houten. *The University in the 1870s.* Berkeley: Center for Studies in Higher Education and Institute for Governmental Studies, University of California, 1996.

Wells, Harry L., Frank Gilbert, and William, L. Chambers. *History of Butte County, California 1882, and Biographical Sketches of Its Prominent Men and Pioneers.* Berkeley: Howell-North Books, 1973.

Wendte, Charles William. *The Wider Fellowship: Memoirs, Friendships, and Endeavours for Religious Unity, 1844–1927*, vol. 1. Boston: Beacon Press, 1927.

Whitman, Walt. *Leaves of Grass.* Brooklyn: n.p., 1855.

Williams, Samuel. *The City of the Golden Gate.* New York: Scribner's Publishers, 1875.

———. *Lights and Shadows of Life on the Pacific Coast.* Whitefish, MT: Kessinger Publishing, 2004.

Wright, Benjamin Cooper. *Banking in America, 1849–1910.* San Francisco: H. S. Crocker, 1910.

NEWSPAPER ARTICLES

Text in these entries that describes article content is indicated by the intials "DC." The rest of any given entry is the original title. A title of a newspaper section is indicated by "Section" before it. Some articles or sections have subtitles, which are marked as such.

Spectator. April 30, 1824. Section: Coroner's Office. DC: John and Charles Farrar.

New York Evening Post. July 3, 1832. Board of Health. DC: Cholera.

Dutch Reformed Christian Intelligencer. April 18, 1835. Section: Married. DC: On Tuesday evening, married by Rev. Thomas de Witt, Minister at the North Dutch Reformed Church at Fulton and Williams Streets: Mr. Peter Sather to Miss Sarah Thompson, both of this city.

Evening Post. March 1840. Section: List of Letters Remaining in the New York Post Office. DC: Letters for Peder Sather.

Evening Post. February 8, 1842. Section: Bankruptcy. DC: Edward W. Church, clerk, to be declared bankrupt.

Evening Post. February 20, 1844. Section: From the Court. DC: Peder Sather and Martin Flowers.

Brooklyn Daily Eagle. November 25, 1844. Section: For Sale. DC: A lot on Willoughby Street, known as no. 82, for sale.

Evening Post. August 22, 1846. Section: Comptroller's Office, State of New York. DC: Notice of the appointment of Messrs. Sather & Church, no. 164 Nassau Street, New York.

Commercial Advertiser. January 8, 1848. Section: City News. DC: Man purchasing a lottery ticket at the office of Sather & Church.

New York Herald. September 15, 1849. Interesting from California.

Portland Daily Advertiser. August 12, 1850. Civilization and Comfort. DC: St. Francis Hotel. Advertisement.

Daily Alta California. March 27, 1851. Sather & Church, Bankers, New York and San Francisco. DC: Dealers in Exchange, Coin and Gold Dust. Also Iron Buildings. Washington Street, San Francisco. Advertisement.

Sacramento Transcript. April 12, 1851. Section: Steamship Isthmus, from Panama. DC: Peder Sather and Theodore Tasheira on the passenger list.

Daily Alta California May 6, 1851. Section: Local Matters: Notice of Removal. DC: Drexel, Sather & Church moving from Washington Street to the Post Office Building.

Daily Alta California. May 18, 1851. Co-partnership. DC: Francis Drexel, Peder Sather, and Edward W. Church certify that they have formed a general partnership under the name of Drexel, Sather & Church, for the transaction of a Banking, Exchange and Commission Business. Location, Post Office Building, in Mr. Atwill's Music Store.

Daily Alta California August 5, 1851. Section: Notice of Removal. DC: Drexel, Sather & Church moving to Montgomery Street.

California Gazette. September 1, 1851. Drexel, Sather & Church. Advertisement.

Sacramento Daily Union. September 2, 1851. Section: Shipment of Gold Dust per Steamer *Tennessee.* DC: Among the shippers, Adams & Co.: $400,000. Drexel, Sather & Church: $20,000.

California Gazette. November 1, 1851. Thomas Tennent: Mathematical and Nautical Instrument Maker. DC: Address: Fire-Proof Building, Montgomery Street, the Banking House of Drexel, Sather & Church. Advertisement.

New York Times. December 2, 1851. Section: Arrival of the Prometheus. DC: Peder Sather on the passenger list.

Daily Alta California. December 5, 1851. Drexel, Sather & Church. DC: James S. Hutchinson, has become manager. Advertisement.

New York Times. January 26, 1852. Arrest of a Bank President.

Daily Alta California. June 8, 1852. William Turnbull & William Walton. Subtitle: Commission Merchants and Wholesale Dealers in Liquors, Provisions cc. Advertisement.

Weekly Herald. June 19, 1852. Section: Ten Days Later from California. Subtitle: Specie List per Steamship *Illinois.* DC: Among the shippers, Adams & Co.: $415,785. Drexel & Co.: $17,600.

New York Times. August 27, 1852. Section: Financial. Subtitle: City Loan—State Guarantee.

Newark Daily Advertiser. March 31, 1853. Section: Local Matters. Subtitle: Charles F. Lott.

Sacramento Daily Union. July 12, 1853. Messrs. Drexel, Sather & Church. DC: Erection of an addition to their banking house, which made their establishment one of the most commodious in the City.

Alta California. November 1, 1853. Destruction of the St. Francis by Fire.

Sacramento Daily Union. August 18, 1853. Section: Arrival of the *John L. Stephens.* DC: Peder Sather on the passenger list.

Public Ledger. January 27, 1854. Letter from California. DC: Banks named with regard to their capital and standing. No. 1: Page, Bacon & Co. and Adams & Co. No. 2: Burgoyne & Co., Davidson & Co. No. 3: Drexel, Sather & Church, Wells, Fargo & Co., and Lucas, Turner & Co.

Daily Placer Times and Transcript. May 1, 1854. Hon. Charles F. Lott.

Daily Placer Times and Transcript. July 22, 1854. Ole Bull at the Metropolitan.

Daily Alta California. August 12, 1854. The Grand Jury.

New York Times. August 25, 1854. Section: California. Subtitle: Ole Bull in San Francisco.

Daily Placer Times and Transcript. September 7, 1854. Anniversary of the Admission of California.

The Sun. October 10, 1854. Section: Two Weeks Later from California. Subtitle: Arrival of the *Northern Light* in New York. DC: Peder Sather and Ole Bull on the passenger list.

The Sun. November 2, 1854. Ole Bull.

Weekly Alta California. December 1, 1854. Section: Importations. DC: Drexel, Sather & Church import a wagon.

Daily Alta California. December 20, 1854: Section: Married. DC: Mr. James S. Hutchinson to Miss Coralie D. Pearsall.

Daily Democratic State Journal. January 24, 1855. Section: Mercantile Library. DC: Speer Riddell is re-elected treasurer.

San Francisco Evening Journal. February 28, 1855. Drexel, Sather & Church Stay the Run.

New York Times. March 20, 1855. The Financial Crisis.

Daily National Intelligencer. March 26, 1855. Section: From California. Arrival of the Steamer *George Law.* DC: Among the principal shippers, Wells, Fargo & Co.: $200,000. Drexel, Sather & Church: $200,000.

Daily Alta California. July 30, 1855. Section: Arrival of Steamship *Sonora.* DC: Left Panama July 15. Peder Sather on the passenger list.

California Farmer and Journal of Useful Sciences. October 12, 1855. Drexel, Sather & Church. DC: Opening of a new branch at the corner of Third and J. Street,

Sacramento. "Their establishment is neat and beautiful and they are now on the road for fame and prosperity. They deserve success."

Sacramento Daily Union. November 2, 1855. Report of the Committee on Farms, Vineyards, Orchards, etc. DC: Reverend Abraham H. Myers and Peder Sather Sather, their orchards in Alameda.

Constitution. November 21, 1855. P. Sather & Co.

Daily Placer Time & Transcript. November 30, 1855. Edwin B. Mastick, Attorney and Counselor, Drexel, Sather & Church. Advertisement.

San Francisco Bulletin. December 5, 1855. Section: Shipment of Treasure per the *Golden Age.* DC: Among the principal shippers: Wells, Fargo & Co.: $273,250. Drexel, Sather & Church: $200,000. Also per *Sierra Nevada*: Drexel, Sather & Church, $190,000.

San Francisco Bulletin. December 18, 1855. A Card.

New York Times. March 24, 1856. To Reverend Francis Vinton. DC: Letter from Benjamin Haxtun and Peter Naylor.

San Francisco Bulletin. May 20, 1856. James Casey, Alias James P. Casey.

New York Times. June 4, 1856: L. S. Lawrence & Co., Bankers. Advertisement. DC: Successors to P. Sather, 164 Nassau Street. Sights drafts on Messrs. Drexel, Sather & Church, San Francisco.

New York Times. June 7, 1856. Section: Financial. Subtitle: A Card. DC: Statement by Peder Sather, recommending Luther S. Lawrence as a banker.

New York Herald. June 29, 1856. The Fate of the Murderers.

San Francisco Bulletin. August 22, 1856. Sisters of Mercy.

New York Herald Tribune. October 1, 1856. Drexel, Sather & Church, Bankers, San Francisco. Advertisement.

Sacramento Daily Union. December 29, 1856. Young Ladies Seminary, Sacramento. DC: Peder Sather is one of six references. Advertisement.

Daily Alta California. January 4, 1857. Section: Importations. DC: Drexel, Sather & Church have imported 3 puncheons rum.

New York Herald. January 16, 1857. The State Debt of California. *San Francisco Bulletin.* January 25, 1857. Drexel, Sather & Church.

Daily Globe. February 6, 1857. Section: Business Affairs. Treasure per Steamer *Sonora.* DC: Among the principal shippers, Drexel, Sather & Church: $250,000. Wells, Fargo & Co.: $229,994. B. Davidson: $200,000.

Daily Globe. February 23, 1857. F. A. Woodward, Esq.

San Francisco Bulletin. March 25, 1857. The Bulkhead.

San Francisco Bulletin. April 6, 1857. Section: Shipment of Treasure per Steamer *John L. Stephens.* DC: Among the principal shippers, Drexel, Sather & Church: $300,000. Wells, Fargo & Co.: $216,406.

San Francisco Bulletin. June 5, 1857. Shipment of Treasure per *John L. Stephens.* DC: Among the principal shippers, Drexel, Sather & Church: $335,354. Wells, Fargo & Co.: $330,000.

San Francisco Bulletin. June 7, 1857. Section: Shipping News.

San Francisco Bulletin. June 23, 1857. Sather & Church Continues without F. Drexel.

New York Herald Tribune. June 24, 1857. Section: Notice of New Firm.

New York Herald Tribune. June 24, 1857. Sather & Church Bankers, San Francisco.

San Francisco Bulletin. June 27, 1857. The Firm of Drexel, Sather & Church.

New York Herald Tribune. June 29, 1857. Dissolution: The Firm of Drexel, Sather & Church.

Daily Globe. June 30, 1857. Dissolution: The Firm of Drexel, Sather & Church.

New York Herald Tribune. July 10, 1857. Dissolution.

San Francisco Bulletin. August 5, 1857. Forgery and Arrest of the Supposed Forger.

San Francisco Bulletin. August 8, 1857. Examination of S. Cohn for Forgery.

The Sun. August 27, 1857. Panic in New York.

The Press. September 25, 1857. The Lost Steamer Central America.

San Francisco Bulletin. October 3, 1857. Financial Convulsions in the East.

San Francisco Bulletin. October 5, 1857. Statistics of the First Baptist Church in San Francisco.

San Francisco Bulletin. October 22, 1857. New York Underwriters Paying Up Lost Treasure of the *Central America*.

Daily Globe. October 23, 1857. List of Treasures Lost on the *Central America*.

Stockton Daily Argus. October 23, 1857. Loss of the Californian Steamship *Central America*.

Daily Alta California. October 24, 1857. Further Particulars of the Loss of the *Central America*.

San Francisco Bulletin. November 2, 1857. Supposed Grand Larceny.

San Francisco Bulletin. November 3, 1857. Financial Troubles of Sather & Co. in New York.

Daily Globe. November 3, 1857. Protests of the Drafts of Sather & Church by the American Exchange Bank.

San Francisco Bulletin. November 3, 1857. Run on Sather & Church.

Daily Globe. November 3, 1857. Sather & Church Attached.

San Francisco Bulletin. November 3, 1857. Statement from Sather & Church.

Daily Democratic State Journal. November 4, 1857. The Panic.

Daily Globe. November 4, 1857. How Stands California?

Daily Globe. November 4, 1857. Suspension of Sather & Church. Subtitle: "Run" on the Banking House.

San Francisco Bulletin. November 4, 1857. Attachment Suits against Sather & Church.

San Francisco Bulletin. November 4, 1857. Our Business Condition.

San Francisco Bulletin. November 4, 1857. Sather & Church Affairs.

San Francisco Bulletin. November 4, 1857. Status Sather & Church.

Daily Globe. November 5, 1857. The Crisis in Sacramento.

Daily Globe. November 5, 1857. Sather & Church Paper.

San Francisco Bulletin. November 5, 1857. Sather & Church's Affairs.

Daily Democratic State Journal. November 6, 1857. Failure of Sather & Church.

Daily Globe. November 6, 1857. Affairs of Sather & Church.

San Francisco Bulletin. November 6, 1857. More of Sather & Church Affairs.

San Francisco Bulletin. November 6, 1857. Sacramento Bank Closed.

San Francisco Bulletin. November 7, 1857. Bank Papers and Brokers.
Sacramento Daily Union. November 14, 1857. Affairs of Sather & Church.
San Francisco Bulletin. November 18, 1857. A Protested Bill of Sather & Church.
San Francisco Bulletin. November 18, 1857. Sather & Church, Wells, Fargo & Co.
Daily Globe. December 1, 1857. Drafts of Sather & Church.
San Francisco Bulletin. December 1, 1857. Sather & Church Affair.
Weekly Herald. December 5, 1857. Section: Arrival of the *Northern Light*. DC: Peder
    Sather on the passenger list.
Weekly Herald. December 5, 1857. Markets.
Daily Missouri Republican. January 8, 1858. Sather & Church of San Francisco.
San Francisco Bulletin. January 21, 1858. Section: Consignee Notices. DC: By
    Clipper Ship *Frigate Bird* from Philadelphia, two boxes of Books for Sather &
    Church.
New York Times. March 12, 1858. Sather & Church of San Francisco.
San Francisco Bulletin. April 2, 1858. Drafts of Sather & Church. Advertisement.
    DC: Drafts drawn on New York, Boston, St. Louis, Baltimore, and Louisville
    will be paid at the office of Peter Naylor, Esq., 76 Broad Street, NY, and drafts
    drawn at all other points, on presentation to Drexel & Co., Philadelphia.
San Francisco Bulletin. April 2, 1858. Sather & Church Affairs.
New York Herald. April 9, 1858. Died. DC: Mercelena Roosevelt of consumption.
Daily Globe. April 23, 1858. Drafts of Sather & Church. DC: All drafts are now being
    Paid at Presentation.
New York Times. April 24, 1858. Sather & Church of San Francisco.
California Farmer and Journal of Useful Sciences. May 7, 1858. Sather & Church,
    Bankers, Opened Their Doors Again.
San Francisco Bulletin. May 19, 1858. To Our Atlantic Readers. DC: Messrs. Sather
    & Church have resumed business at their old place, "under flattering circum-
    stances. The Chamber of Commerce of this city has ordered their funds to be
    deposited with the house."
California Farmer and Useful Sciences. June 25, 1858: Oak Grove Institute. DC:
    Description of the school as equal to any for "its quiet morality and freedom from
    everything that would divert the students from their studies." Advertisement.
San Francisco Bulletin. August 19, 1858. More Private Property Sold under Judg-
    ments against the City.
Daily True Delta. August 23, 1858. Section: From California. Subtitle: The Express
    Robbery.
San Francisco Bulletin. February 15, 1859. Empanelment of the Grand Jury.
San Francisco Bulletin. March 18, 1859. Section: Importations. DC: P. Sather, furni-
    ture, 19 boxes.
San Francisco Bulletin. April 13, 1859. Sather & Church, bankers.
California Farmer and Journal of Useful Sciences. September 23, 1859. Leaves from
    My Journal. By M. A. Sarles. DC: Young Ladies' Seminary, Benicia.
San Francisco Bulletin. December 8, 1859. Scandinavian Officers.
San Francisco Bulletin. January 24, 1860. Classical School. Advertisement.

Daily Alta California. January 31, 1860. State Capital. DC: Petition to the Board of Supervisors in San Francisco, from the largest and principal property owners of the City and County of San Francisco, requesting to remove the State Capital to San Francisco, the underwriters donating a plot of ground valued $50,000 and $100,000 towards improving the same. Peder Sather is among the underwriters.

San Francisco Bulletin. April 4, 1860. Masonic Notice. DC: The funeral of Companion A. L. Tasheira, deceased, late treasurer of the Council.

San Francisco Bulletin. April 4, 1860. Mortuary Notice. DC: Death of A. L. Tasheira.

Daily Alta California. April 23, 1860. The College of California. DC: Peder Sather is elected member of the Board.

San Francisco Bulletin. September 10, 1860. The People Moving! Subtitle: Address to the People's Nominating Committees of 1858 and 1859. DC: The condition of the public affairs in San Francisco is said to be "a source of pride and gratulation to all good citizens." The underwriters "sincerely believe it can only be perpetuated by entirely ignoring all political preferences in making nominations for municipal officers." Peder Sather is among the underwriters.

San Francisco Bulletin. December 21, 1860. Section: Departure of the *Sonora* for Panama. DC: Among the principal shippers, Wells, Fargo & Co.: $227,000. B. Davidson: $144,000. Sather & Church: $75,400. Levi Strauss: $84,000.

San Francisco Bulletin. January 16, 1861. Notice: First Baptist Church.

San Francisco Bulletin. March 11, 1861. Notice: Port Society. *San Francisco Bulletin.* April 18, 1861. Board of Supervisors.

San Francisco Bulletin. April 18, 1861. Nomination for County Recorder.

Daily Alta California. April 30, 1861. Obituary. Edward W. Church.

Commercial Advertiser. April 30, 1861. Mortuary Notice. At San Francisco, April 29, Edward W. Church, of Troy, NY, aged 47 years and 3 months.

San Francisco Bulletin. May 18, 1861. Church Property.

Philadelphia Inquirer. June 20, 1861. Later from California.

San Francisco Bulletin. June 21, 1861. More of Miss Atkins' Seminary at Benicia. DC: Mary Emma Sather has received her Diploma.

San Francisco Bulletin. August 1, 1861. Section: Departure of the *Golden Age.* Among the principal shippers, Wells, Fargo & Co.: $102,000. B. Davidson: $128,000. Sather & Co.: $100,775.

San Francisco Bulletin. November 25, 1861. The National Loan.

San Francisco Bulletin. December 12, 1861. Section: Elections. DC: The Mercantile Library Association.

San Francisco Bulletin. March 1, 1862. A New Attachment Law. DC: Petition to the State Legislature "for a law to inspire confidence between buyer and seller, and afford a proper protection to both." Among the underwriters, Wells, Fargo & Co., Sather & Co., Donohoe & Ralston, and B. Davidson.

San Francisco Bulletin. September 11, 1862. Section: Departure of the *Orizaba.* DC: Principal shippers, Wells, Fargo & Co.: $187,500. Donohoe, Ralston & Co.: $148,894. Sather & Co.: $125,115.

San Francisco Bulletin. October 24, 1862. Sather & Co. Advertisement.

San Francisco Bulletin. December 11, 1862. Section: Departure of the Steamers. DC: The *Golden Age* left for Panama. Principal shippers, Donohoe, Ralson & Co.: $434,600. Wells, Fargo & Co.: $277,500. Sather & Co.: $120,000. Levi Strauss: $68,354.

San Francisco Bulletin. December 29, 1862. Fair Friends of the Orphans.

San Francisco Bulletin. February 21, 1863. Clergymen, Bankers, and Merchants pleading for the Ladies. DC: The underwriters, among them Peder Sather, asking the State Legislature on appropriation for the Ladies' Seamen's Friend Association.

San Francisco Bulletin. March 3, 1863. Internal Revenue Stamps.

New York Herald. June 6, 1863. Death of Mr. Drexel, of Philadelphia.

Philadelphia Inquirer. June 8, 1863. The late Francis M. Drexel.

San Francisco Bulletin. September 15, 1863. Sather & Co. DC: A card by Peder Sather, stating that the co-partnership with Edward W. Church terminated April 23, 1861. The business since then has been carried out by Peder Sather, on his own account.

San Francisco Bulletin. October 2, 1863. The Brigade Encampment.

San Francisco Bulletin. December 4, 1863. The Christian Commission.

San Francisco Bulletin. January 30, 1864. Sather & Co. DC: Partners: Drexel & Co., Philadelphia, George Peabody, London. Advertisement.

Daily Alta California. February 19, 1864. School Accommodation.

Sacramento Daily Union. April 16, 1864. Eastward Bound. DC: P. Sather and "daughter"on the passenger list.

San Francisco Bulletin. June 1, 1864. The Fireman's Fund Insurance Company.

San Francisco Bulletin. July 2, 1864. Sather & Co. DC: The banking house has returned to the corner of Montgomery and Commercial. Advertisement.

Illustrated New Age. Philadelphia, July 6, 1864. Title: United States Christian Commission.

San Francisco Bulletin. July 6, 1864. Sather & Church.

Sacramento Daily Union. August 4, 1864. United States Christian Commission. DC: Article referring a dispatch from the Commission Headquarters in Washington, DC, to Peder Sather: "You have nobly seconded our efforts."

San Francisco Bulletin. August 18, 1864. Marine and War Risks, the California Insurance Company. DC: Among the directors, Peder Sather and Samuel Merritt. Advertisement.

Daily Alta California. October 6, 1864. Marine and Fire Insurance.The California Insurance Company. DC: Among the directors, Peder Sather, Charles F. Lott and Samuel Merritt. Advertisement.

New York Times. October 14, 1864. Christian Commission Fair, San Francisco.

San Francisco Bulletin. November 23, 1864. Enthusiastic Christian Commission Meeting.

Sacramento Daily Union. November 29, 1864. Section: Arrival of the *Constitution.* DC: Peder Sather and "two daughters" have returned from New York.

San Francisco Bulletin. December 4, 1864. The Christian Commission.

San Francisco Bulletin. January 5, 1865. Benevolent Contributions.

San Francisco Bulletin. January 9, 1865. Christian Commission Meeting and Contributions.

San Francisco Chronicle. January 16, 1865. The Mutual Insurance Company. Advertisement.

San Francisco Bulletin. February 6, 1865. Letter from "Verbum Sat."

San Francisco Evening Bulletin. February 6, 1865. The Financial Agent of the Christian Commission Sitting in Judgment on Parlor Theatricals.

San Francisco Evening Bulletin. February 7, 1865. The Parlor Theatricals and Christian Commission Question.

San Francisco Evening Bulletin. February 8, 1865. The Christian Commission and the Parlor Theatricals.

San Francisco Evening Bulletin. February 9, 1865. The Christian Commission and the Parlor Theatricals Again.

San Francisco Morning Call. February 10, 1865. The Christian Commission and the Drama.

Boston Recorder. February 10, 1865. Section: Religious Intelligence. Subtitle: The California Sabbath Convention. DC: A State Sabbath Society is organized, with Peder Sather as treasurer.

San Francisco Morning Call. February 11, 1865. The Christian Commission.

San Francisco Bulletin. February 16, 1865. The Parlor Theatrical Question Again.

San Francisco Bulletin. February 18, 1865. The Christian Commission Continued.

San Francisco Bulletin. February 21, 1865. Incomes in San Francisco.

San Francisco Bulletin. February 25, 1865. The Good of Parlor Theatricals to Our Wounded Soldiers.

New Orleans Times. March 3, 1865. Christian Commission Fair, San Francisco; President Lincoln.

New Orleans Times. March 11, 1865. Christian Commission Fair, San Francisco; President Lincoln.

The Californian. March 18, 1865. An Unbiased Criticism—by Mark Twain. *San Francisco Bulletin.* April 26, 1865. Insurance Company Election.

San Francisco Bulletin. April 26, 1865. Partition of Property.

Daily Alta California. May 11, 1865. Subscribers to the Art Union. DC: Josephine and Mary Emma Sather are members of the Art Union.

San Francisco Bulletin. May 11, 1865. Proceedings of the Annual Meeting of the Chamber of Commerce.

Friend. August 1, 1865. Sanitary Commission.

San Francisco Bulletin. August 12, 1865. Independent Call for Reorganization of the Union Party.

San Francisco Bulletin. September 18, 1865. Section: Sailing of the *Colorado.* DC: Among the principal shippers, Bank of California: $676,429. Donohoe, Kelly & Co.: $271,500. Sather & Co.: $215,000.

San Francisco Bulletin. October 10, 1865. San Francisco Baptist Association.

Daily Alta California. October 19, 1865. Rich Men of Alameda County.

San Francisco Bulletin. November 3, 1865. Valuable Real Estate in Alameda for Sale. DC: Alameda Park Hotel, a few minutes' walk from the elegant residences of Messrs. Sather, Farwell, and Cohen.

San Francisco Bulletin. January 25, 1866. Mass Meeting. The California Branch of the American Freedmen's Aid and Union Commission. DC: Peder Sather, treasurer.

San Francisco Bulletin. January 27, 1866. The Californian Branch of the American Freedman's Aid and Union Commission.

Commercial Advertiser. May 5, 1866. Death Notice. DC: Death of Letitia Church.

San Francisco Bulletin. August 29, 1866. Montgomery Street Property.

Sacramento Daily Union. August 31, 1866. Passengers for the East. DC: Peder Sather and Caroline Sather on the passenger list.

San Francisco Bulletin. September 1, 1866. Internal Revenue Returns of Income.

Sacramento Daily Union. September 6, 1866. Incomes in San Francisco.

New York Times. November 6, 1866. Reverend Granville S. Abbott.

San Francisco Bulletin. November 24, 1866. Section: Arrival of the *Golden City.* DC: Peder Sather and "daughter" arrive from New York.

San Francisco Bulletin. December 15, 1866. Mortuary Notice: Peder Sather Jr.

Harper's New Monthly Magazine. March 1, 1867. A. T. Stewart.

San Francisco Bulletin. April 5, 1867. The Southern Relief Meeting.

San Francisco Bulletin. June 8, 1867. Alameda Seminary. DC: The seminary is Formerly known as the Oak Grove Institute, but since then been occupied as a summer residence by Peder Sather, Esq.

Daily Alta California. July 7, 1867. Fireman's Fund Insurance Company. DC: Peder Sather and William Ralston are among the directors. Advertisement.

Elevator. December 27, 1867. Anniversary of Emancipation.

San Francisco Bulletin. April 23, 1868. Meeting of the Society for the Prevention of Cruelty to Animals. DC: Peder Sather is among the incorporators.

Salt Lake Daily Telegraph. May 30, 1868. Bull in a Flower Garden.

Chicago Republican. August 23, 1868. Letter from Mark Twain.

Daily Alta California. October 6, 1868. Section: Eastward Bound. The Pacific steamship *Colorado* leaves for Panama today. DC: Peder Sather and "wife and three daughters" are on the passenger list.

Anglo-American Times. London, February 13, 1869. Section: Americans registered in Paris. DC: From February 5 to February 12, Mr. P. Sather, San Francisco.

Anglo-American Times. London, February 20, 1869. Section: Americans Registered in Paris. DC: At Drexel, Harjes & Co., No. 3 Rue de Scribe, Paris: Mr. and Mrs. P. Sather, San Francisco.

Anglo-American Times. London, April 24, 1869. Section: Americans registered in Naples. DC: P. Sather and family, San Francisco.

Anglo-American Times. London, June 26, 1969. Section: Americans registered in Dresden. DC: Up to June 22, 1869: Mr. P. Sather.

Anglo-American Times. London, August 28, 1869. Section: Americans Registered in Paris. DC: At Drexel, Harjes & Co. Paris, for the week ending August 19: Mr. P. Sather and family, San Francisco.

Anglo-American Times. London, October 9, 1869. Notice: Mr. Anthony Drexel. DC: Anthony Drexel, the great Philadelphia banker, returns after a few months in Europe.

Anglo-American Times. London, October 30, 1869. Section: Americans registered in Paris. DC: At Drexel, Harjes & Co. for the week ending October 26: Mr. P. Sather and family, San Francisco.

San Francisco Bulletin. January 13, 1870. Fireman's Fund Insurance Company.

San Francisco Bulletin. March 8, 1870. Sather & Co., bankers and dealers. DC: Partners: Drexel, Winthrop & Co., New York. Advertisement.

New York Herald. April 28, 1870. Section: Arrivals. Subtitle: The *SS Cimbria* arrived yesterday from Le Havre and Hamburg. DC: Peder Sather and "daughters" on the passenger list.

New York Herald. July 6, 1870. Obituary. Death of a New York Banker. DC: Luther S. Lawrence is dead.

New York Herald. July 9, 1870. Tribute to the Late Luther S. Lawrence.

San Francisco Bulletin. July 12, 1870. From the National Capital.

Public Ledger. August 15, 1870. Section: Financial, Dividends etc. DC: Co-operation between Drexel, Harjes & Co., Paris, Drexel & Winthrop, New York, Sather & Co., San Francisco, and Drexel & Co., Philadelphia.

California Farmer and Journal of Useful Sciences. November 17, 1870. Where's Alameda? DC: The large landholders in Alameda are Peder Sather and Alfred A. Cohen.

California Academy of Science. January 2, 1872. Meeting Report.

San Francisco Bulletin. January 24, 1872. The Banquet. Ovation for the Japanese.

Trenton State Gazette. April 19, 1872. Great Mass Meeting at Cooper Institute in New York to Endorse President Grant. DC: Among those in attendance, Peter Cooper, Anthony J. Drexel, George Childs and William H. Vanderbilt.

San Francisco Bulletin. May 25, 1872. Into Relief Fund.

Daily Alta California. August 22, 1872. The Solid Men.

New York Times. September 20, 1872. Obituary. Rev. Francis Vinton, of Trinity.

California Academy of Science. November 4, 1872. Meeting Report.

New York Times. January 9, 1873. Letter from the Secretary of War.

San Francisco Bulletin. May 15, 1873. Section: Legislative.

New York Herald Tribune. May 17, 1873. Under the Tribune's Roof: Article of No. 164 Nassau Street.

Jersey Journal. July 17, 1873. Veterans. DC: Colonel E. of The First Battalion held a meeting last evening. Sergeant Tasheira will probably be chosen Lieutenant at the next meeting.

San Francisco Bulletin. August 7, 1873. San Francisco Extends a Helping Hand to Portland.

San Francisco Daily Morning Call. October 24, 1873. Marriage. DC: Mr. Emile Bruguiere and Miss Josephine Sather, in Oakland.

San Francisco Bulletin. January 14, 1874. Finance and Trade.

San Francisco Bulletin. March 31, 1874. Mortuary Notice. DC: Caroline E. Sather dead.

San Francisco Bulletin. April 1, 1874. Section: Oakland Matters. The Death of Miss Sather.

San Francisco Bulletin. April 9, 1874. Second Street Cut Damages.

New York Herald. May 4, 1874. Obituary. Charles Farrar.

San Francisco Bulletin. May 20, 1874. California Insurance Company. DC: Directors, Samuel Merritt, P. Sather.

Oakland Daily Tribune. June 24, 1874. Liquor Sale: Petition to the Board of Supervisors of Alameda County.

San Francisco Bulletin. October 14, 1874. Section: Notable Religious Event. Subtitle: Annual Meeting of the San Francisco Baptist Association.

Daily Graphic. August 6, 1875. The Season at Saratoga. DC: William "Commodore" Vanderbilt and William Turnbull at the United States Hotel, playing card for little and nothing, being to rich to bet.

San Francisco Bulletin. August 27, 1875. The Coin Panic: Scenes on California Street To-day. Subtitle: Peder Sather's House.

Oakland Tribune. October 18, 1875. Remaining Letters. DC: Remaining Letters for Mary Emma Sather.

Sacramento Daily Union. November 30, 1875. Pacific Items. DC: Comments on Peder Sather's orchard in Alameda.

Oakland Tribune. April 18, 1876. Petition from P. Sather.

Oakland Tribune. May 2, 1876. Petition from P. Sather.

Sacramento Daily Union. May 13, 1876. Baptist State Convention. DC: Peder Sather elected member of the Board of Missions.

Daily Alta California. June 16, 1876. Forthcoming Fourth of July Celebrations. DC: On the committee, Leland Stanford and Peder Sather.

Oakland Tribune. July 25, 1876. Petition from Pedar Sather.

San Francisco Bulletin. March 1, 1877. A Second Defalcation.

Oakland Daily Evening Tribune. March 3, 1877. Section: Real Estate. DC: Henry C. Lee to Pedar Sather.

San Francisco Bulletin. June 8, 1877. Ancient and Modern Universities.

San Francisco Bulletin. September 28, 1877. Mysterious Check Transactions.

San Francisco Chronicle. September 28, 1877. Further Inquiry.

Cincinnati Daily Gazette. October 4, 1877. A Stock Operator Commits Forgeries.

San Francisco Bulletin. October 4, 1877. Cooper the Forger.

New York Times. February 3, 1878. Life's Contrasts.

San Francisco Bulletin. May 1, 1879. An Important Banking Case.

San Francisco Bulletin. September 30, 1879. Notorious Forger. Subtitle: Cooper Arrested in London.

San Francisco Bulletin. March 10, 1880. Golden Gate Park Relief Fund.

San Francisco Bulletin. April 19, 1880. Grand Commandery Knights Templar. DC: Charles F. Lott.

San Francisco Bulletin. June 14, 1880. Passengers Passing through Omaha. DC: Peder Sather and wife on the passenger list.

Aftenposten. May 10, 1881. Mortuary Notice. DC: Andreas Christian Johan Encke.

San Francisco Bulletin. June 27, 1881. Attempt to Rob Sather & Co.'s Bank Vault.

New York Times. July 8, 1881. A Burglar's Outfit.

San Francisco Bulletin. October 4, 1881. Hope's Release.

San Francisco Bulletin. October 7, 1881. The Sather Bank Burglary. Trial of Jimmy Hope.

New York Herald October 8, 1881. Meeting of the Trustees of the Peabody Educational Fund. DC: Meeting at the Fifth Avenue Hotel Yesterday. Present: President, Robert Winthrop. Anthony Drexel, and ex-President Grant.

San Francisco Bulletin. November 1, 1881. Died. DC: Death of Mrs. Peder Sather at the Fifth Avenue Hotel, New York.

San Francisco Bulletin. November 10, 1881. Mortuary Notice. DC: The Death of Sarah Sather.

Sacramento Daily Union. November 7, 1881. Omaha, November 5th. DC: Peder Sather on the passenger list.

Daily Alta California. November 30, 1881. Recollections. DC: Peder Sather, William Turnbull, and Ole Bull.

San Francisco Bulletin. March 25, 1882. Life of the Gatherer.

San Francisco Morning Call. November 27, 1882. Marriage. DC: Jane K. Reed marries Peder Sather.

New York Times. February 14, 1883. Imprisoned with the Insane.

New York Times. July 31, 1883. The Rich Men of California.

Daily Alta California. May 19, 1884. The Barker Party at Oakland. DC: Among the 300 guests Samuel Merritt, Mr. and Mrs. Sather.

Daily Alta California. October 24, 1884. Speer Riddell Dead. Subtitle: Seized with a Fatal Fit at the Baldwin Theatre Last Evening.

Daily Alta California. November 16, 1884. Recollections of a Pleasant Social Party.

San Francisco Bulletin. January 15, 1885. Annual Meeting. Subtitle: Election of Officers by the Society for Prevention of Cruelty to Children. DC: Levi Strauss, Joseph Donohoe and Peder Sather elected members of the Board of Directors.

Daily Commercial News. January 21, 1885. California Insurance Company. DC: P. Sather, treasurer.

Salt Lake Tribune. February 19, 1885. A Heavy Failure at the Bay.

San Francisco Bulletin. May 29, 1885. Real Estate Transactions Record.

Daily Times. New Brunswick, June 23, 1885. General Grant and George Childs.

New York Times. July 4, 1885. Obituary. Hans Rees.

New York Tribune. July 4, 1885. Obituary. Hans Rees.

New York Herald. July 5, 1885. Obituary. Hans Rees, Retired Leather Merchant.

San Francisco Chronicle. July 28, 1885. Memorial Day, Oakland.

San Francisco Chronicle. August 16, 1885. Public Sale.

San Francisco Chronicle. March 2, 1886. High Tea.

New York Times. October 26, 1886. Mrs. A. T. Stewart Dead.

Daily Inter Ocean. November 2, 1886. Cornelia M. Stewart.

Cincinnati Commercial Tribune. November 22, 1886. Mr. George Childs.

Oakland Tribune. December 28, 1886. A Dying Millionaire. Subtitle: Pedar Sather, the Banker, at Death's Door: His Property Interest in Alameda County; The Cause of His Sickness.

San Francisco Bulletin. December 28, 1886. Pedar Sather Dying.

Boston Daily Globe. December 29, 1886. Peder Sather, the Well-Known Capitalist, Dead.

Evening Star. Washington DC, December 29, 1886. Death of a San Francisco Banker.

Los Angeles Herald. December 29, 1886. Pedar Sather Dead.

Oakland Tribune. December 29, 1886. The Dead Banker. Subtitle: Death of Pedar Sather Yesterday Afternoon: Reminiscences of the Panic of 1857; Mr. Sather's Wealth and Character; The Funeral To-morrow.

San Francisco Bulletin. December 29, 1886. Death of Peder Sather.

San Francisco Bulletin. December 29, 1886. Finance and Trade.

San Francisco Call. December 29, 1886. Death of Peder Sather.

San Francisco Chronicle. December 29, 1886. Death of Peder Sather.

San Jose Mercury News December 29, 1886. Death of P. Sather.

Trenton Evening Times. Trenton, NJ, December 29, 1886. Pedar Sather, the Well-Known Capitalist dead.

Watertown Daily Times. Watertown, NY, December 29, 1886. Well-Known Banker Dead.

Boston Journal. December 30, 1886. Mr. Pedar Sather Dead.

Daily Inter Ocean. Chicago, December 30, 1886. Peder Sather, Deceased.

Dallas Morning News. Dallas, December 30, 1886. Death of a Well-Known Capitalist.

Decatur Daily Republican. Decatur, IL, December 30, 1886. Sather, a Well-Known Capitalist, Is Dead.

Elyria Daily Telephone. Elyria, OH, December 30, 1886. Pedar Sather Died after Long Illness.

Evansville Courier and Press. Evansville, IN, December 30 1886. Pedar Sather Dead.

Morning Oregonian. Portland, December 30, 1886. Prominent Banker Dead.

Newark Daily Advocat. Newark, OH, December 30, 1886. Death of a California Capitalist.

New York Herald. December 30, 1886. Pedar Sather.

New York Tribune. December 30, 1886. Death of Pedar Sather.

Philadelphia Inquirer. Philadelphia, December 30. Pedar Sather Dead.

Plain Dealer. Cleveland, December 30, 1886. Pedar Sather Dead.

Patriot. Harrison, PA, December 30, 1886. Pedar Sather Dead.

San Diego Union. December 30, 1886. Well-Known Banker Dead.

San Francisco Bulletin. December 30, 1886. The Deceased Banker.

The News. Frederick, MD, December 30, 1886. Pedar Sather, the Well-Known Banker, Dead.

Wisconsin State Journal. Madison, December 31, 1886. Pedar Sather, Deceased.

Petersburg Pike County Democrat. Petersburg, IN, January 7, 1887. Peder Sather Dead.

San Francisco Bulletin. January 27, 1887. Peder Sather's Will.

San Jose Mercury News. January 28, 1887. A Millionaire's Will: How Pedro Sather the Banker Disposed of His Will.

San Francisco Bulletin. April 18, 1887. The Sather Banking Company. Advertisement.

Daily Alta California. September 14, 1887. Peder Sather and His Estate.

San Francisco Chronicle. November 10, 1887. Letters from the Treasurer of the United States, 1887. First Comptroller's Accounts.

Daily Alta California. May 13, 1888. Mrs. Julia Ward Howe at the Residence of Mrs. Peder Sather.

San Francisco Bulletin. May 17, 1888. Assignment of an Interest in the Sather Estate. DC: Petrine Encke.

Daily Alta California. June 12, 1888. Mary Emma Sather.

Daily Alta California. July 25, 1888. Mrs. Pedar Sather Starts for Alaska.

New York Herald. September 8, 1888. Obituary. William Turnbull Dead.

New York Herald. September 24, 1888. Mortuary Notice. DC: Death of Mary J. Farrar. Funeral in Pepperell, Massachusetts.

Oakland Tribune. February 15, 1889. A Temperance Worker. Subtitle: Mrs. Dow Is Spending a Few Weeks at Mrs. Sather's.

San Francisco Bulletin. August 15, 1889. Sale of a Portion of the Estate of Peter Sather.

San Francisco Bulletin. January 6, 1890. Statement of the Sather Banking Company.

Daily Alta California. January 9, 1890. Obituary. Mr. James A. Thompson. DC: Secretary of the Sather bank.

San Francisco Chronicle. October 5, 1890. Ten Years' San Francisco Dead.

San Francisco Chronicle. October 6, 1890. Mrs. Sather in Paris.

Oakland Tribune. October 18, 1890. Mrs. Sather Sailed for New York.

Oakland Tribune. October 23, 1890. Mrs. Sather Expected to Arrive in Three Weeks.

San Francisco Chronicle. October 27, 1890. Mrs. Pedar Sather Will Return from Europe.

San Francisco Chronicle. November 10, 1890. Mrs. Pedar Sather Arrived in New York.

Oakland Tribune. November 24, 1890. Mrs. Pedar Sather Will Soon Be Home from Europe.

San Francisco Chronicle. December 8, 1890. Mrs. Sather Left New York Last Tuesday.

Oakland Tribune. December 15, 1890. Mrs. Sather Has Returned from a Trip to Europe.

Philadelphia Inquirer. December 19, 1890. Mortuary Notice. DC: Mary Emma Sather Died December 17th. Funeral today at Woodland Cemetery, Philadelphia.

Daily Alta California. December 20, 1890. Mary Emma Sather.

Oakland Tribune. December 20, 1890. An Heiress in an Asylum.

Morning Call. December 31, 1890. Obituary. Henry C. Lee.

San Francisco Chronicle. December 31, 1890. Deaths. Henry C. Lee Dead.

Oakland Tribune. January 24, 1891. Mrs. Pedar Sather.

San Francisco Bulletin. April 24, 1891. 38 Residence Lots. Advertisement.

San Francisco Bulletin. September 24, 1891. Estate of Peder Sather.

San Francisco Chronicle. September 24, 1891. Suit Commenced Yesterday.

San Francisco Bulletin. October 27, 1891. Fabiola Hospital Charity Ball.

San Francisco Bulletin. October 27, 1891. Mrs. Sather Will Return from Europe.

Chicago Tribune. November 28, 1891. Death of Mrs. Anthony J. Drexel.

San Francisco Bulletin. December 4, 1891. Across the Bay.

Chicago Tribune. December 18, 1891. Dedication of the Institute.

Chicago Tribune. December 19, 1891. Childs's Collection.

Oakland Tribune. January 16, 1892. An Elaborate Breakfast.

San Francisco Chronicle. April 22, 1892. Mrs. Sather's Narrow Escape.

Worcester Daily Spy. November 7, 1892. Two Grand Old Men.

Hornellsville Weekly Tribune. November 11, 1892. Two Grand Old Men.

San Francisco Chronicle. December 30, 1892. Peder Sather Trustees.

San Francisco Chronicle. May 21, 1893. The Haunted House.

New York Times. July 1, 1893. Anthony J. Drexel Is Dead.

San Francisco Chronicle. July 1, 1893. Anthony Drexel.

Inter Ocean. July 2, 1893. Sorrow Deep: Friends of A. J. Drexel Pay Him Tribute.

San Francisco Chronicle. July 19, 1893. Drexel's Body Arrives.

Hawaiian Gazette. July 25, 1893. James A. Thompson.

San Francisco Chronicle. September 1, 1893. 39 Lots in the Sather Tract. Advertisement.

San Francisco Chronicle. October 30, 1893. Mrs. Pedar Sather Has Returned.

San Francisco Chronicle. December 31, 1893. The Sather Bank.

Chicago Tribune. January 21, 1894. In Memory of Anthony J. Drexel.

New York Times. February 4, 1894. Mourned by a Whole Nation. Subtitle: The Death of George Childs a Bereavement to Humanity.

Chicago Tribune. February 7, 1894. George W. Childs at rest.

Atlanta Constitution. February 24, 1894. George W. Childs.

San Francisco Chronicle. June 2, 1895. Mrs. Pedar Sather.

San Francisco Chronicle. June 21, 1895. Mrs. Pedar Sather.

Oakland Tribune. June 22, 1895. Mrs. Sather Going East.

Oakland Tribune. September 14, 1895. Mrs. Pedar Sather Returned from the East.

San Francisco Call. March 11, 1896. The Sather Bank.

Oakland Tribune. April 28, 1896. Mrs. Pedar Sather.

Oakland Tribune. June 8, 1896. An International Row: A Chinese-Japanese Conflict in Mrs. Pedar Sather's Kitchen.

San Francisco Call. July 21, 1896. Mrs. Pedar Sather at the Fifth Avenue Hotel in New York.

Oakland Tribune. August 3, 1896. The Sather Ranch on San Pablo Creek, Contra Costa County.

Oakland Tribune. November 17, 1896. Mrs. Sather Suspicious.

San Francisco Chronicle. April 11, 1897. The First Schoolhouse.

Brooklyn Daily Eagle. May 14, 1897. Obituary. Charles Farrar Lawrence. DC: Brother of Luther S. Lawrence.

Idaho Statesman. November 6, 1897. More National Banks.

San Francisco Call. November 6, 1897. The Sather Concern to Become the San Francisco National Bank.

San Francisco Call. November 6, 1897. Two Banks Change Names. DC: Subtitle: The Sather Bank to Become San Francisco National Bank. DC: The bank will retain its present capitalization, which is 500,000, the largest capital of any bank west of New York, except the First National Bank of Chicago, whose fortunes are presided over by Lyman Gage, the Secretary of the Treasury.

New York Times. November 7, 1897. The Sather Banking Company.

Oakland Tribune. March 12, 1898. Mrs. Sather.

San Francisco Chronicle. March 27, 1898. One of the Very Rare Luncheons.

Oakland Enquirer. June 28, 1898. Section: Sather Station. DC: Sather Railway Station, located at High Street and San Leandro Street in Oakland.

Mountain Democrat. Placerville, CA, October 15, 1898. The Sather Property. DC: Mound Street, Alameda.

Wall Street Daily News. February 3, 1899. Benjamin Haxtun Is Dead.

Oakland Tribune. April 27, 1899. Section: Alameda News. A Familiar Landmark.

Los Angeles Herald. May 10, 1899. Bought a Farm. DC: Mrs. Josephine Wallace has purchased Sather Farm, near San Leandro, in Alameda County. The Sather Farm is one of the best-known properties in the State. Besides being exceedingly fertile, it is beautifully situated near the foothills. It consists of about 300 acres. The price is said to be about $1,000,000.

San Francisco Chronicle. June 3, 1899. Dingee Sues Mrs. Sather.

Oakland Tribune. November 28, 1899. Mrs. Sather in Ashland, Oregon.

Brooklyn Daily Eagle. February 23, 1900. Obituary. Dr. James L. Watson.

San Francisco Chronicle. September 30, 1900. Emile Bruguiere Is dead.

Los Angeles Herald. October 10, 1900. Endowment of a Generous Woman.

San Francisco Call. October 10, 1900. Munificent Donations to State University. DC: Jane K. Sather gives the following to the establishment and maintenance of a Chair of Classical Literature: Shares from Fireman's Fund Insurance Company, San Francisco National Bank and real estates in Alameda and Oakland.

San Francisco Chronicle. October 27, 1900. Gift of $100,000 to the University of California.

Times Picayune. October 27, 1900. Mrs. Jane Krom Sather of Oakland.

San Jose Mercury News. October 29, 1900. Generous Woman Makes Another Gift.

Philadelphia Inquirer. October 30, 1900. Jersey Jottings.

San Francisco Chronicle. November 6, 1900. Handsome Gift for California.

San Jose Mercury News. November 6, 1900. Third Big Gift.

San Jose Mercury News. November 12, 1900. Mrs. Jane K. Sather.
New York Times. April 6, 1901. University of California at Berkeley.
Oakland Tribune. April 20, 1901. Ebell Society.
San Jose Mercury News. April 26, 1901. Human Bones Pave Roadway.
Oakland Tribune. September 14, 1901. Mrs. Sather Has Returned from Los Gatos.
San Francisco Chronicle. March 6, 1902. Emma Nevada and Pablo Casals.
San Francisco Chronicle. March 17, 1902. The Tea at the Residence of Mrs. William
    E. Sharon.
Oakland Tribune. August 16, 1902. Mrs. Jane K. Sather.
Oakland Tribune. September 13, 1902. A Lady of the Time of Louis XIV.
San Francisco Chronicle. December 15, 1902. Jane K. Sather.
Oakland Tribune. January 5, 1903. Emile Bruguiere and Josephine Sather.
San Francisco Chronicle. January 5, 1903. Dr. Pedar Sather Bruguiere.
Oakland Tribune. March 14, 1903. Reuben Hawk Married in Los Angeles.
Oakland Tribune. May 7, 1903. Suit Sather Tract.
San Francisco Chronicle. May 14, 1903. President Roosevelt Visits Berkeley.
Oakland Tribune. September 12, 1903. Mrs. Pedar Sather Spoke Out in Meeting.
Oakland Tribune. September 26, 1903. Mrs. Sather, Active Patron of Art and
    Learning.
Oakland Tribune. October 13, 1903. At the Home of Mrs. Pedar Sather.
San Francisco Chronicle. February 8, 1905. Sather Tract.
New York Times. June 28, 1905. Sad Isolation of the Rich.
Oakland Tribune. August 30, 1905. Mrs. Jane Sather Would Not Answer.
Oakland Tribune. September 2, 1905. Poor Mrs. Sather.
Oakland Tribune. October 30, 1905. Cosmos Club.
Oakland Tribune. November 16, 1905. Old Mortgage Paid at Last.
Wall Street Daily News. October 3, 1906. William E. Sharon.
Oakland Tribune. October 9, 1907. Owned Much Land.
San Francisco Chronicle. March 30, 1908. 200 Lots in Alameda.
Oakland Tribune. June 10, 1908. Oak Grove Institute, Alameda.
Cedar Rapids Evening Gazette. October 1, 1909. Here's Another "Teddy" in Iowa.
    DC: Theodore Tasheira Roosevelt is said to be a distant relative to Theodore
    Roosevelt, the former president.
San Francisco Chronicle. October 17, 1909. Drexel, Sather & Church.
Grand Forks Herald. April 16, 1910. Nude Figures Must Go.
San Francisco Call. July 8, 1910. Stock Holders Vote for a Big Bank Merger. DC: San
    Francisco National Bank, formerly Sather Banking Company, merges with the
    Bank of California.
New York Times. August 4, 1910. Norman I. Rees.
Oakland Tribune. February 13, 1911. University of California Again Beneficiary.
San Francisco Chronicle. February 18, 1911. Local Ferry Trains to Sather and Melrose.
Oakland Tribune. December 13, 1911. Mrs. Sather's Funeral To-morrow. Subtitle:
    Many Mourn Passing of Noted Benefactress; Will Present to Courts Today.
San Francisco Chronicle. December 13, 1911. Mrs. Jane Sather Called by Death.

San Jose Mercury News. December 13, 1911. Leaves Great Fortune to State University Berkeley.

San Francisco Chronicle. December 14, 1911. Funeral to Be Held Today.

San Francisco Chronicle. December 15, 1911. Funeral of Mrs. Sather Is Held.

Oakland Tribune. December 17, 1911. Mr. Sather's Integrity.

Oakland Tribune. December 28, 1911. Rumored Contest of Mrs. Sather's will.

San Francisco Call. December 28, 1911. Contest of Jane K. Sather's Will.

San Francisco Chronicle. December 28, 1911. Arrives Quietly without Telling New York of Her Departure.

San Francisco Call. January 3, 1912. Coming of Heirs from East.

New York Times. February 25, 1912. Sather Tower.

Oakland Tribune. December 20, 1912. Section: Real Estate. DC: Washington/Fourteenth Street sold.

Oakland Tribune. April 7, 1913. Sather Homestead to Be Razed to Aid Progress.

Oakland Tribune. June 2, 1913. Lakeshore Highlands.

Idaho Statesman. April 4, 1914. Attempt to Break Will.

Philadelphia Inquirer. April 5, 1914. Heirs Fight Gifts to the University.

Oakland Tribune. April 7, 1914. Mrs. Bruguiere's UC Suit.

Aftenposten. April 30, 1914. Dødsfall (Mortuary Notice). Ingeniør Christian Encke er død (Engineer Christian Encke is dead).

New York Times. August 6, 1914. Castlewood. DC: Josephine Sather Bruguiere's Summer Residence.

Fort Worth Star Telegram. September 14, 1914. Sather Campanile.

Duluth News Tribune. November 28, 1914. Campanile Designed to Resist Earthquakes.

Salt Lake Telegram. August 20, 1915. 400 of 423 Passengers Accounted For.

Washington Post. August 21, 1915. Daughter-in-Law Gets News.

Oakland Tribune. August 29, 1915. Incidents in Bruguiere Family History.

Logansport Pharos Reporter. Indiana, September 1, 1915. Josephine S. Bruguiere.

Charlotte Observer. September 26, 1915. Mrs. Bruguiere's Body Found.

Oakland Tribune. April 21, 1916. Sather Funds.

Aftenposten. July 8, 1916. Sæthertårnet (Sather Tower).

Anaconda Standard. October 1, 1917. Huge Chimes Placed in Position. Subtitle: University of California to Have Magnificent Set.

San Francisco Chronicle. November 24, 1918. Rincon Hill.

San Francisco Chronicle. May 25, 1919. Mysterious Figure.

San Francisco Chronicle. August 3, 1919. San Franciscan, 93, Veteran of '49, Dies. DC: James S. Hutchinson.

Oakland Tribune. February 16, 1921. The Campanile.

Oakland Tribune. December 31, 1922. Seems to Be Inexact. DC: Josephine and Emile Bruguiere.

Oakland Tribune. March 11, 1925. Mortuary notice. DC: Mrs. Harriet J. Lee, Berkeley, March 9, 1925. Mrs. Lee was a native of Bridgeport, CT, and widow of the late Henry C. Lee.

Aftenposten. February 23, 1926. Petrine Franzine Encke.

Aftenposten. August 14, 1928. Dødsfall (Mortuary Notice). DC: Petrine Franzine Encke er død (Petrine Franzine Encke is dead).

Oakland Tribune. August 23, 1932. Pedar Sather Bruguiere. DC: Cancer Institute, San Francisco.

Oakland Tribune. April 14, 1935. Pioneers in Human Work.

Oakland Tribune. October 11, 1940. UC Accepts Gifts.

Oakland Tribune. October 27, 1940. Memoirs of a Pioneer.

Oakland Tribune. November 12, 1944. A Word of A. C. Dietz.

Aftenposten. March 17, 1947. Dødsfall (Mortuary Notice). DC: Lege Peter Encke er død (Peter Encke, physician, is dead).

Newport Daily News. January 21, 1948. Louis Sather Bruguiere Dies.

San Francisco Chronicle. February 1, 1950. The Capture of Bandit Jimmy Hope.

Bergens Tidende. December 9, 1957. Sæthers minnetårn ved California Universitet. Amerikabrev frå Hans Aarnes (Sather Memory Tower at California University). Letter from America, by Hans Aarnes.

Oakland Tribune. August 31, 1958. Mrs. Sather and Sather Gate.

Oakland Tribune. May 16, 1965. The Sathers of Oakland.

Vallejo Times Herald. March 10, 1974. Another Old One.

Vallejo Times Herald. March 10, 1974. Trondheim, Vallejo's Sister City.

Nordmanns-Forbundet no. 2, 1975. "Sather Gate." L. Carsten Hatlen.

Glåmdalen. December 18, 1999. I skyggen av Sather Gate (In the Shadow of Sather Gate). By Thor Martinsen.

San Francisco Chronicle. September 4, 2002. Cal's Bells.

UC Berkeley News. May 7, 2003. Sather Gate.

San Francisco Chronicle. December 10, 2007. Sather Gate.

Alameda Sun. March 14, 2008. Sather Mound.

New York Times. April 15, 2008. How Epidemics Helped Shape the Modern Metropolis. By John Noble Wilford.

Berkeley Daily Planet. October 2, 2008. Sather Gate.

ARCHIVES

Aftenposten Arkiv, 1860–Present: www.aftenposten.no/arkivet.

Ancestry: http://home.ancestry.com.

Arkivverket: www.arkivverket.no.

Bancroft Library, University of California, Berkeley.

Brooklyn Daily Eagle, 1841–1902: http://eagle.brooklynpubliclibrary.org.

Brooklyn Historical Society: www.brooklynhistory.org.

Byarkivet, Oslo kommune.

California Bound: Passengers Lists for California, 1848–73: www.sfgenealogy.com/californiabound.

California Digital Newspapers Collection: http://cdnc.ucr.edu/cdnc.

California Historical Society, North Baker Research Library, San Francisco.
California State Library, History Room, Sacramento.
Calisphere, University of California, Berkeley: www.calisphere.universityofcalifornia .edu.
Doe Library, University of California, Berkeley.
Drexel Collection, Drexel University, Philadelphia.
Family Search: https://familysearch.org.
Fold3, Civil War Service Records: www.fold3.com/category_19.
Fold3, History and Genealogy Archives Plus: http://ebscohost.com/archives /history-genealogy/fold3-history-and-genealogy-plus.
Fold3, U.S. City Directories, www.fold3.com/page/122_city_directories.
Genealogy Bank: www.genealogybank.com.
Google Books: http://books.google.com.
Hathi Trust Digital Library: www.hathitrust.org.
Herb Caen Magazines and Newspapers Center, San Francisco Public Library.
History Center, San Francisco Public Library.
Immigrant Ships Transcribers' Guild: www.immigrantships.net.
Internet Archive: http://archive.org.
John Muir Collection, University of the Pacific, Stockton, CA.
Library of Congress, Chronicling America: http://chroniclingamerica.loc.gov.
Maritime Heritage Project: www.maritimeheritage.org.
Michigan Digitization Project: www.lib.umich.edu/michigan-digitization-project.
Mid-Manhattan Picture Collection, New York Public Library, New York.
Nasjonalbiblioteket, Håndskriftsamlingen, Oslo.
Newspaper Archives: http://newspaperarchive.com.
New York Public Library Digital Gallery: http://digitalgallery.nypl.org/nypldigital /index.cfm.
New York Times Article Archive, 1851–present: www.nytimes.com/ref/membercenter /nytarchive.html.
Oakland History Room, Oakland Public Library, Oakland.
Online Archive of California: www.oac.cdlib.org.
Patricia D. Klingenstein Library, New York Historical Society.
Preservation Park Museum, Oakland.
Project Gutenberg: www.gutenberg.org.
Riksarkivet, Oslo.
San Francisco Historical Society, North Baker Research Library, San Francisco.
San Francisco Genealogy: www.sfgenealogy.com.
San Francisco Museum and Historical Society.
Ships' Lists: www.theshipslist.com/ships/passengerlists.
Society of Californian Pioneers: www.californiapioneers.org.
T. W. Norris Collection, Bancroft Library, University of California, Berkeley.
Virtual Museum of the City of San Francisco: www.sfmuseum.org.
Wells Fargo Museum. Montgomery Street, San Francisco.

This section has several subsections, in the following order: Bank Notes; Biographical Sketches; Letters; Passenger and Ships' Lists, 1832–70; Miscellaneous Archival Items

Bank Notes

Check. Drexel, Sather & Church, June 15, 1854. T. W. Norris Collection, Bancroft Library, University of California, Berkeley.

Check. Drexel, Sather & Church, July 3, 1856. California Historical Society, North Baker Research Library, San Francisco.

Bill. Drexel, Sather & Church, June 4, 1858. California Historical Society, North Baker Research Library, San Francisco.

Receipt, Sather & Co, dated June 2, 1886. San Francisco Historical Society, North Baker Research Library, San Francisco.

Biographical Sketches

Haatun, Wenche Sæther. "Sather Gate and Tower: A Norwegian Memorial at Berkeley University of California." Two typewritten pages. Undated and unpublished. Owned by Wenche Sæther Haatun.

Walker, Claudia. "Pedar Sather." Eight typewritten pages. Unpublished and undated. Owned by Kathleen Bruguiere Anderson, Charlotte, North Carolina.

———. "Pedar Sather: A Chronology of His Life and His Estate; Also, His Descendants." Twenty typewritten pages. Includes photos of Peder Sather, Mary Emma Sather, Josephine Frances Sather, and two photos of the farm Nordstun Nedre Sæter in South Odal. Dated April 1, 1945. Unpublished. California Historical Society, North Baker Research Library, San Francisco.

Letters

Anthony Lewis Tasheira Collection, 1849–60. Includes three letters from Peder Sather to Anthony Lewis Tasheira. History Room, California State Library, Sacramento.

Aronson, Barbara Jaffe. "Class of 1958." Undated letter published at www.peekyou.com/barbara_jaffe (accessed in 2008).

Bache, Søren. Letter to E. Backe. Lillesand, Norway, April 1843. Nasjonalbiblioteket, Håndskriftsamlingen, Oslo.

Keith, William. Letter to John Muir. San Francisco, 1909. John Muir Collection, University of the Pacific, Stockton, CA.

Oerne, Inez Odquist Encke. Letter to Ragna Encke. February 27, 1936. Owned by David Prestemon, Skaneateles, New York.

Sather, Jane Krom. Letter to Lyman Gage, Secretary of the Treasury. *San Francisco Chronicle,* June 3, 1899.

Sather, Peder. Two letters to Samuel H. Willey, dated 1860 and 1863. Bancroft Library, University of California, Berkeley.

———. Two letters to his brother Christoffer. San Francisco, 1856 and 1867. A gift from Wenche Sæther Hâtun to Bancroft Library, University of California, Berkeley.

Passenger and Ships' Lists, 1832–70

Captain William H. Samsons' passenger list. Ship *Herald,* Port of New York, October 20, 1832. New York Passenger Lists, 1820–1957, http://search.ancestry.com/search/db.aspx?dbid=7488 (accessed June 25, 2013).

New York Passenger Lists, 1820–1957. New York Public Library, www.nypl.org/collections/articles-databases/new-york-passenger-lists-1820-1957 (accessed June 25, 2013).

Ship Passenger Lists, 1848–73. California Bound, www.sfgenealogy.com/californiabound (accessed June 25, 2013).

Ships Arriving at the Port of San Francisco: 1800s. Maritime Heritage Project. Database on-line. www.maritimeheritage.org.

Miscellaneous Archival Items

Acts of the Ninety-third Legislature of the State of New Jersey. Approved January 14, 1869, Trenton NJ: Henry S. Little, President of the Senate. Leon Abbett, Speaker of the House of Assembly. Marcus L. Ward, Governor. Contains an act to incorporate the Dime Savings Bank of the City of Hudson. Among the incorporators, Theodore Tasheira. New Brunswick, NJ: A. R. Speer, 1869.

Banking House of Drexel, Sather & Church. Photograph. California Historical Society, North Baker Research Library, San Francisco.

Childs, George and Anthony J. Drexel. Double portrait, 1880s. Drexel Collection, Drexel University, Philadelphia.

Døpte i Aker, 1828–34 (Christian baptisms in Aker, 1828–34), p. 117. Church book, handwritten registers. Riksarkivet, Oslo.

Drexel, Francis Martin. Self-portrait as a young painter, ca. 1820. Drexel Collection, Drexel University, Philadelphia.

Letter Book of the College of California, 1849–1867. Letter nos. 16 and 23. Bancroft Library, University of California, Berkeley.

Ministerialbok for Strøm, Sør-Odal, 1804–10, p. 107. Church book, handwritten registers. Statsarkivet, Hamar, Norway.

Morning Call. *Vital Records, 1869–1900.* Herb Caen Magazines and Newspapers Center, San Francisco Public Library, San Francisco.

Nordstun Nedre Sæter. Two photographs, undated. California Historical Society, North Baker Research Library, San Francisco.

North Hall and South Hall. Photograph, 1874. Graves Pictoral Section, 1850–1968, Bancroft Library, University of California, Berkeley.

Passport Application Records, 1795–1905. Applications for Edward W. Church, James Sloan Hutchinson, Hans Rees, Caroline Eugenia Sather, Josephine Frances Sather, Mary Emma Sather, Peder Sather, and Anthony Lewis Tasheira. Fold3, www.fold3.com/title_447/passport_applications_17951905 (accessed June 25, 2013).

Rees, Hans. Certificate of citizenship. Superior Court, New York County, June 5, 1849. Fold3, naturalization records, http://go.fold3.com/results.php?category=n aturalization&links=0&kbid=1274&sub=TextNatStore (accessed June 25, 2013).

Register, University of California, 1906. Report of the Secretary to the Regents of the University of California for the Year Ending June 30, 1906, pp. 69, 81. Information on financial sources for Jane K. Sather's donations. Bancroft Library, University of California, Berkeley.

Sather, Jane Krom. Painting, William Keith, 1892. Graves Pictoral Section, 1850–1968, Bancroft Library, University of California, Berkeley.

Sather, Josephine. Photograph, 1865. William Shew, photographer, 421 Montgomery Street, San Francisco. Owned by Eva Helle, Sør-Odal, Norway.

Sather, Mary Emma. Photograph, 1865. William Shew, photographer, 421 Montgomery Street, San Francisco. Owned by Eva Helle, Sør-Odal, Norway.

Sather, Peder. Certificate of citizenship. Common Pleas Court, New York City, June 17, 1847. Fold3, naturalization records, http://go.fold3.com/results.php?category= naturalization&links=0&kbid=1274&sub=TextNatStore (accessed June 25, 2013).

———. Last Will and Testament, Oakland, 1886. Bancroft Library, University of California, Berkeley.

———. Photograph, 1865. William Shew, photographer, 421 Montgomery Street. California Historical Society, North Baker Research Library, San Francisco.

———. Photograph, 1885. Herb Caen Magazines and Newspapers Center, San Francisco Public Library, San Francisco.

Sather, Peder, and Sarah Thompson. Marriage Certificate. Reformed Protestant Dutch Church, New York, April 14, 1835. Owned by Kathleen Bruguiere Anderson, Charlotte, NC.

Sather, Sarah. Daguerreotype, undated. Owned by Eva Helle, Sør-Odal, Norway.

———. Undated photograph, showing her as an elderly woman. Bancroft Library, University of California, Berkeley.

Sather Banking Company. Semi-annual Statement, January 1, 1890. San Francisco: San Francisco Historical Society, North Baker Research Library, San Francisco.

Sather Family Register. Decorated sheet. Owned by Kathleen Bruguiere Anderson, Charlotte, NC.

Sather House, Rincon Hill. Graves Pictoral Section, 1850–1968, Bancroft Library, University of California, Berkeley.

Sather Mansion, Oakland, Twelfth Street, between Grove and Castro. Undated photograph. Oakland History Room, Oakland Public Library, Oakland. The Sather mansion was located where "Preservation Park Museum" is today.

Stryker, William S. Theodore Tasheira was enrolled May 21, 1861, in Company 1, First Regiment, New Jersey Volunteers. Discharged at U.S. General Hospital, Washington DC, January 27, 1863. Remarks: Disability. Corporal June 4, 1861. Reduced in ranks to private September 1, 1862. New Jersey State Library website, http://slic.njstatelib.org/slic_files/searchable_publications/civilwar.

Tammany Hall. Photograph, New York, 1856. Mid-Manhattan Picture Collection, New York Public Library, New York.

Tasheira, Anthony Louis. Daguerreotype, New York, 1854–56, Peter Welling, New York. Daguerreotype Collection, California History Room, California State Library, Sacramento.

University Chronicle, 1900, p. 350. Information on financial sources for Jane K. Sather's endowments. Bancroft Library, University of California, Berkeley.

CITY DIRECTORIES

Philadelphia City Directory, 1824. Francis Drexel, portrait painter, 40 South Street, corner of Sixth.

New York City Directory, 1827. Farrar, Charles, grocer, 85 South.

New York City Directories, 1832–33. Farrar, John, lottery office, 164 Nassau Street.

New York City Directory, 1836. Sather, Peter, clerk, 46 James Street.

New York City Directories, 1836–38. Farrar, John, exchange office, 164 Nassau Street.

New York City Directory, 1837. Sather, Peter, exchange, 24 Catherine Street. Home: 46 James Street.

New York City Directory, 1838. Sather Peter, broker, 164 Nassau Street.

New York City Directory, 1839–40. Sather Peter, exchange, 164 Nassau Street.

New York City Directory, 1841. Tasheira, James L, cabinetmaker, 23 Downing Street.

New York City Directory, 1842. Sather, Peter, 69 Nassau Street; Leather and Shoe, 49 Ferry. Home: Brooklyn.

New York City Directory, 1845. Rees & Sather, leather, 49 Ferry.

New York City Directory, 1845. Sather, Peder, broker, 164 Nassau Street; Leather, 49. Ferry. Home: 81Pineapple Street, Brooklyn Heights, Brooklyn.

New York City Directory, 1846. Sather & Church, brokers, 164 Nassau Street.

New York City Directory, 1846. Sather, Peder, broker, 164 Nassau Street. Home: Brooklyn.

New York City Directory, 1848. Edward W. Church, broker, 164 Nassau Street. Home: Myrtle Ave., Brooklyn.

New York City Directory, 1848. Sather, Peder, broker, 164 Nassau Street. Home: 82Willoughby, Brooklyn.

New York City Directory, 1848. Tasheira, Anthony Lewis,, iron founder, 63 Centre. Home: 23 Downing Street.

New York City Directory, 1848. Tasheira, Maria, widow of James L.Tasheira, 23 Downing Street.

New York City Directory, 1849. Hans Rees, 67 Frankfort. Home: Williamsburg, Brooklyn.

New York City Directories, 1849-50. Sather & Church, brokers, 164 Nassau Street.

Brooklyn City Directory, 1850–51. Edward Church, broker, 229 Hicks.

Brooklyn City Directory, 1850–51. Sather, Peder, broker, 82 Willoughby.

San Francisco City Directory, 1852. Church, Edward W., 134 Montgomery Street.

San Francisco City Directory, 1852. Drexel, Sather & Church, 134 Montgomery Street.

San Francisco City Directory, 1852. Sather, P. (Drexel, Sather & Church), banker, 129 Montgomery Street.

San Francisco City Directory, 1852. Turnbull & Walton, 83 Front Street, corner of Clay.

San Francisco City Directory, 1852–53. Drexel, Sather & Church, bankers, 134 Montgomery Street.

New York City Directory, 1853. Sather, P., 164 Nassau Street.

New York City Directory, 1853–54. Hans Rees, 37 Spruce. Home: Williamsburg, Brooklyn.

San Francisco City Directory, 1854. Drexel, Sather & Church, corner of Montgomery and Commercial Street.

New York City Directory, 1854. Tasheira, Eliza, 29 Cornelia Street.

New York City Directory, 1854–57. Sather, Peder, broker, 164 Nassau Street. Home: Brooklyn.

San Francisco City Directory, 1855. Drexel, Sather & Church, corner of Battery and Clay Street.

San Francisco City Directory, 1856. Church, E. W., Second Street, between Folsom and Harrison.

San Francisco City Directory, 1856. Drexel, Sather & Church, corner of Battery and Clay.

San Francisco City Directory, 1856. Sather, P., Second Street, corner of Harrison Street.

San Francisco City Directory, 1856–57. Drexel, Sather & Church, corner of Battery and Clay Street.

New York City Directories, 1856–73. Farrar, Charles, banker, 164 Nassau Street. Home: 67 Hicks, Brooklyn.

New York City Directories 1857–58. Lawrence, Luther S, 164 Nassau Street, home: 67 Hicks, Brooklyn.

San Francisco City Directory, 1858. Church, Edward (Sather & Church). Residence: n.e. corner of Harrison and Second.

San Francisco City Directory, 1858. Cook, Nelson, porter with Sather & Church, s.w. corner of Clay and Battery.

San Francisco City Directory, 1858. Day, Henry F., book-keeper with Sather & Church. Residence: 67 Howard.

San Francisco City Directory, 1858. Hutchinson, James S., cashier with Sather & Church. Residence: Harrison/Second.

San Francisco City Directory, 1858. Riddell, de Witt, Charles, teller at Sather & Church, s.w. corner of Battery and Clay.

San Francisco City Directory, 1858. Riddell, Speer, teller at Parrot & Co., n.w. corner Montgomery/Sacramento.

San Francisco City Directory, 1858. Sather, P., Sather & Church, s.w. corner of Battery and Clay. Residence: n.e. corner of Harrison and Second.

San Francisco City Directory, 1858. Taylor, A.J., teller at Sather & Church. Residence: 9 Stevenson.

San Francisco City Directory, 1859. Cook, Nelson, porter at Sather & Church. Residence: corner of Dupont and Green Street.

San Francisco City Directory, 1859. Hutchinson, James S., cashier of Sather & Church. Residence: Harrison between First and Second.

Brooklyn City Directory, 1859. John M. Falconer, painter, 82 Willoughby Street.

San Francisco City Directory, 1859. Lee, Henry C. & Charles Lee, publishers and booksellers, n.w. corner of Montgomery and Merchant, also book-keeper with Sather & Church. Residence: Stockton between Pine and Bush.

San Francisco City Directory, 1859. Nicholson, John Henry, book-keeper with Sather & Church, n.e. corner of Broadway and Montgomery.

San Francisco City Directory, 1859. Sather (Peder) & Church (Edward W.), banker, s.w. corner of Battery and Clay.

San Francisco City Directory, 1859. Taylor, Andrew J., teller at Sather & Church. Residence: 195 California.

Jersey City, City Directories, 1859–60. Roosevelt, William, carpenter and builder, South 4th Street, corner of Prospect.

San Francisco City Directory, 1860. Church, Edward (Sather & Church). Residence: s.e. Second and Harrison.

San Francisco City Directory, 1860. Cook, Nelson, Porter Sather & Church. Residence: s.e. Kearney between Green and Union Street.

San Francisco City Directory, 1860. Hayward, George, clerk with Sather & Church. Residence: s.w. Clay and Battery.

San Francisco City Directory, 1860. Hickox, George C., teller Sather & Church. Residence: n.e. Ellis between Stockton and Powell.

San Francisco City Directory, 1860. Hutchinson, James S., cashier Sather & Church. Residence: Alameda.

San Francisco City Directory, 1860. Nicholson, J.H., book-keeper with Sather & Church. Residence: s.e. corner of Broadway and Stockton.

San Francisco City Directory, 1860. San Francisco Port Society, P. Sather.

San Francisco City Directory, 1860. Sather, Peder (Sather & Church), s.w. corner of Battery and Clay, residence Alameda.

Brooklyn City Directories, 1860–70. Lawrence, Luther, broker, 67 Hicks.

San Francisco City Directory, 1861–62. Sather, Peder, Sather & Church, s.w. corner of Battery and Clay Street. Residence: 346 Second Street.

Jersey City, City Directory, 1861–63. Roosevelt, William, liquors, South 4th Street, corner of Prospect.

New York City Directory, 1862. Tasheira, Maria, widow James L. Tasheira. Home: 25 Cornelia Street.

San Francisco City Directory, 1862. Henry C. Lee, book-keeper Sather & Church, dwelling 422 Second Street.

San Francisco City Directory, 1862. Tasheira, Eliza, widow, 422 Second Street.

San Francisco City Directory, 1862. William Wiskind, coachman with Peter Sather, 346 Second Street.

San Francisco City Directory, 1864. Sather & Co, bankers, n.e. corner of Montgomery and Commercial Street.

San Francisco City Directory, 1865. Eckley, George R., teller with Sather & Co. Residence 826 Folsom.

San Francisco City Directory, 1866. Henry C. Lee, book-keeper with Sather & Co. Residence: 422 Second Street.

San Francisco City Directory, 1867. John Fox, coachman with P. Sather.

San Francisco City Directories, 1867–85. James S. Hutchinson, cashier Sather & Co. Residence: 1910 Howard Street.

San Francisco City Directory, 1869. Sather, Peder, Sather & Co. Residence: 346 Second Street.

San Francisco City Directory, 1870–86. Peder Sather (Sather & Co). Residence: Oakland, Twelfth Street, between Grove and Castro.

Oakland City Directory, 1873. Maloney, David, gardener with P. Sather.

San Francisco City Directory, 1873. Henderson, David M., book-keeper, Sather & Co.

San Francisco City Directory, 1873. Martin, Albert, paying teller with Sather & Co.

San Francisco City Directory, 1874. Edwards, Edward, porter with Sather & Co. Residence: 17 Diamond Street.

San Francisco City Directory, 1874. William H. Harnden, note teller with Sather & Co. Residence: Oakland.

San Francisco City Directory, 1875. William H. Harnden, note teller, Sather & Co. Residence: Alameda.

San Francisco City Directory, 1876. Edwards, Edward, collector, Sather & Co. Res.: Diamond/17th.

San Francisco City Directory, 1876. Henderson, David, book-keeper, Sather & Co. Res.: Oakland.

San Francisco City Directory, 1876. Kelley, Luke, paying teller, Sather & Co. Res.: Oakland.

San Francisco City Directory, 1876. Mann, Albert, clerk Sather & Co.. Res.: Oakland.

San Francisco City Directory, 1876. Tasheira, Eliza, widow, 606 Folsom.

San Francisco City Directory, 1876. Thompson, James Alden, book-keeper. Res.: 534 Bush.

San Francisco City Directory, 1879. Edwards, Edward, collector Sather & Co. Res.: 1104 Clay.

San Francisco City Directory, 1879. Kelley, Luke C., teller Sather & Co. Res.: Oakland.

San Francisco City Directory, 1879. Mann Albert W., clerk Sather & Co. Residence: Oakland.

San Francisco City Directory, 1879. Thompson, James Alden, book-keeper. Res.: 2107 Jones.

Oakland City Directory, 1879–81. Anderson, David M., book-keeper, Sather & Co.

San Francisco City Directory, 1879–80. Anderson, David W., book-keeper, Sather & Co.

San Francisco City Directory, 1880. Edwards, Charles, messenger, Sather & Co.

San Francisco City Directory, 1880. Emile Bruguiere, Sather & Co. Residence: 1800 Franklin.

San Francisco City Directory, 1880. James A. Thompson, book-keeper, Sather & Co. Residence: Abbotsford House.

Oakland City Directory, 1881–82. John Fox, coachman with Peder Sather, 621 13th Street.

Oakland City Directory, 1881–82. Miss Louise Clason, domestic with Peder Sather.

Oakland City Directory, 1881–84. William Stuart, gardener with P. Sather 664 12th.

Oakland City Directory, 1881–84. Marie Otahal, domestic with Peder Sather, 664 12th.

San Francisco City Directory, 1883. Tasheira, George, manager. Residence: Sausalito.

San Francisco City Directory, 1883. Tasheira, Lewis, civil engineer. Residence: Oakland.

Oakland City Directory, 1884. Luke C. Kelly, paying teller with Sather's bank.

San Francisco City Directory, 1884. Thompson, James A., book-keeper, Sather & Co. Res.: San Mateo.

Providence, RI, City Directory, 1884–87. Tasheira, Theodore, night clerk, Freeman House.

Oakland City Directory, 1887. Luke C. Kelley, paying teller, Sather Banking Co. Res.: 1214 Brush.

Oakland City Directory, 1887. Samuel Nelsen, gardener with Mrs. Peder Sather.

Oakland City Directory, 1887–88. Peter Anderson, coachman with Mrs. P. Sather, s.e. corner of Grove and 13th.

Oakland City Directory, 1887–88. William H. Harden, with Sather & Co., Broadway near the Bay.

Oakland City Directory, 1889–91. Charles F. Baker, receiving teller, Sather Bank. Home: 1215 Chestnut.

Providence, RI, City Directory, 1890. Tasheira, Theodore, night clerk, Hotel St. George, dwelling do. Removed to Woodstock, Connecticut.

1840. Peter Sather, New York Ward 4.

1845. Peter Sather, 81 Pineapple Street, Brooklyn Heights.

1850. Mary Dooner, domestic with Peder Sather, Brooklyn, Ward 11.

1850. Jane Krom, Marbletown, Ulster, New York.

1850. William Roosevelt and Mercelena Tasheira, Jersey City, NJ.

1850–51. Sather, Peder, 82 Willoughby, Brooklyn, Ward 11.

1860. Caroline Eugenia Sather, Poughkeepsie City, Ward 2.

1860. Peder Sather, Alameda.

1860. Sarah and Abraham Myers, Alameda.

1860. William Roosevelt, Jersey City, NJ.

1870. Charles Tasheira, brass moulder, 23 Downing Street, New York.

1870. Eliza Tasheira, b. 1814, London, England; c/o Henry and Harriet Lee, San Francisco, Ward 9.

1870. Jane Krom, Landis, Cumberland, New Jersey.

1870. Peder Sather, San Francisco.

1875. Theodore Tasheira, farm laborer, single, Canaan, Columbia County, New York.

1880. Christian Encke, engineer, born in Norway, c/o Tinius Olsen, Philadelphia.

1880. Mary Emma Sather, Clifton Heights, Delaware, Pennsylvania.

1880. Peder Sather, Oakland.

1880. Theodore Tasheira, Canaan, Columbia, New York, farm laborer, 44 years, single. Household: Alton Bradley, farmer, 44 years, single. Eliza Bradley, 79 years, his mother.

1895. Peter David Encke, physician, St. Paul, Minnesota.

1900. Jane K. Sather, 664 12th Street, Oakland. Servants: Rosa Moser 31 years, house keeper; Christine Kull, 29 years, Ohio, in the kitchen; Isabelle Garvun, 30 years, Ireland, chambermaid.

1900. Josephine Bruguiere, San Francisco.

1910. Jane K. Sather, 664 12th Street, Oakland. Servants: Marie Ahrensberg, 53 years, Germany, house keeper; Margaret Jorgenson, 30 years, Denmark, servant; Annie Adelhof, 50 years, Sweden, nurse.

1910. Josephine Bruguiere. Newport, Rhode Island.

1920. Claudia Walker, Oakland. Teacher, born 1884, Indiana.

ORAL SOURCES

Anderson, Kathleen Bruguiere. Peder Sather's great-great grandchild. Lafayette, CA. Spring 2008.

Helle, Eva. Christoffer Sæther's great-great grandchild. Sør-Odal, Norway. Summer 2011.

Richardson, Leon Joseph. *Berkeley Culture, University of California Highlights, and University Extension, 1892–1960: Oral History Transcript and Related Material.* Typescript of an oral history conducted 1959 by Amelia Fry, pp. 82–84. Berkeley: Regional Cultural History Project, General Library, University of California, 1962.

Sæther Håtun, Wenche. Christoffer Sæther's great-great grandchild. Slependen, Norway. Spring 2011.

Thornton, Sigvor Hamre. Berkeley. Spring 2005.

INDEX

125, 141, 191; Sather's friendship with, 88, 107–8, 111

Cook, Sara, 107, 111

Coolbrith, Ina, 227

Cooper, Peter, 149–50

Cooper Union, Lincoln's 1860 speech at, 148–49

Cox, Aaron, 42, 43

"Crossing Brooklyn Ferry" (Whitman), 55

Dandini, Countess, 226–27

Darwin, Charles, 138

Davidson & Co., 100

Davidson, Benjamin, 182

De Witt, Thomas, 30

Dickens, Charles, 55, 97

Didion, Joan, 179–80

Dingee, Mr. (Jane Sather's agent), 234

Domestic Manners of the Americans (Trollope), 27–29, 65

Dometius, Captain, 68–69

Dow, Sterling, 193

Drexel & Co., 168; and Bank of California silver crisis, 219–20; New York office, 123, 136, 168, 204, 214; Paris office, 207; Philadelphia office, 37–38, 79, 95. *See also* Drexel, Anthony; Drexel, Francis

Drexel, Anthony Joseph, 36, 56*fig.*, 120, 207; appointed Mary Emma's guardian, 229, 232; career, 79, 95, 136, 150, 168; and 1875 Bank of California crisis, 219–20; and George Childs, 56*fig.*, 150, 187; and Grant, 203, 218; and J. P. Morgan, 213–14; and Sather's passport application, 204, 205*fig.*, 206; Sather's relationship with, 56*fig.*, 79, 136, 150, 184, 203, 214, 232, 234; and Sather's will, 229, 231, 232. *See also* Drexel & Co.

Drexel, Catherine, 36

Drexel, Francis Martin, 35–38, 37*fig.*, 40, 93, 95, 96; death, 167–68; and Drexel, Sather & Church, 79, 86, 110, 120, 121, 140; Mexican War financing, 79, 98; Sather and, 34, 38. *See also* Drexel & Co.; Drexel, Sather & Church

Drexel Institute (Drexel University), 150

Drexel, Sather & Church, 87*fig.*, 91*fig.*, 119, 130, 136; after Church's death, 167,

183–84, 189, 200, 207; bad loan to Meiggs, 121; *Central America* shipwreck and its aftermath, 133–36, 140; contract with Drexel, 79, 110, 120, 121; first Montgomery Street location, 89, 90, 91*fig.*, 95–96, 101; founding and early operations, 78–80, 86, 89–91, 95–96, 100; insurance business, 142; later locations, 123, 133, 184, 190; operations after expiration of Drexel contract, 110–11, 120–21, 123–27, 133–36, 140–41; Sacramento branch, 123, 134, 135; Sather's concerns about Church, 108, 111, 127; social relations among staff and owners, 100, 108, 187–88. *See also specific staff members*

Dumas, Alexandre, père, 114

Dysterud, Anne (Sather's sister), 15, 41, 47, 119

Dysterud, Bernt, 119, 121–22, 128, 199

Dysterud, Ole Olsen, 13–14, 15, 41, 119; correspondence with Sather, 35, 49, 57

Dysterud, Peder Olsen, 41–43, 119, 185

earthquakes, 88–89, 133

education, 137, 143, 152–54, 162; Peter Cooper's work, 149; of Sather's children, 143, 176; Sather's own education, 14–15, 16. *See also* University of California

Elevator (newspaper), 132–33

emigration, Norwegian, 16, 17, 58–59

Encke, Aagot, 199

Encke, Christian, 199, 230

Encke, Johan, 123, 199, 230

Encke, Peter David, 199, 230

Encke, Petrine, 18–19, 47, 123, 190, 199–200, 230

Encke, Ragna, 199

Erie Canal, 40

Ethington, Philip, 63

Europe: Jane Sather's European travel, 234; Josephine Bruguiere's European residence, 240; Sather family's 1869–1870 visit, 206–7, 213

Falconer, John, 93

Fargo, William, 70, 72, 73, 140. *See also* Wells, Fargo & Co.

Sather, Peder *(continued)*
conscience, 56–57, 131, 182–83; trust, 121;
views on race and slavery, 132, 167, 182;
views on women's rights, 143. *See also*
—CIVIC PARTICIPATION; —FAMILY
LIFE AND RELATIONSHIPS
—CIVIC PARTICIPATION: in the 1840s,
56–57; in the 1850s, 110, 132–33, 137–38,
142; in the 1860s, 147, 162, 164, 166, 167,
169–73, 182; in the 1870s–1880s, 215,
228, 229. *See also* Baptist Church;
University of California; *other institutions and organizations*
—FAMILY LIFE AND RELATIONSHIPS:
Alameda home, 143–45, 175–78, 180–82,
188; children's births, 33, 44, 45, 47,
50–51, 53; contact and relations with
Norwegian family members, 15, 38, 49,
119, 122–23, 183, 190, 192, 196, 197, 199;
correspondence with his brother, 14, 15,
122–23, 183, 194, 197; correspondence
with his brother-in-law, 35, 49, 57; family
life in the 1860s, 164–65, 174–82; family's move to California, 108, 110, 119, 136,
142–43; Josephine's marriage, 215–17;
marriage to and life with Jane Krom,
225–26, 228–29, 236; marriage to Sarah
Thompson, 29–33, 31*fig.*, 33, 35; Mary
Emma's mental illness, 174, 178–81,
184–85, 211, 217, 221, 228; Mary Emma's
sweetheart, 164, 172–73; nephews' visits,
41–43, 46, 119, 121–22, 128, 199; New
York homes, 33, 38, 45, 46, 48–49, 50, 53,
59, 93; Oakland home, 208–11, 209*fig.*,
228, 233; Peder Jr.'s death, 185; relationships with Sarah and his children, 30,
145, 164, 177–78; San Francisco home,
108–10, 109*fig.*, 136–37, 142, 144, 145,
180–81, 188, 194–95; separation from
family during the 1850s, 94–95, 136, 145.
See also *specific family members*
—FRIENDSHIPS AND ACQUAINTANCES, 51,
70, 197–98, 214–15, 226–27; Alexander
Stewart, 202–3; Anthony Drexel, 56*fig.*,
79, 136, 150, 184, 203, 214, 232, 234; Benjamin Haxtun, 204; class divisions and,
65–66, 74, 110, 112; Eliza Tasheira, 70;
with fellow Scandinavians, 49, 53, 114,

115, 197, 198–99, 211, 224; Freemasonry
and, 98–100, 146, 188; George Childs,
56*fig.*, 150–51, 234; H. H. Bancroft,
157–58; Jane Krom, 52, 211, 214, 223–24;
Nelson Cook, 88, 107–8, 111; with the
Roosevelts, 76–78; Theodore Tasheira,
76, 78, 90, 104; William Tecumseh
Sherman, 129. *See also* Drexel, Anthony;
Merritt, Samuel; Rees, Hans; Tasheira,
Anthony; *other specific individuals*
—HEALTH AND DEATH: death and burial,
229–30, 239; health in the 1840s, 60, 61,
63, 68, 70, 71, 78; health in the 1850s,
89–90, 92, 94, 97, 108. *See also* —WILLS
AND ESTATE
—TRAVELS: 1851 return to New York,
90–92; 1868–70 family trip to New
York and Europe, 196, 197–98, 200–
207, 213; first trip to California, 78–80,
81–84, 85–92; returns to New York,
115–17, 136, 139; Sarah's death and return
to California with Jane, 221, 223–25
—WILLS AND ESTATE, 229, 231–34; assets,
232; 1866 bequest to the University of
California, 238; Jane Sather's inheritance, 232–33, 236–38; Josephine Bruguiere and, 230, 232, 233–34, 239; Mary
Emma's inheritance, 234; press reports
and speculation, 230, 234; provisions for
Mary Emma, 229, 232; settlement with
Petrine, 230
Sather, Peder Dysterud (Sather's son), 44,
53, 80, 137, 206; in California, 142, 143,
144, 164, 176; death and burial, 185, 217
Sather Professorships, 6, 193, 236–37, 238
Sather Ranch, 213, 228
Sather, Sarah Thompson, 29–33, 32*fig.*, 47;
after move to Oakland, 211; in Alameda,
142–45, 176, 177–78; before Peder's
move to California, 47, 50–51, 52, 80;
children, 33, 44, 45, 47, 50–51, 53;
church membership, 30, 164; death, 221,
223–25; during Peder's stays in California, 94–95, 108, 110, 119; on 1868–1870
trip to New York and Europe, 201,
206–7, 213; family's move to California,
108, 110, 119, 136, 142–43; and Josephine's marriage, 216; personal qualities,

www.ingramcontent.com/pod-product-compliance
Lightning Source LLC
Chambersburg PA
CBHW020338100426

42812CB00029B/3174/J